NEWS

NEWS

Postcards from the
Four Directions

Drew Hayden Taylor

Talonbooks

Talonbooks
Box 2076, Vancouver, British Columbia, Canada V6B 3S3
www.talonbooks.com

Typeset in Monotype Joanna and printed and bound in Canada.
Printed on 100% post-consumer recycled paper.

First Printing: 2010

The publisher gratefully acknowledges the financial support of the Canada Council for the Arts;
the Government of Canada through the Book Publishing Industry Development Program; and
the Province of British Columbia through the British Columbia Arts Council and the Book
Publishing Tax Credit for our publishing activities.

Library and Archives Canada Cataloguing in Publication

Taylor, Drew Hayden, 1962–
         NEWS : postcards from the four directions / Drew Hayden Taylor.

ISBN 978-0-88922-643-2

         I. Title.

PS8589.A885N48 2010   C814'.54   C2010-902236-X

Many of these articles and essays have been previously published in *Now Magazine*, *Windspeaker*, the *Peterborough Examiner*, *Off-Centre*, the *Globe and Mail*, *prairie dog*, *Planet S*, *Canadian Geographic*, *Spirit Magazine* and broadcast on CBC Radio.

CONTENTS

West

South

INTRODUCTION

Welcome. I bring you greetings from my people, all the blue-eyed, *Star Trek*-obsessed, can-make-chicken-cacciatore-from-scratch, playwright/novelist/screenwritering Anishnaabe.

This is a book of thoughts and perceptions divided into four sections. The Four Directions are an important part of many traditional First Nations teachings. To the initiated, they are more than just the cardinal points on a compass. They encompass (no pun intended) philosophy, culture, spirituality, and identity. Each of the Four Directions even has its own colour, thought by some to represent one of the four races of humanity—Red, Yellow, Black, and White. While their attributes and even their colours vary from nation to nation, these directions and their teachings are at the core of many Aboriginal ceremonies and beliefs.

That being said, this is not specifically a book of traditional teachings or Aboriginal spirituality—far from it. Instead, this is a book of my personal musings, wanderings, impressions of the Native community, as well as many other communities in Canada and the world, inspired by these, the Four Directions. Within these pages are several dozen essays, commentaries, articles, speculations—postcards, for lack of a better term—exploring the complexites of Native identity and perceptions of Native people by others. Their topics range from experiences and perceptions gathered while travelling the world and travelling Canada's Native communities. There are controversial articles here, dealing with how to argue with an Elder(!), to the representation of Native people in the media, to economics, to politics, to history, to the environment, to the just plain silly—did you know, for example, they have moose in Finland, domesticated ones, and they actually milk them to make very expensive cheese? These ponderings, collected over the past few years, reflect some issues that have been on the tips of people's tongues for as long as centuries, for years, and sometimes for even as little as days. Hopefully, some of the topics will make you go, "I remember that!" Others will perhaps remain timeless and ever-present.

Please keep in mind that in setting up these four sections, I have tried as much as possible to adhere to the actual characteristics of each Direction, within the framework of my own people. However, the Four Directions are a broad, variously expressed, and much-disputed part of Aboriginal culture, so there can be both ambiguity and overlap in what they represent, depending on whose particular teachings you are embracing. There are even contradictory beliefs as to which colour represents which direction from one nation to the next. As among Bible-believers and wine and cheese regions in France, every hundred kilometres, one will inevitably encounter interesting variations in the culture. So please forgive me if there appears to be discrepancies in my classifications. For the sake of this book, I have used references from many different sources, including *The Sacred Circle*, a book that came out in 1984, but I have also consulted on these matters thoroughly with Douglas Williams, an Elder from my beloved Curve Lake First Nation.

After reading some of the pieces, you may agree with some of the things I have to say, or you might not. You may not even believe some of things I've come across in my travels—not to worry, sometimes even I don't. However, very few things are more interesting than a good discussion. Above all else, I have tried to view these things with a good sense of humour. Sometimes that's the only way to get through life.

So read on, my curious friends, and stick your big toe in Lake Indigena. Hopefully, you will enjoy the water and find some things in here you didn't know, or didn't know enough about. Enjoy.

—Drew Hayden Taylor, Curve Lake, Ontario, 2010

North

North is the direction of winter, and the element of rock, and is typically represented by the colour white. It is also the direction of getting older—thus spiritual processes, contemplation, reflection, and wisdom are some of its important characteristics. Elders figure prominently here, as does the transfer of knowledge. From the north come purity and storytelling—something very important to me—and also travel. It is the most spiritual of the directions, one that's responsible for going home—both physically and metaphorically. The bear and medicine come from the north.

THE ABORIGINAL TIME CONUNDRUM

Let me run a theory by you. One dealing with Aboriginal time perceptions. And Elders. But first, some background.

If I've heard my mother say it once, I've heard her say it a thousand times ... things are sure bad in the world today. Maybe true, maybe not. Personally I don't think things were much better back in the 1930s during the Depression, or at any other time. The world is a tough place at the best of times. But this does introduce an interesting concept: the way we view time. As the Rolling Stones used to say, "Time Is on My Side." But then again, maybe Bob Dylan put it more succinctly: "The Times They Are a-Changin'." And as Native people, our relationship with time is quite unique.

Native people have always looked to the past for instruction. The future was often viewed as the past that hadn't happened yet. We've always looked back to our ancient teachings to guide our way. More importantly, we always looked to our Elders for much of that guidance and teaching, because they were and are wise in the ways of the world, and are put on this Earth to try and make our lives a little easier. Their world was a world we were all familiar with. They already had experienced it, and could share that experience. But I fear the times are a-changin'.

In the world outside our windows, we have all witnessed the disintegration of many Native families and communities, often because of modern issues like alcohol, land and water pollution, residential schools, and a host of other unfortunate things. But I believe there may be other reasons, ones that lead to our own doorstep, that are contributing to our modern troubles. It is, quite possibly, that descriptive term left over from the sixties, the "Generation Gap." I propose to rename it the "Elder/Information Gap."

The world has turned topsy-turvy. For the first time in our history, today's generation of youth is in the unique position of having to instruct, that is to say, be the teachers of, the Elders in our communities. The proverbial table has been turned, and community chaos and confusion are arising from it. By this I mean the worlds our Elders knew are remarkably different from the world our kids know today. The technology of our day is overwhelming and alluring, and like any new language, it's best taught to a person when they are young. Computer and video games are quickly becoming like a new language—Ojibway is giving way to Dreamweaver. Cree is losing ground to Acrobat. And there's more Javascript being utilized by our youth out there than Haida.

I have seen computer classes where Elders are trying to make sense of email and downloading, while kids young enough to have been born when the Elders were already Elders are going through it like it was water. They are becoming the keepers of information. Our Elders look fondly back at their youth and still listen to the music of their childhoods (often country in flavour), and recall the first car they ever owned. They are remembering their past, whereas the youths of today are looking forward to the future, to their next computer upgrade or DVD. They live for tomorrow. The world is in constant change and that is normal for them. Different perceptions of reality from those of the Elders, it seems.

What's worse, in our past it was natural for our children to grow up dreaming of becoming wise and loving like their grandparents. It may be sacrilege to say, but it requires no stretch of the imagination to understand that most kids today would not want the lifestyles their Elders enjoyed as children. It would be too alien, too rustic. Too boring. Kids today probably couldn't tell the difference between a clothesline and an outboard motor cord (here's a clue: the clothesline is longer).

There was a time when we believed the Elders knew everything. Nowadays, it's impossible to know everything. Today we're lucky if we know anything. When I was in high school, I remember reading about some White man back in seventeenth-century Europe whom historians considered the last man to know "everything." With our Elders, that was only a few decades back.

Of course the wisdom the Elders do command can never be replaced. Theirs is a wisdom of life, of experience, of knowing what's right and what's wrong. That kind of wisdom will never go out of style. Chances are though, that things are just gonna get worse and worse. More technology changing faster and faster, till only a very few can keep up with it. And because of this, when these kids of today become Elders, it's possible the "Elder/Information Gap" will be bigger and harder to bridge. We won't be able to talk to our grandkids.

I hope I'm wrong, but in case I'm not ... welcome to the twenty-first century.

FEELING THOSE MANY WINTERS

Every time you go home, it happens. You find you are getting older, yet the world seems to be getting younger. You don't know your iPods from your IHOPs. Kids today just don't seem to know or care about the "old days." This is nowhere more evident than in the Native community. I grew up on a small Ojibway Reserve in Central Ontario during the sixties and seventies. Luckily, during those years on the Reserve, I was safely insulated against such dubious non-Reserve creations as the disco phenomenon and managed to emerge from those polyester years with only one set of tight Jordache jeans. Though oddly enough, the older I get, the tighter my jeans seem to become.

And as the decades continue to pass by with increasing speed, I can't help but notice that everything I grew up knowing about life on the Reserve is now the stuff of ancient history and engenders blank, confused looks when you bring it up. I have discovered that those younger than me have no idea what television show the character Joe Two Rivers was on. Or the difference between the White Paper and The White Album.

Once when I was home for Christmas, I found myself sitting around the kitchen table with a like-minded group of people I tend to call the Generation Ex-ers. I call us that because we are all of the same generation who, a thousand years ago, used to drink Molson Ex all the time. Nowadays, since I've moved to the city, our beverages of choice have become Alexander Keith's or a nice Australian pinot noir. You know you've become a comfortable urban Indian when your idea of roughing it involves ordering the house wine, and accepting Atlantic instead of Pacific salmon. The savages ...

Basically, when you talk to anybody under thirty or thirty-five, and you start to reminisce about anything before the nineties, they roll their eyes. I understand that's pretty universal in most cultures. For instance, most Native people in that age range have no idea who Kahliga was, even though every Native garage band in North America knew that old Hank Williams Sr. song by heart, which isn't easy in a culture that didn't have garages. For those not in the know, Kahliga was a wooden Indian standing by the door. He had a heart of knotted pine and he was in love with another wooden Indian across ... well, it gets kind of silly after that.

Add to that the fact that over the years, the nostalgic, personal, and intimate connection between the Eaton's summer (or winter) catalogue and outhouses seems to have been lost in the mists of time. Alas, Eaton's is now but a fond memory, the outhouse has become a happily distant memory, and catalogues have gone virtual. Good taste prevents me from going into any further details regarding the symbiotic relationship and the decline in selection among publicly available reading materials in our society generally, but I think you can make the connection. Just try mentioning these associations to young folks and notice the shocked looks you just might get. Kids today …

Now I'm the first to admit this lack of understanding can be a two-way street. I fully admit that there is a generation or two ahead of me with whom I occasionally don't see things eye to eye. Take pork fat, for example. During that same Christmas, I distinctly remember several older members of my family sitting around the kitchen table fondly remembering the days of yore. They were saying that when they were young, there was no junk food that the kids of today seemed so hooked on. No hamburgers or potato chips or stuff like that. And if there was, they couldn't afford them. "Yep," one woman said, "we sure ate a lot better." It was then I reminded them of all the stories I'd heard, from years gone by, about those fabulous slices of white bread with liberal amounts of lard spread on top—and for the more adventurous, with a sprinkling of white sugar to top it off. Yum. In my mind's eye I could see them crumbling up some hard lard and sprinkling it over their morning cereal. Maybe adding a drop or two in their coffee to make it heartier. So, like Kahliga and outhouse-catalogues for those with a few less years under their belts, I look at those older than me with a look of something that can only be best described as mystified revulsion.

Then again, it could just all be me. Call it cultural or generational paranoia. As Thomas Wolfe once wrote so accurately, you can't go home again. Wolfe … was he Native?

SOUTH OF BOTH BORDERS

Mexico City is a fascinating place. I'm told it's a city of over twenty million people—that's almost two-thirds of Canada in one single place. Lesser known is the fact that like the city of Venice, it's sinking in places. Many venerable old buildings have huge cracks in them, not because of the well-known devastating earthquakes that frequently shake the country, but because different parts of the city are sinking at different rates. The city itself is built on the original remains of the Aztec capital, which was established on a series of islands connected with causeways. In post-contact times, parts of the lake and marsh were filled in so the Spanish could erect more and more buildings until the lake practically vanished under a sea of buildings. But as we all know, Mother Nature has a way of getting her revenge on those who don't show her an appropriate degree of respect.

I was in Mexico City for a PEN International Congress on disappearing Indigenous languages. As an Ojibway writer who does not speak his mother's tongue, I had been asked to speak about having to write in English. It's a subject of real concern in Mexico. Of the sixty-two acknowledged Indigenous languages in the country, nineteen are currently threatened, and if Mexico is like Canada, more are likely to follow. Above and beyond the language issues, it was an eye-opening experience for me. Most of us only know Mexico through Cancun or Acapulco ... and nobody likes a nice sandy beach better than me. Like most Canadians, I arrived with only the Spanish provided by such venerable language instructors as Speedy Gonzales, but despite these language barriers I learned a lot about the country and its people at a non-verbal level.

For instance, it was a rude shock being driven from the airport to arrive forty-five minutes later at our hotel ... right beside a Scotiabank, across the road from a KFC and a Dunkin' Donuts, and just down the street from a Sears. It didn't look all that different from my neighbourhood in Toronto. A little later, many of the Canadian writers were invited to a reception at the Canadian Embassy. I was expecting the typical array of red and white wine, with maybe some champagne thrown in. But I must admit, it was my first high-class wine and cheese function where they also served trays full of tequila shooters. More importantly, they encouraged you to try them: "after all, it is Mexico's national drink." I don't remember anything like this in Italy. In fact, after a while, I didn't remember much of this in Mexico.

But I do remember having a detailed conversation with the Mexican government's chief negotiator with the Chiapas Zapatistas, from whom I got the official low-down on Subcomandante Marcos and the gang. A bit later we moved on to a local hangout, a cantina where the revolutionary Pancho Villa had once had dinner a hundred years or so ago, and somebody dared to interrupt him. His response was to take out his gun and shoot a bullet into the ceiling, setting the stage for many subsequent customer/ waiter exchanges. The bullet hole is still there today, somewhat of a tourist attraction.

Amongst some of the local Mexican delegates, there was a genuine surprise and interest in the popularity of Native theatre in Canada. Evidently such an interest in Mexican Indigenous theatre was unthinkable down there. I was told by several different people how highly unlikely it was that any domestic Native theatre of substance would get produced in Mexico, other than some sanitized traditional legends or innocuous "value-neutral" historical pieces. The possibility of any real Indigenous theatre was considered too provocative, its topics too politicized, especially in the wake of the Chiapas uprising. As an Aboriginal playwright, this story reminded me of that old sales story. Two shoe salesmen go to an African country looking to sell shoes. One sends a telegram back saying: "Bad news. Nobody here wears shoes." The other salesman sends a telegram back saying: "Good news. Nobody here has shoes."

That's as good a segue as any to what I saw on television there. On all the Mexican commercials, soap operas, game shows, etc., practically anybody and everybody looked White. Or more specifically, European. Fair-skinned, blondish. Yet everybody I met on the streets, in the restaurants, at that KFC, looked a lot darker ... and dare I say it—more Mexican. A friend of mine who is a frequent visitor to the country told me the image of people on television is how most middle-class Mexicans would prefer to see themselves. And how they want the rest of the world to see them too. And since the middle-class has most of the buying power, this is translated directly into television programming, which is funded by advertising aimed at the desires of those who watch it.

At the other end of the economic spectrum, a particularly powerful image that will stay with me is of all the impoverished kids who rushed to the cars at stop lights trying to sell candy, flowers, and lottery tickets. They looked a lot worse off than our own squeegee kids, but somewhat better off than some of the other ragamuffins begging on the streets, sometimes with what looked like their grandparents. I don't know if it was the children or the elderly that elicited the most sympathy in me. The irony struck me hard one morning as I ate breakfast on the hotel's twenty-fourth-floor boardroom, with its panoramic view of the city, where I enjoyed the sumptuous feast laid out for the delegates. On my way to help myself to a second helping at the buffet, I noticed a poster for a theatre show painted on the entire wall of a small, nearby building. It was for the musical Los Miserables, and staring at me was the image of that familiar hungry-looking waif we are all acquainted with. I recognized the look. I decided against the second helping.

One of the most revealing non-Mexican moments occurred in a conversation I had with an American PEN delegate. He was amazed to learn that PEN Canada and PEN Québec had arranged to send down fourteen Canadian writers to the congress, courtesy of the Canada Council and the Department of Foreign Affairs. Inspired, he contacted the American Embassy to inquire if they might be interested in sponsoring some American writers to attend. He was told, "Possibly ... but it depends on which writers," in a concerned tone. My new friend said he ended the conversation right there, not liking the direction it was going. They had managed to find alternate funding to allow a few delegates to attend.

In the end I came away from my trip to Mexico City with two resolutions. First, I must remember to send all those Canadian government organizations a "thank you" for not being concerned about my politics. And second, I must see what a humble Ojibway writer can do about breaking the Native theatre barrier in Mexico. I like a challenge.

HOW EXOTIC CAN HOME BE?

Not that long ago, I was at a book launch in Toronto. There I was in the audience, listening to the first line of this novel written by a writer from the other side of the world. It began, "The monsoons came early that year ..."

It was a wonderfully evocative, descriptive, and exotic way to begin a novel, and I thought to myself enviously, I wish I could start one of my stories that way. But when you live on a Reserve, the opportunity to be that exotic is rather limited. Yes, there are many fabulous and interesting things that happen all the time in a Native community, but somehow they seem more ... everyday. There's a sense of otherworldliness lacking. Oh, I'm sure many Native writers and academics would dispute that and possibly quite rightly. But as somebody who grew up on the Reserve, and has spent his entire life in the Native community, starting a book with the line, "Indian summer was early that year ..." or, "The fogs were early that year ..." or even, "The mosquitoes came early that year ..." just doesn't have the same caché.

Let's take another example: "Somewhere in the deep humid jungle, a lion's hungry roar split the dank night and the villagers cowered in their huts."

It paints quite an interesting picture. Now compare that to: "Somewhere in the muggy, blackfly-filled bush, a squirrel could be heard scolding a house cat, and nobody cared."

Maybe I'm a little jaded. I am well aware that to many authors from the other side of the world, a novel that starts with a comment about the monsoons coming early isn't too exciting from their perspective. Or anything with lions. Or giant lizards that can eat a Rez dog in one gulp. Exoticism is in the eye of the beholder I guess. I remember escorting a bunch of Maori, the Indigenous people of New Zealand, around Toronto and southern Ontario. One of the most exciting and interesting things they came across was squirrels. I distinctly remember half a dozen of them standing at the base of a tree looking up into the branches and pointing eagerly at a little furry creature chattering away at them. So maybe squirrels *are* exotic.

But unfortunately, I also get the same sense of literary frustration when I see the movies *Cyrano* and *Pirates of the Caribbean*, or take in a Shakespeare play at Stratford. I will admit it—I am dazzled by a good sword fight. Alas, the opportunity to write a decent and exciting sword fight into a Native play has been somewhat limited. The best that's been done so far has been two guys poking sharp sticks at each other. Again, a noticeable lack of exoticism. Maybe some sort of hockey stick fight could be choreographed, or a three-day-old bannock-tossing showdown could be staged. I've heard you can take an eye out with one of those.

On that same theme, I just can't picture a James Bond film taking place in a Native community. Can you? While many Native communities have their share of megalomaniacs (please send your nominees to the editor of this paper), those with plans for world domination are still a little rare. It's too time-consuming and the Department of Indian Affairs doesn't have the proper paperwork for it.

"I like my rye and Coke shaken, not stirred."

Somehow, it just doesn't fit. Bond in a Rez car. Bond in an immaculately tailored ribbon shirt. Okay, playing baccarat or poker in a casino might be feasible these days, but call me crazy, dealing with the evils of land claims or cigarette smuggling is not something Bond would be interested in tackling professionally.

At the other end of the literary spectrum are those popular historical romance novels that excel in exoticizing Native/White sexual/romantic relationships in the 1800s. Some would call it a sort of Métis Genesis story: a big handsome brave comes out of the windswept plains and somehow sweeps up a naive White chick wandering the wilds of the Prairies. And, after some plot-heavy and hickey-inducing adventures, they end up living happily ever after. Somehow, kidnapping and genocide have never seemed so sexy and attractive since.

Oh well, part of the journey of a writer is to find those quintessential elements of true exoticism in our own everyday world. That's part of the fun. They say that you should write what you know ... that's good up to a point. Then you must make up what you know. Or take what you know, wash it, spin-dry it, fluff it, and hang it out to dry. That's where the real talent begins.

WOULD YOU SPRINKLE THIS ON YOUR SPAGHETTI?

File this under: "Just when you thought you've seen and heard everything"; subsection "Unusual things you have eaten or heard about eating."

In my travels, I've had tea mixed with buffalo milk in India—very rich and sweet. I've had coffee sweetened with maple syrup—interesting, sort of an Indigenous flavoured coffee. I've even heard of a Native woman roasting a chicken stuffed with sweetgrass, just to see if the meat would have the same sweet flavour she loved. She ended up throwing it out the window— oddly enough, it seems chicken and sweetgrass don't mix. But this story has got to be a new one. On several different fronts. First of all, there are moose in Scandinavia. I did not know that. They may be blonde-haired, blue-eyed moose for all I know. Even more unusual, there's a small town 650 kilometres north of Sweden's capital of Stockholm that has a unique dairy farm where they make cheese from moose milk. And if you're the curious type, it costs about $1,370 per kilogram, or over $500 a pound. Now that's some pretty expensive cheese.

This farm is run by Christer Johansson and his wife, Ulla, who claim it's the only moose dairy and cheese farm in Europe ... dare I say the world? And they mostly sell their cheese to upscale hotels and restaurants in Sweden. "Waiter, why is my grilled cheese sandwich $73? And my milkshake $55?" Evidently there's a similar dairy establishment in eastern Russia but they only make moose milk. There are moose in Russia too?

And while you may think making moose cheese is probably easy and wonder, "Why didn't I think of that? Especially at $1,370 a kilogram!" evidently it isn't that easy. Of the fourteen moose owned by the Swedish farm, logically called Moose House, only three are working, milkable moose. And they only produce milk between May and September, from the time when they calve to when they are in heat again. It takes about two hours to milk a moose (now's there's the ultimate Trivial Pursuit question), and each moose, when so inclined, produces up to four litres of milk a day. Now, multiply that by three and the end product is twelve litres a day. "That's one of the reasons why the cheese is so expensive," Christer Johansson says. The milk is then refrigerated, and curdled into cheese only three times a year. Still, the farm manages to turn out about 300 kilograms of the moose cheese a year. Johansson adds: "We hope later on to be able to export more of the cheese."

The moose cheese is substantially healthier than cow cheese, and comes in three varieties, with only 12 percent fat and 12 percent protein. And if you're wondering just what moose cheese taste likes, the owners claim it has a "somewhat sour feta-type" flavour. I wonder if feeding in a swamp might have something to do with that. As of yet, there are no plans to introduce fat-free moose cheese, or moose curds, or moose cheese singles, or even moose Cheez Whiz. I guess if they used the moose milk or cream to make a chocolate mousse, then it would technically be a moose mousse.

One woman, on discovering this unique money-making venture, decided to see if it could be done here in North America, where of course, all the better moose live. Apparently, she contacted the State Fish and Game Department in New Hampshire to investigate the possibility of starting such a business. The sergeant in charge told her that in order to milk a moose, she "would have to be in legal possession of the moose." And since New Hampshire is probably not that different from your local municipality, this means that it is probably illegal to own a moose. Also, there is little precedent for owning a moose in this country. Therefore, it would be illegal to milk a moose. I bet you didn't know that.

It is, however, legal in many towns to own elk and several varieties of deer for certain agricultural purposes. That, of course, means the possibility of elk and deer cheeses (though deer seem a bit too skittish to have their teats milked). But who knows, maybe your local Band Council or municipality does allow private moose ownership. If so, some hot-shot Aboriginal entrepreneur could make a killing. If the Wahta Reserve can market spring water and cranberries, there's a moose cheese fortune waiting out there for the taking. Just keep in mind, $1,370 per kilogram, and remember that White people will eat anything.

This story reminds me of an interesting book I read a long time ago, by Arthur C. Clarke, I think called *The Deep Range*. In typical science fiction style, he told a story that takes place about a hundred years in the future. It's about a man who works in an ocean farm where whales are domesticated, raised for both meat and milk. Boy, when milking animals that size, you better hope your hands are really warm.

AN INDIAN IN INDIA

It was not an auspicious beginning. The gods of Air Canada had deemed it necessary to place me in the most uncomfortable seat possible, in one of the middle seats of four. There I sat, all six feet, 200 pounds of me, for sixteen hours, including the two hours we spent on the runway waiting to take off. Over half a day and half a world away, fighting claustrophobia all the way, we landed in Delhi, India. I was travelling with three companions, two York University professors of South Asian heritage—Alok and Arun Mukherjee—and Janine Willie, a Native PhD student and employee of the Equity Office at Ryerson University. We were all there to attend several conferences, as well as an arranged lecture tour regarding the wonders of Native Canadian literature.

Three weeks earlier, I had been offered a chance to visit India, the country after which, for some reason, my ancestors had been named. While I had travelled to many other parts of the world, I was assured India would be a completely different experience.

In a mad rush, I had to get a travel visa as well as visit a travel clinic for the first time in my life. There I got several expensive shots and pills, but considering the alternative of what exotic diseases I could conceivably come down with, I swallowed the cost. Maybe they're tax deductible. With my bloodstream and suitcase full of science's best defence against the nastiest little bugs India could throw at me, I was given a medical brochure to read. My complacency quickly evaporated as I read that several thousand people a year die of rabies in India. I suddenly had visions of rabid elephants and tigers running rampant through the streets.

Somehow, I knew already, this was going to be an interesting trip.

This is a journal of my adventures.

July 31
The minute I stepped off the plane in Delhi, I was assailed by India's unique aroma—kind of a burnt smell, reminiscent of smoked leather combined with an exotic spice. I also assumed the crowded airplane seats had been designed to acclimatize the passengers to a country with approximately 1.4 billion people. And one of them, an Indian teenager beside us in the customs line, was wearing a t-shirt with Sitting Bull on it. It seems I wasn't that far from home after all.

The country, still in monsoon season, was quite hot and humid, with the departure/parking/taxi area of the airport awash in people. It was about 9:30 at night, dark, and we were tired, having been awake for thirty hours. During the drive from the airport, I nervously looked out the window, searching for all those rabid tigers and elephants. Instead, I saw the famous herds of cows wandering the streets, sleeping wherever they desired. Being considered sacred definitely has its advantages. According to my friends, there aren't nearly as many cows in Delhi as there once were. Due to a beautification plan by the municipal government, most of the cows have been removed to the outskirts of the city. But it reminded me of the story of a Native man who, for one reason or another, was at the Banff School of the Arts. He was sitting in a boardroom when he casually looked out the window at the stunning beauty of the Rockies and he noticed, a scant two or three metres away, a big, juicy, well-fed elk calmly eating grass on the front lawn. This man leaned over to the guy next to him and said, "Let me guess, we can't touch them, right?" As a man who loves a good steak but also respects other cultures' beliefs, that's pretty much how I felt.

We arrived at the university guest house, where we were greeted by tiny salamanders scurrying all about. After years of living in Toronto, the sight of anything scurrying about makes me nervous, but Janine thought they were cute. Inside the humid room was the most essential piece of equipment you can find in India, the air conditioner. And this particular AC made me feel nostalgic. The brand name on the ancient machine said "Arctic." It was another touch of home (though I've never actually been to the Arctic) in the tropics.

My first evening in India. This is where Columbus had thought he'd landed all those years ago, and why we were called Indians. I don't see how he could have been confused. It doesn't look anything like home.

August 1
We left Delhi early the next morning for our first conference, in a town called Jaipur, about five hours away by car. Such a long trip so soon after arriving was not exactly high on my list of things to do, but I never say no to a good adventure. During the trip, we saw more wildlife ... if it can be called that: donkeys, monkeys in the trees, goats, pigs, camels, and eventually elephants. Curve Lake First Nation was never like this.

One of the first things I noticed is that in such a hot country, practically nobody wears shorts. All the men wear drab cotton pants, and buttoned shirts, regardless of their social or economic status. Office wear, practically. Yet in interesting juxtaposition, the women continue to wear their traditional, brightly-coloured, gorgeous saris, again regardless of their background. It's an odd by-product of the British influence—the men dress like the colonizers, whereas the women were under no such pressure.

Driving on the highways is an experience unto itself—suffice it to say the lines on the road are there merely for decoration, and the national sport is playing "chicken." The horn is the dominant form of communication on the highway. I saw a family of four riding on a scooter, with the woman riding side-saddle for modesty's sake.

Jaipur is a fascinating city. It translates as "pink city" because of the colour of the stone used in its construction. It really is pink. At the Contemporary Drama in English conference at the University of Jaipur, I was introduced as Professor Drew Hayden Taylor, which was news to me. Maybe I did go to university after all and had just forgotten about those years. Hard to say, but I didn't bother to correct them. I liked the respect the title gave me. I tried to act smarter.

It was at this conference I was introduced to the Dalit literature debate. The Dalits are what used to be called "the untouchables," the lowest caste of Hindi society. They used to clean the toilets and do all the menial work for the higher castes. And they were considered unclean. They weren't allowed to live in the towns; they had to live outside the walls. Some had to walk with a broom tied to their backs so it would sweep the ground clean after they walked on it. Their shadows weren't allowed to touch upper caste shadows. They constitute approximately 50 percent of the population. And much like Native people of this continent, they have discovered the sword of literature as a means of liberation. Dalits are beginning to write their own stories, tragic survival narratives—a classic example of an oppressed people getting their voice back and writing about being oppressed. The caste system was officially abolished in the Indian constitution back in the 1950s, but things like this die hard.

Alok Mukherjee, a high-caste Brahman (though it's not something he boasts about), had translated the book *Towards an Aesthetic of Dalit Literature*, by Sharankumar Limbale, into English and was discussing it at the conference. It was *déjà vu* for me as a Native person when a woman stood up and asked Alok, "Now that they are being appeased by the government, why are they still complaining and upset?!" Boy, did this sound familiar from the Aboriginal perspective. Even on the other side of the world, some things show their universality.

At this conference I was introduced to my first real unique taste of India, the tea. After hearing about the superiority of Indian tea, I was surprised to discover how they serve it. It comes in a vat, already premixed with sugar and buffalo milk. Buffalo milk is a lot sweeter and richer than cow's milk. I wasn't sure if I liked it or not. But after my first full twenty-four hours in the country, I was beginning to appreciate the food and the people. But it was becoming obvious that the best description for Indian food is vegetarian ... and I was wondering how long it would be before I began to crave a steak. Pretty soon those cows along the highway would start looking pretty good.

August 2

When I woke up this morning and went for breakfast, I noticed something: the rooms in India are constantly noisy. There is always a ceiling or desk fan or an air conditioner going. Then we took a tour of the town of Jaipur. It was there I began to develop a strange feeling, a sense of "otherness." I obviously did not belong. I didn't look like everybody else, I didn't dress like them, I didn't talk like them. I was, for all intents and purposes, a tourist. Even worse, after fifteen years of writing about my Native heritage (a heritage not obviously apparent, due to my blue-eyes) and titling a series of books Funny, You Don't Look Like One, I was indistinguishable from any other White tourist. I saw a Caucasian couple riding an elephant. They looked and dressed like me—completely out of place. They even waved at me. I began to have flashbacks to my childhood when we used to watch tourists, who were obviously more well off than us, come to the Reserve to shop at the arts and crafts store. We looked at them like they were from another planet. Evidently I, too, now had a cottage on that planet. I was a stranger in a strange land.

And as the world knows, all White people have money. On the drive up to see a fort, a man came running up to the car and literally banged on my window shoving his guide's licence against the glass, begging us to hire him. He picked my window because Alok and Arun were obviously South Asian, and Janine looked Native enough not to be so obviously White. My companions told me, "Get used to it. You're White here." I pondered the philosophical implications of this while we returned to Delhi. Did this mean I was suddenly in the market for a Jetta?

August 3

Woke up in the Delhi YMCA, gradually getting used to a steady, three-meals-a-day diet of excellent Indian food, and that is a serious adaptation. In the Native community, the only spices worth mentioning are salt and pepper—garlic is still considered a new fad that will take some time to get used to. Indian food is a completely different ball game. In fact, it's called cricket. But I still had fried eggs for breakfast. I prefer to slip into the lake slowly, not jump off the dock.

Today was a slow day so I managed to catch up on my Bollywood education. Actually it had started with two films on the plane when I was flying over, and of course there's practically nothing but Bollywood musicals on local television. I was surprised to be informed that most of the performers are from the Punjab region of the country, up in the northwest. This is primarily because they are lighter skinned. That is part of the country that the Indo-Europeans invaded and later Western armies flooded through, resulting in a population of lighter complexion in that region. And as is the case in many parts of the world, the lighter your skin is, the more social advantage you have. It had been the same with Mexican television—everybody looked more European than Mexican. Ironically, I was informed I could possibly have a successful career as a Bollywood actor. But I just couldn't master the choreography.

August 4

Oh my god, what a day. Janine and I decided to explore a bit more. She'd
been to India seven years ago and was somewhat familiar with the area.
She told me of Connaught Place, a sort of outdoor shopping mall, India
style. We left the safety of the Y and went forth like Lewis and Clark amongst
the Indians. Bad idea. We were about two blocks away when a gentleman
stopped to chat with us. He was very amiable and told us of a nearby
emporium, a place of good shopping. He said Connaught Place was under
construction. Wanting to shop, we thought, "What the hell." He led us
through the winding streets of Delhi to a building where, once we entered,
we were assailed by waves and waves of attendants wanting to sell us stuff.
And we're talking hard sell. Pressure. They wouldn't leave us alone. Buy! Buy!
Buy! By the time we left, having bought two carpets, we were exhausted.

Waiting outside was a three-wheeled cab and driver that had tried to
pick us up earlier. He had followed us there. We had said no, we wanted to
walk, but he was very persistent. Again, he followed us down the street,
practically begging us to hire him. "What, you don't like me?" We were in
such a hurry to get away, we managed to get lost. Then another person
came up to us asking if he could help. We told him where we were staying
and he said he was going in that direction. So we followed him, and as we
walked along the street, he casually mentioned that we would be passing
by an emporium that had the best deals in Delhi. We should stop in for a
few minutes. We said no, but he was rather persistent. It finally occurred to
us that these so-called "people in the streets" probably get commissions
for bringing people in. He left, annoyed, when we refused to enter his
emporium. Luckily we thought we saw a familiar building in the distance.
Triangulating, we went in a straight line and somehow ended up in what
appeared to be the Indian equivalent of a shopping market frequented by
the locals, not by us tourist-like people. We looked and felt completely out
of place.

We were getting worried. A shoe-shine boy took pity on us and showed
us the way out. As we were leaving, we were swarmed by at least a dozen
children of various ages, all asking for rupees, dollars, or chapati (bread).
They were skinny, wore ragged clothes, and tugged on us incessantly.
Walking as fast as we could, they followed us for about six blocks like flies
after honey. Just as the Y appeared in the distance, our young shoe-shine
friend mentioned that nearby was an emporium that maybe we'd like to
visit. We practically ran back to the Y. It had been two of the most stressful
hours in our lives. I began to appreciate the wonders of the fetal position
as a recreational endeavour.

To offset the experience, Alok took pity on us and took us to lunch at the
five-star Hotel Imperial. It was magnificent, a complete opposite to what
had happened that morning. Poverty gave way to opulence, starving kids
gave way to immaculately dressed waiters. I was beginning to understand
India as a bipolar country in search of lithium.

August 5

It's monsoon season here and I'm beginning to wonder if all the stories I've heard about the burning sun and sweltering heat have been largely fictional. It's been overcast and rainy for most of the trip. Muggy, but tolerable. Today we flew to Hyderabad, the location of the conference on postcolonial Commonwealth literature in English. What the hell I'm doing here, I don't know ... as an Aboriginal person, there's a train of thought that says Native people are not postcolonial because in many ways we are still colonized. So I'm a sheep in wolf's clothing ... or more accurately, a colonized person in a postcolonized environment. I just hope I have the proper paperwork.

We were scheduled to be picked up at the airport, but were having difficulty locating our driver. Once outside the safety of the airport, I was immediately approached by a man asking for money. Then a young boy appeared, saying, "Mister, Mister," wanting money. He literally followed us across the parking lot, and hovered nearby, constantly calling to us as we waited for our car. We had been warned not to give kids anything, or, much like in Delhi, word would get out and every kid within a mile would be on us. I managed to concentrate on looking for our driver but Janine, being the soft heart she is, gave in. She had squirreled away a bag of candy in her purse. The boy disappeared with the candy and Janine seemed quite satisfied with the solution to our little dilemma—that is until I pointed out that being a street kid, the boy probably didn't have a very good dental plan and in fifteen years, he's going to hate her for all that candy.

We checked into the Taj Banjara, a five-star hotel. It was gorgeous. It had a pool. It had a gym. It had four restaurants with food from around the world. It was quite an experience. But I began to notice something unusual. Both in Delhi and here, when we were approached, people, specifically men, would talk to me. It was like they were ignoring Janine. I was told it was a cultural thing. It's impolite or improper for a man to address or harass a woman. According to Janine, being invisible can be both annoying and a relief, depending on the circumstances.

Luckily no sign of any rabid elephants or tigers so far.

August 6

After a great night's sleep, I was concerned when I woke up with a sore throat. I was hoping it wasn't serious, just a side effect of going from the air-conditioned rooms and hotels outside into the humid Indian summer. I've had the same thing happen in Canada. Nothing worse than being sick in a foreign country.

There's a lot to be said for five-star hospitality after staying at the Y. As we were having breakfast, I noticed another unusual characteristic of life in India. The restaurant had a ratio of about one waiter for every two tables. It was ridiculously overstaffed. And the meal was a buffet, requiring almost no serving staff! This is quite common in high-end establishments in India because of the ample workforce and its low wage demands. The situation approached the ridiculous when I wasn't allowed to carry my own toast or soup to my table from the buffet. They were literally taken out of my hands. There were always way more bodies to serve you than you would find in any Canadian establishment. Uncomfortably so.

I couldn't help remembering that my mother, for most of her life, until her mid-fifties, made her living by cooking and cleaning for White people. She was a domestic in the USA and Canada, in resorts, camps, and nursing homes. Supposedly during her early years she could make a hell of a martini. I kept seeing my mother amongst the working staff here, catering to all the White people.

Today was the first day of papers and lectures, and I found myself in a room surrounded by academics. Homi Bhabha was speaking. Evidently he's the Brad Pitt or Wayne Gretzky in the world of postcolonial theory. He sure sounded smart. I've always found that academics are like people who eat in restaurants all the time but never bother to cook. I passed the time by counting the ceiling tiles.

On touring the city, I again noticed that most of the signs are in English. In a country with twenty-two official languages (not including a host of other unofficial languages and dialects), I've heard it said that one of the only useful things the British left behind was their language. Without a unifying tongue, the country would be much more divided. I found this contrary to how Canada's Native people view the English language—as more of a weed, slowly making its way onto the lawns of Indigenous languages, slowly choking out the Aboriginal plants until there's practically nothing left of them. Yet, exactly how unifying English actually is to the country is open to question, as only about 2 percent of India's population can speak, read, and write English. Another interesting contradiction.

August 7

Today, after getting my pancakes and fighting off a waiter's attempt to carry my plate, I knew that where there are pancakes, there must be syrup. When I found it, I was slightly amused by the label, which proudly proclaimed it contained 2 percent real maple syrup! Ninety-eight percent of me was disappointed, but what can you do. Eight days into the trip and I hadn't seen a single maple tree.

Today was the day I paid for my supper. I did a half-hour reading and lecture about the nature of First Nations theatre and humour, and it went over amazingly well—after two days of dry academic lectures, they appreciated a little fun, though one woman had an issue with a comment I had made about what I do: I had described my multi-genre writing career as "being married to theatre, but having many mistresses." She was offended by the term "mistress," considering it to be derogatory towards women. It was later pointed out to me that she was Dalit and that in this country mistresses were often Dalit women. While I disagreed with her interpretation of my comment, I understood where she was coming from.

The first inkling of controversy hit us today—it seems no Dalit writers had been invited to present a paper or read at the conference. Emails were flying all over the place like bats on an insect frenzy. There was talk of a protest materializing, but nothing happened. Later that night, at the official book launch of Alok's translation, it was pointed out that the author, a Dalit writer, had not been invited. Kind of awkward to say the least, though not something I haven't experienced many times before as a member of a colonized people: being talked about, rather than listened to.

August 8

It was the end of the conference and things were winding down. Janine, Alok, and I ended up having drinks with a very well-known Dalit writer who had been part of the anticipated protest. He happened to be in town and had read about the conference in the newspaper. For some reason I can't quite remember, we all ended up singing Bob Marley's "Buffalo Soldier," and discussing its political significance with respect to First Nations and Dalit issues.

As we were getting ready to go back to the hotel, one of the conference volunteers came up and asked us if we needed a ride. I asked if he was our driver and he laughed, saying, "No, I'm upper caste." As they say, you can cut the tree down, but the roots run pretty deep.

August 9

Today we got to visit the University of Hyderabad, about forty minutes outside of town, where we all lectured on various aspects of Native/Dalit literature. Got to see more of the rural landscape—lots of scrub land and big, almost artistic-looking, rock outcroppings. The countryside is unique.

I'm beginning to get a little tired of Indian food. It's absolutely no comment on the quality or taste of it, it's just that in Toronto I would have Italian food on a Monday, Chinese on Tuesday, Greek on Wednesday, Thai on Thursday, and so on. Not since growing up on the Reserve have I been used to one type of cuisine constantly. I remember being in Turin, Italy, eating some of the best Italian food on the planet, but after eight days of it finding it too rich and complicated—literally too much of a good thing. Oddly enough, I felt the need for comfort food—simple, uncomplicated sustenance that I had grown up with. On the cab ride back from the airport in Canada, I stopped in at a Swiss Chalet. Maybe this is why Native people didn't discover any other countries. We need our bannock and moose meat too much.

August 10

Today we all flew to Chennai, formally known as Madras, on the Eastern shore. Like many First Nations communities, Indian cities are changing their names back to their original, pre-colonized forms. Bombay is now

Mumbai. Calcutta is now Kolkata. Just like in Ontario where Cape Crocker is now Nawash and Gibsons is now Wahta. Curve Lake is still, however, just Curve Lake.

I was really looking forward to visiting Chennai and, specifically, the University of Madras, for a very special reason. Even before I had arrived in the country, this local university had been desperately trying to arrange for me to visit. It seems several of my plays were on the curriculum there and they wanted to produce selected scenes from Someday and Education Is Our Right with me in the audience. It was quite surreal to see what M.G. Vassenji and I had called each other one night: dot (as in the dot on their foreheads) Indians playing feather Indians. There was plenty of heart up on stage, but I couldn't help wondering how much of the back-story and the issues they understood of my plays. In a post-performance discussion, my concerns were laid to rest. The reason they had chosen to study my work was due to a sense of alienation they said they shared with the First Nations of Canada. Many of the students and teachers were Dalits and who understood the message in both plays—about government and the larger society's cruel and unfair manipulation of a powerless segment of its population. If possible, I felt even more flattered. The amazing thing is there's talk of doing a full-scale production of Someday in Chennai in February.

Still no sign of rabid elephants or tigers. My luck is holding up.

August 11
We had a really early morning today. Up at 5:15 A.M. to grab our 8:15 flight to Trivandrum, only to discover I was short a ticket. The people at the Chennai University had asked for my plane ticket to make a photocopy for administrative reasons, and had neglected to give it back. And experience has taught me airlines tend to actually want to see the ticket before letting you board the plane. After a few panicked 7:00 A.M. phone calls, the man who had access to the ticket said he had to go to his office at the university, pick it up, and bring it to the airport. All within one hour. Highly unlikely in early-morning Chennai traffic. We waited as long as we could before realizing he wasn't going to make it in time and bought another ticket at 8:00 A.M. in order to make the flight. Thus began the long, tiresome, aggravating administrative process of cancelling the first ticket and purchasing a new one, getting hold of the original ticket, cashing it in, and seeking reimbursement for the other ticket, all while we were on the road ... I sometimes believe the only true universal constants are the speed of light and administrative headaches.

Landing near the tip of southern India, we were picked up by a student whose PhD thesis was on Canadian Aboriginal oral tradition and short stories. That's normally not the kind of thing you expect to encounter in India. After doing my lecture, I got the opportunity to see the university. This was definitely one of my favourites so far. The landscaping was lush;

palm trees and luxurious ferns were everywhere. It looked truly tropical and more rural than Chennai or Delhi.

From there we drove to Kovalam, a small town on the coast of the Arabian Sea. After eleven days of being on the road and working, we were tired and wanted a little down time. So we rented rooms at a gorgeous hotel, Uday Samudra, right on the beach. It was classically tropical: crashing waves, coconuts about to fall, sandy shores … It's interesting that the beaches directly in front of the hotel are semi-public, but the hotel property itself has security guards. This seems to be because there are people patrolling the hotel beaches trying to sell a variety of objects such as sarongs, shirts, skirts, and boat trips to a nearby lagoon. The guards are there to prevent any hassling of guests on hotel grounds, but these capitalists hovered literally on the edge of the hotel property waiting for unsuspecting patrons to wander out onto the beach. And like in Delhi, they don't take no for an answer. They will follow you into the ocean trying to make a sale. I know that for a fact.

While most of the beach was taken up by private hotels, it wasn't long before we came upon a public beach where the local residents hang out. It's a stunningly beautiful landscape, lush and fertile. I can't speak for the whole country, but in this part of India, people go into the ocean fully clothed. I saw local men entering the water in long pants and shirts, and women dressed completely in their saris. And having a great time. It looked uncomfortable but again, I'm supposedly just a White tourist in this country, and am in no position to judge …

Today is my mother's birthday, so I tried calling her from one of the international phone lines that seem to dot every fourth or fifth store in every town we've been to. For some reason, they're called STDs, which makes using one to call my mother vaguely uncomfortable. However, I find out, via email that for my mother's birthday our family took her to the Buckhorn garbage dump in Ontario to watch the bears forage. Today I saw Janine chased by a water buffalo.

Kovalam is one of the oldest Christian towns in India. This is where St. Thomas, better known as Doubting Thomas, travelled to and died. I was surprised to learn that though Christianity supposedly teaches equality amongst people, that doesn't seem to be the case here. In an attempt to convert higher caste Hindus, the Church decided arbitrarily to incorporate aspects of the caste system into its doctrines. The church cemetery has a wall that physically separates the upper-caste graves from the those of the lower castes.

August 12

We are officially on vacation. No thoughts of Dalit or First Nations literature.

At night, out on the ocean's horizon, you can see the fishing boats. They leave in late afternoon, heading out towards Africa. They each have a lantern and they hug where the sky meets the ocean, the light appearing and disappearing with each successive wave. It's a very serene image, and one no doubt thousands of years old. You can sit on the beach for hours watching them fish the ocean, knowing that tomorrow, if you are so inclined, there's fresh seafood waiting, with your name on it. It's a land of plenty, with coconuts and other fruits ripening on the trees around us. The word bountiful comes to mind.

August 13
It's still monsoon season. The rain today gave me time to reflect on some of my experiences and observations. I've noticed that besides the English language, the Indian people took various English traditions, like gin and cricket to heart. Canada's Native people seem to have had more of an affinity for Scottish influences, typified by bannock, golf, and whiskey.

For something to do, we took a trip back to the tourist strip of Kovalam. There, like practically everywhere, we once again had to run the commercial gauntlet. Women on the boardwalk accosting you trying to sell fresh pineapple or bananas. Men carrying shirts and sandals, or trying to entice you into their restaurant. By chance we found a clothing store that also sold used books, in English, German, French, and Italian. Evidently that's one way backpackers make extra money passing through: selling books they've read on the road.

On the ride back, we couldn't help notice a lot of road construction. But it was the way the road was being constructed that gave me pause. Underneath huge woven palm fronds acting as protection against the rain or the sun were women sitting at the side of the road with huge chunks of what appeared to be limestone. In their hands were hammers. Their job was to turn these several-hundred-pound mini-boulders into gravel. By hand. Chipping away at them until they were reduced to rubble. All day. Every day. Another example of the multitudinous labour force available, and what people will do for work. These are basically public works projects. Much like the over-supply of waiters, it's technically a very inefficient way of doing things. But it is said to spread the wealth.

August 14
Because of the continuing rain, today was another slow day.

We asked Alok and Arun, "What do cars do when they are on a road and it becomes impassible due to an influx of cattle casually taking their time, hanging out cow-gossiping?" If you've ever seen them, they actually do have an attitude or expression that says, "Hey, I'm sacred. You can't do anything. Take a detour." Alok said that if necessary a driver will try to "persuade" them to leave the road and if worse comes to worst, will "kindly" move or direct them with a long stick.

If the situation should ever arise, I offered to "move" them using a fork and knife.

August 15

Happy Independence Day. Today is a holiday celebrating the day India got its independence from Britain. It still rained. Occasionally the sun would peek out, merely to taunt us, I'm convinced.

We finally decided to give in to the local pressure and go see the famous lagoons that half a dozen guides had tried to interest us in. Needless to say, finding a guide was not difficult. A short taxi drive later, we were languishing in a boat as we were given a three-hour tour of this island—population 4,000. Gorgeous trees, kids playing in the water while some adults fished. We visited a community where they make coconut rope. Some poisonous avocado-looking fruit trees were pointed out to us. We passed a shrine to Krishna and sometime later a Christian church, but our guide proudly informed us that the island had no "bin Ladens," meaning no Muslims. Interesting choice of words.

At the end of the trip things got a little tension-filled. The guide had promised us a two-hour boat trip, but he had taken his time and as a result we had been out cruising for an hour longer. For this, he demanded we pay triple the rate. A potentially nasty confrontation was brewing as Alok argued with the man, saying they had agreed on a fixed price. Again we got the feeling it was another game of "fleece the tourists." After some discussion, a compromise was reached and we called it a day. Back at the hotel, due to the presence of one of India's larger Christian populations, we got into a discussion of, "What would Jesus do?" in regards to the situation with the boatman. But being primarily a Hindu country, the conversation quickly turned to, "What would Shiva do?" in answer to which I was informed, "Probably burn everything to the ground, Shiva being their god of Destruction. In the end I thought, "What would Nanabush do?" Probably order room service, charge it to somebody else's room, then go off and have some sex. Sometimes I really like being Native ... It's our last full day in this paradise.

August 16

Today we flew back to Delhi on the last leg of the journey. Once there we checked into the Claridges Hotel, yet another five-star hotel modelled on, and catering to, the British elite. How I ended up here I'll never know. I am beginning to feel spoiled, and it's not just me. Already Janine is forgetting how to open her own doors—not good in an Equity officer. That night, I decide to have a tenderloin burger, my first in three weeks, in an attempt to start the re-acclimatization process with North America. Also had some domestic Indian wine. Both were divine.

Up in the hotel room, we watched some of the Olympics. In this era of political correctness, I sometimes forget how we are all taught to be uncomfortable around certain word usages. Little did I think this would be a factor in watching a badminton match in India. As per usual, the local

station was showing only the matches that featured their country's participants, and we kept doing mental double takes every time the announcer
would say something like "Good shot for the Indian." "Ooh, the Indian
just wasn't fast enough there." Or "The Indian went to the ground for that
one, and is still there."

August 17

Today was our last full day in India and there was still much to do and
things to buy. We went to a couple of reputable emporiums and eventually
found ourselves at Connaught Place where, in the name of culinary and
cultural experimentation, we decided to see what a Delhi McDonald's
looked like—just another story to tell the family. As expected, no such
animal as beef there. In fact, I remembered a controversy that made the
news back in Canada some years ago, about the rumour McDonald's was
cooking its fries in beef tallow, something the faithful Hindus in Canada
found severely objectionable. They did however have something called a
McAloo Tika burger … essentially a spicy potato burger. This reminded me
of the famous "Royale with Cheese" monologue in *Pulp Fiction*. On our way
out of the restaurant, Janine was still working on her fries and Coke when
this little girl immediately appeared out of nowhere, miming a hungry,
eating action. Janine, always a soft touch, readily gave up her fries to the
child, which must have seemed to the locals like she'd turned on the
starting lights at the Indianapolis 500—a woman instantly grabbed her
Coke and disappeared, leaving a very surprised and empty-handed Janine
standing on the sidewalk.

Later, we stopped off for some margaritas in a Mexican restaurant called
Rodeo. It was truly surreal. South Asians, dressed in pseudo-cowboy/
Mexican outfits, including cowboy hats, in what appeared to be a Western-
themed room, making tacos. For those familiar with the famous Buffy
Sainte-Marie song, they were literally "Indian Cowboys in the Rodeo."
There was even a moth-eaten medicine wheel/mandala in the showcase
beside our table. Leaving this theme-restaurant was also my last opportunity to see an unfortunate and darker aspect of Indian society—beggars
and, more specifically, lame, crippled, or, the more politically correct term
would be disabled, ones, though I'm not sure if that term is used all that
frequently in this country. Adults and kids, many with withered limbs,
jostled for our attention and rupees. Rohinton Mistry's book *A Fine Balance*
lurked somewhere in the back of my consciousness.

August 18

We left today. The Mukherjees stayed behind to tend to various family
concerns. They were not due back until the beginning of the university
semester. Janine was exceedingly reluctant to leave. India had become a
special place for her and even though this was her second trip to the far-

off land, the country had firmly cemented itself in her heart. If India's monsoon season needed another dark cloud, there it was, hanging over Janine. But it was time to go home. She had a job and some credit card bills to pay off, and I had a book launch in a few days in Toronto.

The plane left India at 10:00 that night. From my window seat, though it was dark, I was sure I could see a rabid elephant chasing the plane as we took off.

I came back as an Indian who'd actually been to India.

WASHINGTON AND THE MUSEUM

Toronto and Washington, DC, have surprisingly much in common. Both cities have muddy, dirty rivers; ours being the Don (and let's not forget the Humber); and theirs being the Potomac. Theirs is bigger. Each city has its own large phallic symbol looking down benignly over the city—the CN Tower and the Washington Monument. Ours is bigger (not that it matters, I'm told). And as with any proper Freudian phallic symbol, there is an equally large mammary symbol close by—the SkyDome and the Capitol Building. I don't know which is bigger, but ours is large and flat while theirs is more conical and pointy in shape. Again not that it matters. And finally, as Manifest Destiny would dictate, both are obviously of a White tint, or perhaps off-white would be the more accurate description.

Washington also has something we don't have. It now has a museum dedicated to Indigenous people. And what's even better, they threw a large party to celebrate its opening. On September 21, the Smithsonian National Museum of the American Indian opened with a bang. Anybody who was anybody in the First Nations community (American, Canadian, Mexican—contrary to what the official title may say, borders were irrelevant) was there to celebrate. Over 1,800 people from several dozen Nations/tribes and assorted Aboriginal organizations across Turtle Island participated in the grand entry, a parade-like procession that took at least two hours to make its way to the stage. It was reported that over 80,000 people were there in what is called the "Mall" to observe the opening day festivities.

The museum building itself has several of its own Canadian connections. Originally designed by world-renowned Métis architect Douglas Cardinal, its distinctively rounded and smooth surface reminded everybody of the Cardinal-designed Museum of Civilization in Ottawa. Mired in controversy, Cardinal and the Smithsonian parted ways in disagreement just before construction of the actual museum began. Another architectural firm was hired to complete the construction based on his original design. But bad blood still exists between the two parties, and he was not there to bask in the glory of the completed monumental edifice.

Briefly, a week or so before the opening, emails began flying across the Internet talking about a possible boycott of the museum opening, because of the disrespect shown Douglas Cardinal. Calls for letters of protest were heard but apparently not heeded. The whole thing was reminiscent of a similar call concerning the Mohegan Sun Casino, located on the Mohegan Reservation in Connecticut. Last year, Tim McGraw was performing at the casino and several Native organizations tried to orchestrate a boycott of the performance. Evidently, some of the more politically correct Native people were still annoyed by a song he released a good number of years ago titled

"Indian Outlaw." It goes something like, "You can find me in my wigwam, I'll be beatin' on my tom-tom, pull out the pipe and smoke you some. Hey and pass it around. I'm an Indian outlaw, half Cherokee-Chocktaw. My baby, she's a Chippawa. She's one of a kind." However, I'm told the show was pretty packed.

To celebrate the official opening of the museum, organizers planned a week-long series of cultural and artistic events showcasing the continent's Aboriginal people. Canadian Cree funny man Don Burnstick, American comedy icon Charlie Hill, and I started the week off with an evening of Native comedy at, of all places, the famous Kennedy Center. Despite two shows with standing room only, the real fun was being stuck in a car for thirty minutes with the both of them in a traffic jam on our way to the show. The one-liners were flying fast and furious and our poor driver didn't know what was going on.

The following day brought the aforementioned Native Nations procession, and for the next six days, Washington was treated to an exhilarating festival of Native talent. Oneida singer Joanne Shenandoah sang in her folk-tinged style on the mainstage, and practically every performance ended with an impromptu round dance in the audience. Buffy Sainte-Marie, the St. Laurent Métis Dancers, the Six Nations Singers (traditional Iroquois singers from down near Brantford way), War Party (a hip-hop rap group from Hobbema, Alberta), and Pappy Johns Band with Murray Porter all represented Canada well.

Ulali, Rita Coolidge, Ledward Ka'apana (from Hawaii), Suya (from Brazil), Dene' Tah Navajo Dancers (from Arizona) and Pamyua—the best damn Alaskan Inuit/Yup'ik jazz-blues fusion band (including an Australian didgeridoo) you would hear that week, were other well-travelled participants in the festivities. We were all a little concerned watching the Suurimmaanitchuat Dance Group, an Inupiat group from northern Alaska, dancing in full regalia (meaning heavy clothing) in eighty-seven-degree weather.

But perhaps the best event of the festival happened in a place where only a precious few got the chance to watch and participate. An ancient, or some would say contemporary, social event known as a 49er that spontaneously erupted one evening back at the hotel, in one of the conference rooms. A 49er is a social event where people sing culturally based songs, other people join in, dance, or just listen. You can't have a pow wow without having a 49er after the sun goes down. And it now seems like you can't have a museum opening without one either. At this particular one, for instance, a traditional Iroquois water drum group sang social songs while people from around North America danced. People from the Four Directions took turns entertaining and sharing, in a much more intimate setting. It was the kind of magic you can't plan for.

The museum itself was very interesting. It's no secret that Native people have a strained relationship with most museums. They're sometimes perceived as a future mortuary for our ancestors and there was some concern about how this particular museum would represent Native people. But it seems its mandate is quite different. Most of the curators are Native. The focus seems to be on today's Native people, not on hundred-year-old totem poles or boxes of bones—living Indians are more interesting than dead ones at the Smithsonian National Museum of the American Indian, it seems. Profiles of several different contemporary Native communities across the Americas were highlighted, including Kahnawake, Igloolik, and several Métis communities out west.

And it seemed fitting that on my final day in Washington I was invited, along with a host of other Canadians, to the Canadian Embassy for a wine and cheese party celebrating the opening of a Native art show located on the premises. But there was more than wine and cheese there—they had lovely "Canadian" munchies consisting of caribou and muskox tenderloin. As a loyal Canadian, I can't recall ever finding that at my local Loblaws. It was at the embassy that I heard the best Canadian joke from an American: A seal pup walks into a bar. He looks at the drink menu trying to decide. The bartender gets a little frustrated and says to the seal pup, "Hey, what do you want to drink?" The seal pup puts the drink menu down and says, "I don't know yet. Anything but a Canadian Club."

As the night drew to a close and we were all leaving the Embassy, I noticed a group of Native people hanging around the front of the museum building. There, jutting out, part of the structure seemed to be an intentionally constructed mini-amphitheatre—a circular, concrete, porch-like structure. The roof was circular, creating a unique echoing effect. One of the noted Aboriginal artists being honoured, a gentleman named Ahmoo Angeconeb, took out his hand drum and began to drum out and sing. One by one, two dozen or more people started to round dance, with him in the centre. This went on for about fifteen minutes, the dancers holding hands, feet moving side by side, bellies stuffed with blueberry bannock and muskox tenderloin. Then eventually the song ended, as all songs must, and we all went home. They just don't hold museum openings like that anymore.

COMRADES IN ARMS

On July 12, 2004, the Ontario government opened an official inquiry into the death of Native protester Dudley George. Dudley was an unassuming Ojibway man who was better with a joke than with a political manifesto. From what I understand, he was not the type of man who made a regular habit of upsetting the status quo or rocking the political boat. He was more interested in visiting with his family than having guns pointed at him. That's easy to understand. But as the old adage goes, sometimes you just gotta do what you gotta do. And it killed him.

It was nearly nine years ago when the unarmed Kettle Point First Nations resident came face to face with the Ontario Provincial Police at Ipperwash, a small park on the shores of Lake Huron. He had been there in support of his community's attempt to convince the authorities to return land appropriated by the government during World War II to his community. The demonstration was peaceful. Dudley was peaceful. The morning everything happened was peaceful. A few days later, his funeral was peaceful.

And the end result was one less living Native protester to annoy the authorities.

As the long-anticipated inquiry approached, I couldn't help pondering this man's brief existence. I never met him. Never met the family. I've never even been to Kettle and Stony Points. But there was something achingly familiar about the whole situation—the scenario had a familiar ring of sadness about it. There's something ominous about a person who becomes more famous in death than in life. This was a person who, if not for the accuracy of a trained OPP sniper, probably would have been more than content to live in relative obscurity. That's how I have always thought of Anne Frank.

On the one hand, they are strikingly dissimilar in age, race, geography, and cause of death. Yet on the other hand, it occurrs to me, they are sacred kin. People in faraway places decided whether they lived or died without having even met them. And, it could be said, directly and indirectly, they died because of their race. If Anne Frank had not perished in a German concentration camp, would she still be a household name today? Hard to say, but highly unlikely. A good friend of mine praised the quality of the writing in her diary, but when asked if Anne Frank had lived, would the diary still be recommended reading in many school curriculums, she couldn't say. At some level, it was Anne Frank's death that made her diary so memorable. From her own account, she was a very ordinary girl with ordinary aspirations thrust onto centre stage by actions above and beyond her understanding and control. In fact, it was her very ability to remain a "typical" young girl in an atypical situation that lies at the very heart of her fame.

Same with Dudley. In reading *One Dead Indian* by Peter Edwards, I get the distinct impression Dudley George was not meant for greatness. I do not say this to be malicious or cruel. Dudley seemed to be one of the thousands upon thousands of guys who were born on the Reserve, and were content to spend their lives being good sons, brothers, husbands, and fathers. Those were probably the only rewards he was looking for in life. Instead, his name has become a rallying cry for busloads of social and political activists. And a royal pain in the ass for Mike Harris, the former Ontario premier, on whose watch Dudley inconveniently chose to end his days. Many claim the blood from the OPP bullet splashed onto his hands—thus one of the reasons for the inquiry.

Dudley George and Anne Frank, two names you don't normally expect to see linked together. Yet Dudley George and Anne Frank's place in history came not from how they lived, but how they died. Both, I'm sure, would have been content to live to a ripe old age in anonymity, with bundles of grandkids fighting for their attention. Instead, their names have become synonymous with great tragedies and injustices. It's also ironic that both their deaths, over fifty years apart, have their roots in government policies from the Second World War.

Repercussions of another recent war come to mind, like the 1970 massacre at Kent State University in Ohio, where multitudes of unarmed students protesting the Vietnam War came face to face with the National Guard. This confrontation resulted in four fewer people to send to Vietnam. They were too busy being dead. Except this time it was White people killing White people. Maybe that's why nobody remembers their names. They weren't "oppressed" enough.

Postscript

The official inquiry came and went with some impact. Mr. Justice Sidney Linden reported it was his belief that then-Premier Mike Harris misled the provincial legislature when he denied telling high-level police and government officials, "I want the fucking Indians out of the park." He also dismissed the denial of the former minister of natural resources, Chris Hodgson, who was accused of telling a government meeting to "get the fucking Indians out of my park." Notice a theme here?

"I have found that both the former premier and minister of natural resources made racist comments," Linden added. While I have great respect for people of Sidney Linden's achievements, education, and position, I can't help but say, "Duh!"

Another positive thing that came out of the Ipperwash Inquiry was the recommendation that the Stony Point First Nation should get their land back with compensation. The good news is the people of Stony Point did get their land back. But at what price?

Still, we can only hope Dudley George didn't die in vain. He wasn't the first "fucking Indian" to die for his land. We can only hope he will be the last.

AN OJIBWAY DOWN UNDER

Australia is a gorgeous and fascinating continent. There is no other place like it. In the early part of this year I had the unique opportunity to visit there and spend some time in the Brisbane area on the eastern coast. Occasionally I would look northeast and know that somewhere off in that direction, several thousand miles away, was the land we Native people call Turtle Island, but geographers and cartographers prefer to call North America. The Land Down Under had beckoned to me, as both an artist and as a person of Indigenous ancestry. And who am I to say no to a good beckoning? So I decided to explore what this country had to offer, and this is my abbreviated journal, a sort of First Nations hitchhiker's guide to Australia.

January 3
Not the best beginning to a life-changing journey. I get to the airport to check in and am asked, "Where's your travel visa? You need one to enter Australia." Air Canada had neglected to tell me that when they booked my ticket. The ticket agent at the airport said that we should be able to apply, then and there, over the Internet. But he was unable to give me anything concrete, like a piece of paper. He said, and I quote, "Hopefully it will be there in the computer when you arrive." It was the word "hopefully" that left me uncomfortable. So I spent the next twenty hours on the plane, fearful that the moment I stepped off the plane, there would be no visa and I would be refused entry. I had visions of being deported back another twenty hours to Canada, and didn't sleep easy on that flight.

January 5
Lost a whole day somewhere over the Pacific. I think it was when they served what appeared to be a breakfast omelette on the plane. Slept maybe four hours during the entire trip. Finally landed in Sydney and was incredibly relieved to find out there was indeed a travel visa with my name on it in the computer. In my love/hate relationship with computers, this was definitely a love day.

Had to take a shuttle from the international to the domestic airport to get to Brisbane. It was hot, twenty-six degrees in fact. Shorts and a t-shirt might have been a better fashion choice than my winter coat. On the shuttle, I noticed a small canal of water and a row of trees running parallel to the road, and I couldn't help but imagine there were platypuses in the water and koalas in the trees. Then I realized tourists to Canada probably think their own versions of the same thing: are there any beavers in Toronto's Don River, or any polar bears in Vancouver's Stanley Park?

Flew the final leg of the journey to Brisbane, and felt remarkably well and coherent for someone who'd been awake for roughly thirty-two hours altogether. If only the voices in my head weren't screaming so loud. At the airport I was picked up by Nadine Macdonald, the artistic director of Kooemba Jdarra, the Aboriginal theatre company I'd travelled all this way to work with. A lovely and smart woman, she had arranged for me to stay in a great apartment in the arts building where Kooemba's office is located. It was a spacious, air-conditioned studio space—actually better than my place in Toronto. It was here I saw the first Australian interpretation of North American Aboriginal life. On a television commercial, a woman is putting lipstick on. She changes her mind and starts drawing lines horizontally under her eyes, like war paint. She then starts dancing around, whooping it up with that familiar rhythmic palm-of-her-hand-over-her-mouth gesture from 1940s Westerns. The tag line "Release your hidden warrior!" is for a jewellery store.

The first thing I learn about Australia's Indigenous people? An Aboriginal who has been assimilated into the dominant culture is called a coconut— black on the outside, white on the inside. Yet in the Samoan culture, it can mean a warrior, because those nuts are so tough and hard to crack. Either way, the expression can get you in a fight. *Australian Idol* had just finished, and the winner was an Aboriginal woman named Casey Donovan. Everybody was quite proud of her achievement and was bragging about her. It suddenly reminded me that when I came through Australian customs, they went through my luggage looking for eggs and other farm products, ostensibly to protect their unique Australian ecosystem. As delightful as Casey's win was, I thought the government should have spent some of that prophylactic energy preventing shows like *Australian Idol* from spreading into their country like a foreign plague.

However, I was not surprised to learn Casey Donovan was actively encouraged not to mention her Aboriginal heritage, and it was certainly downplayed in the publicity, in the belief that it might limit the "universality" of her popularity.

January 6
Nadine gave me six scripts by local Aboriginal writers (they hate being called Aborigines) to familiarize myself with their work. Kooemba Jdarra is one of the leading Australian Aboriginal theatre companies, and the only one in Brisbane. Their name means "good ground, sweet earth," and they are at the forefront of Indigenous theatre. They were formed in 1993 as a response to the United Nations International Year for Indigenous People. One of the scripts given to me was about the "Stolen Children," generations of Aboriginal children that were taken away by the state and raised in missions to be domestics for the White population. I found it very reminiscent of the residential school issues we are facing in Canada—in

fact, the similarities gave me the willies: a legacy of abuse, deculturalization, etc. Most people would be familiar with the Australian mission system through the popular movie *Rabbit-Proof Fence*, but I was very surprised to learn most Aboriginals didn't quite care for the movie. They felt the settlement the kids came from was too tidy, the children seemed too clean and well fed, and the White officials just a little too gentle and concerned. I guess their reaction was similar to the mixed feelings most North American Native people have about the film *Dances with Wolves*.

Luckily the Australian "Stolen Children" system came to an end around 1969, when Aboriginals were finally recognized by their government as being human beings and given the right to vote. Prior to this, they had been the responsibility of the Federal Department of Flora and Fauna. They were either plants or animals. Sometime later, the government launched a commission to investigate those "Stolen Generations." Today, several years later, not one of the recommendations put forth by the commission to redress the harm and deal with the many issues the system had raised has yet been adopted. Speaking as a Canadian Aboriginal, this all sounds suspiciously familiar.

To welcome me to their lovely country, my hosts took me out for a social evening—just me and a bunch of Aboriginal artists. That night I noticed two things. In one corner of the bar, bolted on the wall, was a small brass plaque. It read "Jodie's Corner"—in memory of a local woman who was killed, along with a lot of other vacationing Australians, in the 2002 bombing in Bali. The second unsettling surprise occurred when I looked up into the wide-open Australian sky, where I saw huge black things flying across the stars. I'm talking huge. At first it freaked me out because I still hadn't recovered fully from the flight. But these large, dark, menacing images turned out to be fruit bats, with wing-spans of four or five feet! It all looked very eerie, especially to a weary Canadian.

January 7

I got up this morning and looked out my window to check the weather. It was then that I noticed, just below my fifth-storey apartment, a huge sign painted on the side of the next building over, evidently advertizing the company located there. It was called Colour Chiefs Digital Imaging. The reason I noticed it was its twelve-foot logo: a huge Indian chief in profile, wearing a stereotypical Sioux headdress, with feathers of different shades radiating out dramatically. I couldn't help but find it interesting how North American Native people are used worldwide to advertise goods and services. Are we the only race of people, other than maybe the Inuit, that can be recognized and utilized any place in the world in advertisements? I don't think I've ever seen any advertising utilizing Australian Aboriginals, or bushmen of the Kalahari, or Laplanders in North America or Europe. I guess there's very little that's marketable, and therefore internationally interesting, about them. I guess that's a good thing. I'd hate to see an Australian Aboriginal in a Canadian magazine selling weekends in Whistler.

Today I discovered that brothels/bordellos are legal in Queensland. Unfortunately, the Canada Council Arts Grant I was given didn't include per diem for conducting research in this exotic cultural niche. Though oddly enough, right next door to such an establishment was a bar that advertised "Jugs for $5.00." Nothing like a good price war.

Today's interesting Aboriginal fact: the term "Minnehaha," a name North Americans are familiar with from the famous poem "Hiawatha," translates in the local dialect as vagina. *The Minnehaha Monologues.* One wonders if Henry Wadsworth Longfellow had this in mind when he wrote his famous poem.

January 8

Had a puzzling metaphorical wake-up call this morning. But in order to understand the irony of the situation, I have to give you some background. There is a big movement in Australia to encourage its citizenry to utilize as many local and indigenous plants in landscaping as possible. Over the centuries, the British and other immigrants have brought over a lot of their own country's plant life to make the country more familiar and homey for themselves. As a result, some local species are threatened. So, special nurseries have been set up to grow and sell indigenous flora—called "native nurseries" because they carry native plants. So there I am, at about 7:30 in the morning, listening to the radio, when all of a sudden I hear a blaring, obnoxious radio commercial come on—a guy with a thick Australian accent is practically screaming out at me: "Natives?! You want Natives?! We've got thousands of Natives. Just come on down!!" My first semi-conscious reaction, as a Native Canadian was: "Nobody told me! Where are my pants? I'll be right there." It was a few moments before I realized he was talking flora, not fauna.

Visited North Stradbroke Island today with some people from Kooemba's board of directors. It's a gorgeous island, with three communities on it (one Aboriginal). Saw dolphins, sea turtles, manta rays, and echidnas—my first taste of Australian wildlife (except for those freaky bats the other night). We came upon a plaque commemorating Captain Cook's landing on the island in 1770, "Proudly erected in 1970 by the local inhabitants," which prompted Avril, one of the Aboriginal board members to mumble to herself, "Not the local inhabitants we know." It reminded me of all the celebrations in Newfoundland and Labrador in 1997 to celebrate the 500th anniversary of the landing of John Cabot, which elicited more than a few similar disgruntled Native reactions.

Heading up to the bar, located on a ledge overlooking the beach, I was introduced to some locals, and that's where the theory of six degrees of separation was given an Indigenous touch. Amongst North American Native people, it's called the two teepees of separation. At any gathering of First

Nations people, you are bound to have relatives, friends, former or current partners in common. Up until then, I wasn't aware Australia was to become a third teepee. This Aboriginal man had lived in Ontario's Six Nations Reserve for six months with a woman I used to know, and we caught up on the latest Reserve gossip over a beer.

When I finally got back to my apartment, I was delighted to find out that I had found a cure for the jet lag and insomnia that had been plaguing me since I arrived. It's called sunstroke. I discovered this when I woke up in the morning, at a reasonable hour, refreshed from a night of uninterrupted sleep ... half-way between the door and the bed. On the floor.

Today's interesting Aboriginal fact: depending where you are in the country, the Aboriginals tend to call themselves either Kooris or Murris.

January 9

Day one of sunburn—the bane of every travelling Canadian, regardless of heritage. Even my hair hurt. That huge hole in the ozone layer, directly overhead down here, might have something to do with it. Later that day I saw an ad on television stating Australia has the highest rates of skin cancer. Lovely.

So I spent the day recovering, and getting more familiar with Australian television. I was in the middle of a documentary on Jewish ritual and religion when, lo and behold, there was Toronto's own master playwright, Jason Sherman, talking about his own perception of ritual. At least he wasn't dancing around in a yarmulke trying to sell jewellery.

The kitchen unit in my apartment was a little under-equipped, so I went shopping. I found myself in the Australian equivalent of a dollar store looking for a spatula, and I found one, right next to a rack of dreamcatchers. Two whole racks of them actually. All with tags saying, "Made in China." I stood there for a few minutes looking at them, wondering what the Chinese labourers thought of these strange circular webbed objects they were making by the ton. Somehow I doubt making these things in a sweatshop for pennies a day represents a form of Chinese spirituality. On inquiry, I found out that the inukshuks from Taiwan were scheduled to arrive the following week.

January 10

Today seemed to be my day of learning about Canada from Australian television. During the morning show on one of the network channels, there was an eight-minute piece on cottaging in the Muskokas! "Australians go to the beach to get away. Canadians go to a place they call Cottage Country. A place they call the Muskokas." Personally, I prefer the beach—fewer mosquitoes and the water's warmer. Around lunch time, I turned on the television and there before me was the smiling face of Cree actor Gordon Tootoosis, in a documentary about the Prairie Chief Poundmaker. As an added bonus, Tom Jackson was narrating it. A little slice of home, albeit about a place several thousand miles from where I actually live. It was during this show I saw another commercial with a suited man in a Plains headdress dancing around his dirty car, making that familiar "whooping" sound with his hand over his mouth. He was trying to make it rain—it was an ad for a car wash.

Today's interesting Australian Aboriginal fact: Aboriginals (Murris) down here refer to each other as "blackfellas." Even the women. Now there's a dandy racism/sexism discussion waiting to happen.

January 11

Went to the Brisbane Museum today for a behind-the-scenes tour of the place by one of the Murri curators. As part of an effort by the board of directors, the museum hired several Murris to develop and install exhibits about their people. But they had been instructed, unofficially of course, "Don't do any exhibits that might be considered confrontational or controversial—like nothing about the Stolen Generation/Children, for instance." Needless to say, the Murri curators were not pleased. They felt their hands were tied. Regardless, it was fascinating. I saw thousands—and I'm not exaggerating—and thousands of boomerangs, filed in endless rows, of every size, shape, and design you could imagine. More than I could imagine, and I have a very good imagination. Some had that wide "V" shape we all know, while others only had a slight curve, almost a straight piece of painted wood.

While I felt a certain kinship with the Koori of this country, it was becoming increasingly obvious that there were several noticeable differences between our people. And it was looking increasingly unlikely to me that a Canadian Native person could live here. The first and most obvious reason is that there is no such animal as baloney here. It is nonexistent. Also, when I was doing a reading from one of my books, a Koori woman put up her hand to ask me what Kraft Dinner was. I went three weeks without either ... it must have been all my White blood that allowed me to survive.

January 12

Today I went to the local museum where I saw a small exhibit of Murri art. The longer I stay in this country, the more obvious it becomes how each region has its own style of art, much like Native art does in Canada (West Coast, Inuit, Eastern Woodlands, etc.). Some Murri artists prefer the intricate use of overlapping imagery, while others like utilizing sequential dots to illustrate their ideas. Because a lot of the paintings are created with the canvases spread out on the ground, many of them have sand and various bits of things like grass and fibres scattered over them. Some even have paw prints from dogs on them.

I spent the evening watching the reality show *Outback Jack* with Nadine and her husband, Philip. I had heard about it when it aired in North America several months earlier, but I hadn't watched it. For obvious reasons, it was quite popular here. It's a cross between *Crocodile Dundee* and *The Bachelorette*. A hunky outdoorsman takes a bunch of city women into the outback to survive with him and, one by one, they are voted off. But according to Nadine, Jack isn't all that outdoorsy. Evidently, the gossip is he's a preppy, from a private school. After seeing Outback Jack without his shirt on, I came to the conclusion that there must be fully equipped gyms out there in the bush. Most Aussies find the show outrageously funny.

January 13

Two kookaburras nearby started their loud wake-up call at about 6:00 this morning. As much as I like to support and encourage local flora and fauna, I was not pleased. However, I did get my chuckle later in the day. I got an email from a friend in Edmonton, who sent me the Environment Canada report for that Albertan city, where it was a balmy minus forty. It's plus thirty in Brisbane. When I read the report aloud to the Kooemba office staff, it was the first time I saw a collective shiver amongst a group of Aboriginals. "How can you live in an environment like that?" they asked. I explained the concept of a double-double, an homage to the great god Tim Horton, to keep warm. They were just as bemused and intrigued by the concept of plugging in your car at night.

During a meeting with the company's board of directors, I discovered that the terms half-breed, mixed blood, and half-caste are all considered very naughty, if not downright inappropriate words. Using them is almost like swearing. I write a lot about identity, and my experiences as somebody of both Native and non-Native blood, and I was shocked and a little embarrassed to discover that every time I used either mixed blood or half-breed, the people I was talking to became uncomfortable. This aversion to certain figures of speech is derived from the government keeping records of the Indigenous people, and its fondness for classifying them. So when you were listed as a half-breed or half-caste by the government, it meant you were polluted. They just about had a fit when I told them about Maria Campbell's biography *Halfbreed*. "She willingly calls herself that?!" Murri philosophy says that either you are something, or you aren't. Maybe I have something to learn from them.

January 14

First Murri fact of the day: at time of contact, it was estimated that there were approximately 600 languages and dialects spoken in Australia. Today, about 200 can still be heard with varying levels of competency, and at least fifty are still spoken well.

Second Murri fact of the day: the Indigenous population can be classified between Fresh-Water people, Salt-Water people, and Desert people.

Third Murri fact of the day: they love country music.

Today I saw the flags for the Torres Strait Islanders (a series of islands just north of the mainland) and the Aboriginals of Australia. They are quite different. In the TSI one, there is a large white section in the middle of the flag that represents the Christian influence on the islands. This was considered a positive influence, because the Islanders have melded that religion to suit the particular needs of their island culture, not the other way around. On the other hand, the Aboriginal flag reflects the earth, the people on it, and the sun shining down on them.

January 15

Today I got to see a little more of the country than just the Brisbane area. Nadine invited me and a few friends up to her parents' house in Gympie, about a hundred or so kilometres north, along the Sunshine Coast. We were going from a temperate climate to a more tropical, rainforest one, the difference becoming gradually more obvious. Along the way, we stopped at Aussieworld, a tacky tourist spot with your typical selection of kitsch. Over one store there was a sign that said, "Souvenirs and Aborigine Outlet." "Excellent," I said—I was hoping to get my mother some cheap Aborigines.

Finally we arrived in Gympie. It was a lovely house, reflecting the gracious warmth of Nadine's parents. And, if you can believe it, in their very back yard I saw my first kangaroos! Evidently a pack of them hangs around the area and they popped in for a visit. I felt like an official Australian, until that night at the barbecue, when they put some kangaroo steaks on—presumably not cut from the ones I had seen earlier. I looked deep into my Indigenous heritage to find that fondness for wild, bouncing meat, but alas, I groped in vain, and finally passed on that unique opportunity. That night, as we sat watching the sun set, drinking our beer—contrary to market belief, in all the time I was there, I never saw one person drink a Foster's; everybody drinks the local favourite, called XXXX (Four X)—I heard the kookaburra sing. According to legend, whenever you hear a kookaburra sing, it means somebody just got pregnant. I can safely say of that night though, "Hey man, it wasn't me."

Interesting Murri fact of the day: it is commonly believed here that South Africa's apartheid system was directly derived from Queensland's treatment of Aboriginals. But I've also heard the theory that it came from Canada's treatment of Native people. I must remember to ask a South African this question at my earliest opportunity.

January 16

Woke up to the sound of parrots just outside my window. I swear to god the aural atmosphere sounded like a *Tarzan* movie. We spent the day in the pool, sunning ourselves and gossiping about Indigenous theatre and film all over the world. I was surprised and delighted to find out that producers in New Zealand, in an attempt to cash in on all the tourism derived from *Xena* and *The Lord of the Rings*, are planning to turn *Whalerider* into a musical play. I was dismayed, however, to find out that some other producers want to do the same to *Once Were Warriors*. Could it only be me? I'm having great difficulty imagining that film as a musical. What kind of ballad do you sing during the rape of a thirteen-year-old girl?

The scariest part of my trip happened today. It was hot, nothing much to do, so everybody stayed inside and watched cricket on television. Five hours of it. And now ... gulp ... I actually believe I understand the game. It's quite simple really ...

January 17
Had another media flashback today. Turned on the television this morning and saw my good friend Cree actor Billy Merasty as Black Hawk in a dramatized documentary. Then it occurred to me, I had yet to see any Murris on television. I'm told, "If it isn't a documentary where they stand around in a loincloth waving a boomerang, there's not much work for Murri actors." And for what seemed the ten thousandth time, I heard that familiar phrase: "You guys over there are a thousand years ahead of us here in Australia." They mean in regards to politics, representation, public acceptance, media visibility, public relations, etc. The fact we have our own Native television cable network in Canada seems awesome to them.

Read some more of their plays. They read like the early years of Canadian Native theatre: angry, accusatory, stories of oppression and survival, but excellent writing.

January 18
Went for coffee at the local café today. The owner told me that Americans have put together some kind of travel kit to disguise themselves as Canadians when they are on the road. Evidently, worldwide, Canadians are better liked than Americans, and are less of a target. And since many of us speak and look roughly the same, the camouflage works. So, as a proud Canadian, I have devised a way of weeding out fake Canadians. They must be able to answer correctly three of the four following questions:
1. What was the last year the Toronto Maple Leafs won the Stanley Cup?
2. Who was René Simard?
3. What is the generally accepted approximate ratio of maple sap to maple syrup?
4. Where did *The Beachcombers* television series take place?

January 19

Spent the morning watching the Australian Open tennis match on television when I heard the most bizarre comment. One of the announcers said during the highlight reel that, much to everyone's surprise, a particular top-seeded player who lost a match was "scalped" today. Luckily, I was out of town.

A certain sense of universality occurred to me when I learned about an incident on Palm Island that had happened about a month before. It seems a young Murri man was arrested for drunk and disorderly conduct or something like that, and he hanged himself that night. Only there were a few problems with that story. Evidently he had several broken bones and a ruptured spleen and liver. The police said it came from falling down a flight of stairs. There's also word that the man was too drunk to walk, let alone manage to hang himself. And supposedly there were witnesses in other cells who saw the assault on him. So, a little annoyed, the local community of Palm Island rioted, attacked the local police station, and burned it down. And as is usually the case, the media covered the riot, not the inciting incident. This sense of the universality of the human condition was reinforced when I also discovered that, fairly recently, an Aboriginal boy was attacked by several non-Aboriginal men, had a rope wrapped around him, and was dragged some distance by a truck while being beaten with a stick. It went under-reported because of all the news coverage concerning the Indian Ocean tsunami disaster. The spirit of Neil Stonechild must have been on a couple of walkabouts.

This evening, as part of my grant, I lectured to about twenty interested individuals about the nature of First Nations humour, and I am happy to say the lecture went well. The anatomical similarities of each of our funny bones abounded. All the Murris got the Indian jokes, and I even got a few of the Murri jokes.

January 20

Today the Aboriginal Centre for the Performing Arts beckoned. It's a fabulous educational institution that provides a three-year program where Murri students learn all three disciplines; dance, music, and theatre. In fact, one of their recent graduates just made it into the prestigious Australian Academy of Drama (*alma mater* of Cate Blanchett and Mel Gibson).

Had my second lecture this evening, this time on the history of Native theatre in Canada. It went very nicely, until for some reason I asked a completely out of context question: "Has anybody in this room, besides me, ever thrown a snowball?" Of the fifteen people in the room, only one had. And she had lived in London, England, for six months when they had a freak snowstorm ... That's where she threw her first and only snowball. Suddenly, it all seemed so un-Canadian to me.

January 21

As a writer of theatre for young audiences, I was taken to lunch and invited to participate in a children's theatre festival a fair ways up the coast near a place called Townsville. Asking the typical Canadian question, "How's the beach up there?" I was told: "Fine, but you'd have to watch out for jellyfish, it's their mating season. And there are sharks and crocodiles too." And they send their children up there?

And to top off a very interesting day, we all went out for a night of Murri karaoke (or as they like to call it, Murri-oke) in an Irish bar called Shamrocks. I swear it was just like being home. A lot of dark-skinned people singing country ballads and thirty-year-old rock classics. Another unique bond was forged.

January 22

Went for a walk today, down by the river that winds through Brisbane. Sitting under a tree, I saw four Murris, possibly street people, minding their own business. Hovering directly over them were three imposing White cops, waiting expectantly in a semi-circle. Without a word, the Murris started getting their things together. In the five minutes or so it took me to approach and pass them, neither party said a single word. But the message was clear.

Today was National Australian Day. But the Murri have a more ironic title for it, "Survivor Day" or "Invasion Day." Got me thinking that maybe we should think of something similar for this year's Canada Day. Except July 1 is my birthday too. Don't want it to be too much of a downer.

I decided to contribute to the local economy and went shopping as the end of my Australian sojourn slowly draws near. I bought a couple of t-shirts in a Murri-flavoured shop, and I couldn't help wondering how much of my local economic contribution will actually make it into local Murri pockets. I also visited Kumquats, "Modern dining. Native flair." It was a Native Australian restaurant that "celebrates the flavours of Australia." Some of the delicacies included smoked emu, wallaby chipolatas, wallaby salami, pepperberry crocodile and couscous, braised Tasmanian possum bomb, and my favourite, Moreton Bay bugs (this one comes with a lovely rainforest lime beurre blanc!) I also found a flyer advertising, along with a wildlife cruise, "a day of Aboriginal culture." For $49 ($29 for children), you too can experience boomerang throwing, try the didgeridoo, take in an artifacts display, go for a bush-tucker walk, learn storytelling, and visit a nudgee waterhole. And, best of all, you get a free boomerang! Who could turn down a deal like that?

January 23

I decided that today, on one of my final days in this fabulous city and country, I would take a brief walkabout of my own, ending up downtown where I saw some Murri street performers at an outdoor mall. They were dressed very scantily, and covered in body paint in what I assume was a traditional manner. They were playing the didgeridoo and, for percussion, one man was banging two boomerangs together to keep the beat. A dozen or so people listened for a few minutes, then dropped some coins on a blanket. For a moment I tried to imagine a Canadian First Nations drum group, in full pow wow regalia performing on Toronto's Queen Street or Vancouver's Granville Island. I had difficulty drawing that picture.

January 24

To say good-bye to this fair land, I made one last trip to North Stradbroke Island to deepen my tan. It rained all day. But I did find a new beach listed on the map. It was called Deadman's Beach, but I could never find anybody who had ever been there. Or come back.

January 25

Today, starting at 4:00 in the morning, I began my journey home. Twenty-two hours later I made it to my front doorstep. During my journey, I was shocked to discover I had picked up a few Australianisms that I was unaware of. I tended to say "no worries, mate" a lot. Read my first *Globe and Mail* in a while and was surprised to find Paul Martin was still our prime minister. I was equally surprised to find out Adrienne Clarkson was still our governor general. I was not surprised to learn Stephen Harper was still annoyed about practically everything.

Final Murri fact of the day: supposedly, there are about a hundred or so people of North American Native heritage living in or around the Brisbane area. And I bet they all come from that Native nursery place.

THE KIND OF IMPORTS OUR GOVERNMENTS NEED

It almost makes you believe there's hope. And of all places, it's coming from Down Under. Evidently there's more then just excellent shiraz and those slick oily jackets that come from there.

I was in Australia last summer attending the Australian National Playwright's Conference (ANPC) when I observed something very unusual during the opening festivities. Dr. Chris Mead, the curator (similar to the artistic director of the event), opened the conference with a simple acknowledgement. Before anything else began, he said, "We would like to acknowledge the traditional owners of this land, the Awabakal people who were the custodians of this land until colonization." Afterwards, practically everybody of importance had a go at thanking the traditional owners; the chair of the conference, the mayor of Newcastle (where the conference was held), and the local member of the state government. How progressive, I thought.

It made me think of my own country called Canada whose citizens often pat themselves on the back for Canada's relationship with its First Nations. Oh sure, people say it could always be better I suppose. There could always be more money for health and education costs, housing, etc., but essentially there's a certain smugness from Canadians when it comes to the recognition of its first inhabitants. At least we're not like the Americans or other countries. We like our Native people and indulge them. We have the Assembly of First Nations, the Aboriginal People's Television Network, and the Royal Commission on Aboriginal Peoples (commonly known as R-CAP) to name some notable back-pattable successes.

But at every conference, event, festival, and meeting that takes place from Newfoundland to Vancouver Island and up to Ellesmere Island, do they remember us? The Indige-who? Most people probably believe Native people did not wander the vast expanse of Scarborough since Time Immemorial. Why should we acknowledge them? After all, didn't they come with the Vikings?

Australia is a fabulous country with equally fabulous people, both Indigenous and non-Indigenous. But in a country that's still coming to grips with how to deal with its Aboriginal population—up until the late sixties, the administration of their First Nations came under the charter of the Department of Flora and Fauna, they were either animals or plants. I wonder if they got to pick which?—organizations and governments now acknowledge the people who roamed the hills long before all those home-less White folk showed up. It's embarrassing that Canada, so proud of its Aboriginal program, still barely acknowledges Native people unless they are protesting, dying, or opening a casino. Sometimes all three.

In that country called Australia, things are different in many ways. What I witnessed that day at the opening was the rule, not the exception. "At most arts events these days, where people from different geographical areas are gathered together in one place, it is increasingly common to follow this protocol. Indeed if it doesn't happen, it feels like a breach of accepted norm. I can't say who else does it (outside the arts, that is) though it is fairly standard for centre and left political parties to include it in their standard welcome to visitors," added Dr. Mead. As always, that stubborn right wing of the political spectrum (in whatever country) refuses to acknowledge the fact that Indigenous people can mark a ballot.

To be honest, I have been to gatherings, normally Aboriginal- or arts-oriented, where whomever's territory we happen to be on at that time is acknowledged. But this is usually only at small gatherings of a predominately Aboriginal attendance or function. The idea of a non-Native organization, let alone a federal, state, or municipal political member offering up such recognition of their own volition at non-Native functions is amazing. At the ANPC, I and a handful of Aboriginal performers were the only members of a darker hue there. So it was definitely not for our benefit. It was wonderful.

When I asked Dr. Mead why such recognition is given, his answer was quite simple: "Because it's important. Because it's the right thing to do. Because for many, many years we lived under the belief that the Indigenous population did not legally own the land on which we now find ourselves. Since Prime Ministers Hawke and then Keating highlighted social questions of reconciliation with our Indigenous people, Native title, and the Stolen Generation, along with a new history that told of massacres and resistance, the legal cases granting Native title, and a number of other triggers, often generated by Indigenous peoples themselves, there has been a change with respect to attitudes, education, and action."

Australia was settled by prisoners as a penal colony. Canada was settled by people looking for gold and the skins of dead animals. It seems the prisoners are on their way to being rehabilitated. And while fewer people in Canada are looking for furs and gold, there's still a little recognition to be dealt with here. Maybe if we all drank more Australian shiraz, it wouldn't hurt.

It's interesting how often progress seems to come from the arts.

ON BEING A HOUSEHOLD WORD WHEN THE HOUSE IS IN THE WRONG PART OF TOWN

Just the other day I was sitting around musing about the irony of being famous ... or semi-famous, as the case may be. If you've ever read the *National Enquirer* or *People* magazine, you know how rough and tragic it can be. My heart goes out to Brad Pitt and Angelina Jolie. Really, it does. But try being semi-famous. That's my cross to bear. People always kinda know my name, or think I look familiar, and they always spend about thirty seconds standing there after we've been introduced, trying to figure out where exactly we met before—was it at a cousin's wedding or a police line-up? And once you help them connect the mental dots, seeing their reactions can be quite disconcerting: at worst, "Never heard of ya"; or at best, "I think I've heard of you somewhere."

Luckily, I did some early training with far more famous people. I called it Public Recognition Boot Camp. That's where I began to learn about the double-edged sword of being a national icon, an idol for millions. For instance, I remember once riding down an escalator with Erica Ehm, former Much Music VJ, at the Calgary airport. On the other escalator heading upwards, a guy yelled out loudly, while pointing vigorously with his finger, "Hey, you're Erica Ehm!" Somehow I'm sure she was aware of that. She said she hates it when people just yell out her name in public.

This kind of thing doesn't happen to me often, except for that one time I was at some conference, and a guy a few feet away suddenly yelled out in a room full of people, "Hey, funny, you don't look like one," referring to the title of one of my books. How do you react to that? "Neither do you"? "Haven't heard that one before"? "No hablo English. ¿Qué?" It's not that I or anybody else resents being recognized, but I have a hard time believing everybody standing around these excitable people is just as excited to know that they happen to be standing there at that very moment too. A quieter approach would be much appreciated. That, and gifts.

Now, there are both pros and cons of being semi-famous. And both reflect the often inaccurate image the public eye can present of you. One of the better examples I know of got me a girlfriend. Several years back, I used to write frequently for the *Globe and Mail* and the *Toronto Star*. This lovely lady would read my articles every couple months and said they made her laugh and think. She wanted to get to know me. So, through a friend, she managed to organize a meeting and, to make a long story short, we ended up as a couple for three years. The sad part is, it didn't take her long to realize why I wrote an article for these two papers every couple of months. That's how long it took me to have an original idea. And write it down. Silly girl thought we'd be having scintillating conversations over breakfast about the state of the world and other political issues. That would have left me no time to watch *Star Trek*.

Unfortunately one of the cons of being a public figure is that anybody can take a shot at you and your family, at will. Amazon.ca sells books on-line. One of the unique things Amazon does is allow people to write personal reviews of books. One person who called himself "Cousin From Turttle Island" had a rather strong reaction to one of my *Funny, You Don't Look Like One* books: "This in no way represents the true life of anyone but another lost breed cashing in on his C-31 mom. He grew up in Toronto and occasionally came to Curve Lake. Hey, Drew, have another glass of stereotype, pal." How about that? I've been called a lot of things in my life but a "lost breed" is a new one. When much of what you do involves writing your opinions down and getting them published, you get used to contradictory views and harsh responses. But is it just me who thinks there's definitely something wrong about picking on a guy's mother—who, by the way, like me, was born and raised on the Reserve. Oh well, freedom of speech and all that. The only thing that gives me solace is the fact this gentleman of refinement and knowledge misspelled the word "Turtle" as "Turttle."

Speaking of my mother, it's always been a fear of hers that all this success and media exposure will go to my head and make me completely impossible to live with. After all, in the last year or so I've been to Belgium, Italy, France, Washington, DC, California, and Fort Frances, if you can believe it, and if all goes well, I'll be visiting Australia and New Zealand this fall—all this in support and promotion of Native theatre and literature in Canada. The first-class trip to Mexico spoiled me so bad, it almost made me insufferable.

But as anybody familiar with the workings of family and Reserve dynamics knows, whatever goes up, just might come down. The other day I was in Ottawa giving two lectures. One was at a place of higher learning, Carleton University. The other was for Health Canada. There was an older lady in the audience, who happened to be from my Reserve, who worked for Health Canada and, as luck would have it, was taking classes at Carleton. So there I am, pontificating on the brilliance of Native theatre and my humble contributions to the genre and she's in both audiences listening intently.

Afterwards, as I'm proudly signing books, she's busy telling people around me that she used to baby-sit me when I was a toddler. And, she proudly adds, she used to change my diapers. Thus ended the momentary glory of my auspicious lectures. And at that moment, I realized, no matter what you do, or where you travel, or who knows your name, in reality, you're just another boob in the porn film of life.

IF ALL THE WORLD'S A STAGE, I WANT BETTER LIGHTING

In my almost twenty years of working in the arts, I have come to some very interesting conclusions. First of all, no play, film, television, or book/magazine project is complete until the cheque clears. You've heard of Murphy's Law? This is now Taylor's Law. Second (and indirectly related to Law #1), attempting to become rich in the world of Native arts is like trying to fly while parachuting. You can pretend and fake it all you want, but eventually the reality of the situation will come rushing at you at approximately 250 kilometres an hour, as you're flapping your arms in vain screaming, "Why isn't this working?"

But the third law I have learned is that, should I ever wish to be a world-famous Indigenous actor, I would quite probably have to move to another country. That's because I don't look Native enough—not a good thing in the North American film industry, except for what's called the Val Kilmer Effect. I say this because on his MySpace page, he identifies his ethnicity as Native American; other research says he's a whopping one-sixteenth, and he's proven to be quite successful with that. His official website even sells Navajo blankets. Still, on shows highlighting the Native experience in Canada and the USA, darker is better, and definitely preferred.

While I'm primarily known as a Native writer, I have dabbled over the years in various pools of the performance arts. When I was younger, I had a cameo role on the television series *Spirit Bay*. Look for a blue jacket changing scores at an outdoor hockey game. I was also an extra in several films including the Cher/Liam Neeson/Dennis Quaid courtroom drama *Suspect*. I'm the blur over Cher's left shoulder as she stands in the court room, telling the judge she was going on vacation. The casting director had originally phoned me looking for a Native guy to sit in the defendant's box. I showed up, they looked at me, and I was put in the visitor's gallery. It seemed I looked too White to be a believable defendant. I guess I should have taken that as a compliment.

Over the years I've also appeared in a few public service announcements and related advertorials. I was in a Native comedy improv troupe for a year as well, and once did a lone stand-up gig (with Don Burnstick and Charlie Hill) at the Kennedy Center in Washington, DC, for the opening of the Smithsonian Museum of the American Indian. I've been interviewed by the media a million times, so I've grown comfortable with all their electronic paraphernalia and sound-studio environments. But that's about the extent of my acting resume. No starring roles in *Hamlet*. No *Death of a Salesman*. No *North of 60*.

In recent years however, I've been travelling the world, and that involves staying in a lot of hotels, which in turn involves watching a lot of television at three in the morning as you try to get over the jet lag. Television can be a window into the soul of a country. In many European countries, I was shocked to discover, there is a definite propensity to televise strippers and extreme nudity at those wee hours of the night. Several hours of nothing but women taking their clothes off almost makes the jet lag worthwhile, but eventually even more difficult to recover from. What that says about the soul of the new European Union ... I'm not sure. But it sure beats all those infomercials they show on late-night television at home.

In countries like Australia, Mexico, and India however, the television tells a different story. In Mexico, I couldn't help notice all the people starring in the soap operas, the commercials, etc., looked very European—that is to say, very pale and very White. There is a noticeable lack of Mexican-looking people on Mexican television—let alone any representation of its Indigenous people at the level of programming. With the sound off in Mexico, you could be watching Canadian television. Provided they don't go outside. Mexico City does not look like Toronto.

There's something similar going on in India. It seems the lighter your skin is, the better chance you have of a successful career in Bollywood, and that's not just my opinion. I asked around while I was there. I was told that the majority of the performers come from the Punjab, a region in the north-western part of the country. That's where most of the successive waves of European invaders came through for thousands of years, lightening up the skin colour of the locals as they pillaged and plundered the land. From what I understand and saw, the Bollywood film and television representation of South Asian people is not very reflective of the vast majority of the subcontinent's population. No big surprise there.

On the other hand, in three weeks in Australia, I literally saw more television programming about Canada's Native people than I did about Murris or Kooris (Australian Aboriginals). I think I saw one dark-skinned Aboriginal face once on one half-hour Australian drama. That was about it. But I saw at least three documentaries about Canadian First Nations on one of the channels—on their multicultural channel. Granted I did not watch every single television show, twenty-four hours a day for twenty-one straight days while in Australia—just when I was home in my suite. Still, the Murri and Koori people I was working with said that what I'd seen was an accurate representation of the state of Australian television. Australian Aboriginals practically do not exist, unless it's a period documentary you're watching, and they are made to shake a boomerang at the camera. Evidently, White is right Down Under.

But here in Canada, I find the opposite is true. The few times I've auditioned for television or movie roles—and it's only been for Indigenous roles because of my connections—I am always too light-skinned to be considered seriously. Damn these blue eyes. It's not that I have any great ambition to be the next Graham Greene or Gary Farmer—in fact I get a little stage fright just thinking about it. But as the government and the Assembly of First Nations assiduously repeats to our youth, we should always remember we have the option of being whatever we want to be when we grow up, not just what people tell us we could or should be. So, someday when I grow up, I may want to be an actor.

So should I decide to explore this thespian career path, I may have to contemplate moving to either Australia, Mexico, or India to do so. At least there, perhaps, I could become successful—these blue eyes would be an asset, not a hindrance. I could conceivably revolutionize Bollywood by introducing some inter-tribal pow wow moves to their dancing style. Mexican soap operas might also never be the same once they opened up a role or two for me—I wonder if they've ever heard of an Indian taco? Australia? Well, remember that classic line from *A Cry in the Dark*: "A dingo ate my baby!" I think it would add poignancy to the movie if it went something like: "A beaver ate my baby."

But once again, perhaps I'm being a bit hypersensitive on this subject. Perhaps what's really at issue here is not culture, but technology. Anybody who's worked in the video production industry knows that before the video camera can record scenes accurately, it has to be focused on and "read" a blank, white piece of paper. For some technical reason this sets the colour levels for the camera, and is called "doing a white balance." Where's the balance, is what I want to know?

IT DOES SEEM LIKE YESTERDAY

It was in China of all places that I discovered something quite disturbing. Believe it or not, I found myself being in the unique position of disagreeing with the views of our beloved federal government. Shocking ... Yes, I know. A Native person with a difference of opinion from that of the Canadian government ... I almost alerted the media. And, equally surprising, it had nothing to do with land claims, residential schools, public inquiries, or money. It had to do with history in this country, and publicity on the other side of the world.

I was in Chengdu, China, with several other Native artists for a kind of "Canada's Aboriginal People Meet China's Minorities" symposium. Red Sky Performance was there, showcasing a dance theatre piece written by Tomson Highway, along with singer/guitarist George Leach and traditional dancer and drummer Lorne Doucette. While there, we were treated to a variety of cultural performances from many of China's fifty-six recognized cultural minorities. These were images and memories I will carry with me for the rest of my life.

I was also fortunate enough to see and experience a lot of other fabulous and interesting things that country had to offer, including a sandstorm that blew in from the Mongolian desert. However, ironically enough, my most startling discovery came from the press release issued by the Canadian ambassador to China praising our appearance in Chengdu, and later in the cities of Yinchuan and Nanjing. It was all summed up in the document's first line: "Canadian First Nations have inhabited what is now Canada for centuries." I stopped reading there. Did he say centuries ... like a couple of hundred years?

Those centuries? Perhaps the Canadian ambassador was thinking of these centuries in terms of dog years.

Was the paint still wet on all our teepees when Columbus and Cabot first arrived? Had we had time to unpack our pow wow outfits yet? Maybe our canoes were even still under warranty. Gee, was that only a couple hundred years ago ... seems like yesterday. Granted, Native people and government people have always viewed the concept of time differently, but I think this is getting a little ridiculous.

Our Traditional Knowledge tells us that we've been here as long as the winds have blown, rivers flowed, grass grown—all that Time Immemorial stuff. And there are some people who rightly or wrongly believe we crossed over into Canada from China and Siberia, on a land bridge across the Bering Strait. I can understand that because there don't appear to be any Tim Hortons in China.

Now, admittedly, I might be a little inaccurate in my judgment here because I don't work for the government, and as we know the government is never wrong. But because we who find ourselves kicking stones around our local Reserves have always believed, silly us, that it was people like the ambassador and his relatives that have enjoyed the benefits of Canada for those last scant few centuries, not us. Oh well, I guess I could blame that misinformation on the notoriously bad education available in Native communities.

Luckily though, in gratitude for the fine treatment we received over there, I managed to warn the Chinese about the ambassador and his people. They'll show up on your doorstep for a cup of tea, usually to prevent scurvy, end up staying for a "few centuries," and then, before you know it, you're knee-deep in Starbucks, *Star Trek* series, and *Toronto Star* telemarketers. Next time you look, they'll be telling you that the Chinese have only been in Asia for a couple of centuries too. The whole scene reminded me of that famous George Orwell novel, 1984, where he wrote about a big centralized government with a yen to rewrite history, as it felt necessary.

Of course the whole "inhabited what is now Canada for centuries" thing could just have been a misprint. An honest mistake, a typo, if you will. I could even be just a little culturally paranoid. I considered all these possibilities as I tasted a local Chinese delicacy. Something called a "10,000-year-old quail egg." Apparently they are as popular over there as they are on this side of the Pacific. I was pondering its unusual name when a member of the Canadian Embassy leaned over and quietly informed me that, actually, they were only about 500 years old—a couple of centuries at best.

It was then that I started telling people I was actually just thirty years old. Hey, when in Rome … I mean China …

THE REPAVED ROAD HOME

I left home, the small Ojibway First Nation of Curve Lake in Central Ontario, way back in 1980. The reason: college and a desire to see if there was more to life than country music, mosquitoes, and baloney. Twenty-six years later, it looks like I will be returning home, leaving a city of over three million people for a First Nations community of considerably fewer inhabitants, depending on if it's the weekend or not, of course. Much has changed in that intervening time—both in my community and in me.

When I left home, I was young, thinner, more impressionable, trying to understand the appeal of disco, and still believed in the Maple Leafs. Now I'm old, still impressionable, trying to understand the appeal of rap, and the less said about my weight and/or the Maple Leafs the better. I know I'm old now: I read the *Globe and Mail* and listen to CBC Radio faithfully. That's a better indicator than what it says on your birth certificate.

Why I originally left should be no surprise to anybody who grew up on a small Reserve, or even in a small non-Native town, for that matter—it's all a matter of statistical probability. My mother is the oldest of fourteen siblings, and in a village of about eight hundred or so at the time, it didn't take my adolescent brain very long to do the math and discover that I was related to practically every girl on the Reserve. This rather awkward situation is surprisingly common on many Reserves. I'm surprised more colleges and universities don't exploit this fact as a potential recruiting opportunity.

That said, I decided after all this time that life in Toronto holds no more mystery for me. I've done the restaurants, the theatres, the bars, the museums, and the transit system. Basically, I'm Toronto'd out. I'm urban'd out. I want to be able to build a fire without filling out a permit. I want to be able to take a deep breath without immediately recognizing by its exhaust the type of vehicle that just passed by. I want my "rush hour" to be more of a "rush minute." A lot of my family thinks I won't take the transition well, but then, most of them have never spent a thirty-five-degree summer in Toronto. Somehow, I think I'll survive. I love the city, but let's face it, the novelty has worn off. Now, the salmon must return home to spawn ... Well, perhaps that's not exactly the best metaphor to use ...

In the two and a half decades I've been away, I've done more than just live in Toronto. I have travelled the world, published a whole pile of books, tiptoed my way through a half-dozen different forms of media expression, and had my heart broken a few times (nothing new there, that happens to practically everyone everywhere). But, as I said, my community and I have both changed, hopefully for the better. I am reminded of Brian Maracle's wonderful book, *Back on the Rez*. In it, he describes the trials and tribulations of an Urban Indian taking up residence back "home." I just hope the transition won't be too difficult for me.

Needless to say, my experiences in those intervening years have changed me somewhat. Two years ago when I was in India on my mother's birthday, I emailed her via my aunt, wishing her a happy birthday and saying that I'd just taken a tour of a city called Jaipur where I'd seen camels, monkeys, and elephants walking the streets. My aunt later emailed me back saying that for my mother's birthday, her sisters took her to a nearby garbage dump to watch the bears. I'm going to have to reconcile these two realities. Still, I'm sure the people of Jaipur would find bears and a First Nations garbage dump as fascinating as I found their charming city.

When I left all those years ago, I thought I'd never return—the anger of youth and all. There was a world to be explored out there and god damn it if I wasn't going to do that. Since then, I've chased kangaroos in Australia, gotten drunk with Finnish university students, battled sandstorms in northern China, sampled asparagus ice cream in Germany, got seasick in Cuba, stuck my finger in a bullet hole left by Pancho Villa in the ceiling of a cantina in Mexico City, seen plays in the West End of London, and swam in the oceans off the coast of Sicily while trying to avoid the jellyfish. And that's just a sampling of my adventures away from home.

A small part of me would love the opportunity to ... say ... return to a small island I found off the coast of Fiji. As a writer in the Internet age, that is conceivably possible ... though my writing could lose its authenticity. Instead of Molson Canadian, my characters would end up drinking kava, a narcotic drink Polynesians imbibe, made from the roots of an island plant. Again, not a lot of kava on my Reserve.

On the positive side, while I have gone out to the world, the world has also come to my Reserve. When I went to China a few months ago, I asked some cousins what they wanted me to bring back for them. They all asked for green tea, which amazed me. I brought back as much as I could. I don't even drink green tea. So maybe the move back won't be so traumatic.

I'll also be going from a street address to a rural route address. However, walking to the store for a quart of milk will require packing a sleeping bag. I will be leaving behind in the city a sincere love of lemongrass soup for the smell of sweetgrass in a field. That will be the most intense regret I will have about leaving Toronto—the food. Let's face it, most Native communities I have travelled to don't excel in excellent international cuisine. Over the years I've found myself preferring mortadella to baloney and wonder if that will be a problem. It doesn't fry as well. I don't know if that makes me elitist or what. Common knowledge dictates I won't be enjoying Korean bulgogi and kimchee at Chad's, a local culinary establishment on my Reserve—unfortunately, there aren't a lot of Koreans in the 'hood. Enjoying some excellent Vietnamese pho at Rosie's, another fine eatery down the road from Chad's, is highly unlikely. I don't think I can expect any superb saganaki at the Tea Room either. Luckily there's a place down the road from where I'll be living that actually makes pizza from scratch, they say—but I really don't want to know what they scratch.

What Curve Lake does offer is peace and quiet. Family. Fresh air. And lots and lots of trees. Unfortunately most of those trees hide alarming numbers of mosquitoes, but on the other hand, in Toronto most of the trees hide squirrels, many of them with bald patches.

It's green at home. Very green. I can't forget the relatives who know everything you are doing, even before you do, which is a bit unnerving. But it's home. The pace is slower, stress is definitely lower, and I've got a lovely house surrounded by several acres of trees to hide in, should the going get tough. So maybe it won't be all bad. I have purchased an authentic Chinese/Korean cookbook. And the satellite dish I have will keep me more connected with the television stations in Newfoundland and Alberta than Toronto cable service ever could.

Admittedly, it's been a very long time since I so fully embraced the rural lifestyle—over half my life—but I definitely am looking forward to it. The peace, the quiet—I'll finally get a chance to write the Great Canadian Aboriginal Novel. I've already got a title: *The Norval Morrisseau Code*, about a secret message hidden in the Peterborough petroglyphs ...

And who knows, maybe in those faraway foreign countries, saying I live on a Native Reserve will make me seem a lot more exotic and interesting than saying I live in a split-level bungalow in Toronto.

ONE YEAR LATER!!!!

It's been over a year now since I moved back to my home community of Curve Lake from the big city of Toronto and, as I expected, I've noticed some changes since I left over two decades ago, both in the community and in me. Let's just say it's taken some getting used to. You can't order a pizza, or Chinese food, or anything else unless you have it delivered by Purolator. I'm still scanning the Reserve for a good dry cleaner. And I've given up waiting for any form of rapid transit system to stop at my place.

Obviously I think it's me that's changed the most, not my community. I've been infected with a disease called urbanization. I have to go back to being an Anishnaabe from being an Ani-snob. Believe it or not, wine doesn't always have to come from France. Spam is more than unsolicited email. And pick-up trucks can be status symbols.

As a man who made his career in the theatre arts, I've come to grips with the fact that the Reserve doesn't have a sizeable theatre district. Evidently me and my house are it. But it's home and, like all homes, it has its own set of lovable quirks. Last December the community had a Santa Claus parade that was delightful to watch. About a dozen trucks and flatbeds rolled past a sizeable showing of Curve Lakers, showcasing the community spirit. But when Chinese New Year came around, let's just say I was severely disappointed by the lack of community participation. Same with the Oktoberfest and St. Patrick's Day festivities. Not a single float or parader to be seen. Again, I was it. And don't get me started on the Gay Pride Parade. I waited around all day for that, but nobody else showed up.

Living in Toronto has obviously affected my homegrown taste buds too. While I'm cognizant of the fact Curve Lake doesn't have a decent Thai restaurant, there is still a rather severe learning curve to be acknowledged on my part. Not that long ago I was making dinner and realized I'd run out of flour. So I hopped in my car and drove to Buckhorn, a nearby small town, to pick up a bag of said ingredient. The woman behind the counter, whom I believe is from Curve Lake, recognized me and we had a nice little chat. As I was paying for the flour, she casually commented, "Oh, flour; frying some fish?" I looked back at her rather puzzled. "No," I said, "making a nice chicken piccata." Now it was her turn to be puzzled. Evidently back home, flour's only good for frying fish and making Indian bread. I just wish I liked fish. It might make my reintegration much smoother.

And while on the topic of food, there was this other incident. I had stopped for lunch at a little roadside fast-food joint on the Reserve. I always believe in contributing to the local economy whenever possible, especially since it might be run by relatives. I noticed the menu had that iconic symbol of Aboriginal delicacies, fried baloney on a saucegun (fried bread). It had never been a favourite of mine, though my mother to this day still enjoys a good pan-fried hunk of baloney. In some circles it's referred to as Indian steak. But I long ago decided that I don't think I could ever be that "Indian." I prefer my baloney raw and unprepared—still bleeding if possible.

Be that as it may, I ordered an Indian taco, a hearty and tasty concoction of fried bread, chili, tomatoes, lettuce, cheese, and hot sauce. As I waited patiently in line, a gentleman came up behind me and ordered the fried baloney special. So there I stood, watching this teenager pull out a thick roll of baloney, cut off a sizable slice, grab it with tongs, and hold it in the deep fryer. She was deep frying baloney. I've been to sixteen countries around the world and that was a new one on me.

I wondered if maybe, during my time in Toronto, I had somehow been kept in the dark regarding the latest technological advancements and developments in the culinary art of preparing baloney in Curve Lake. However, even my mother shuddered at the thought, so I wasn't alone.

I know there's still a long journey ahead of me before I feel truly at home, but I believe I'm half-way there—I just need to find that middle ground. How about something like ... baloney tartar. I bet that would go over big. Even with me.

I WENT TO AN AA MEETING (ABORIGINALS IN AUSTRIA)

Once more the world beckoned, titillated by dreams of Canadian Aboriginal people, and of course I answered the call. This time, it was the far-off land called Austria. As is becoming far more common, I found myself at a conference in Vienna where I was expounding on the humour and literature of Canada's Native people. Yes, Austria—the hills were indeed alive with the sound of drumming. Last March I went to a similar conference on Native people in Helsinki, Finland, and then a month later to a conference in China. I've already been invited to one in Poland and another in Germany in the next few months. The study of Native people seems to be quickly becoming one of our major exports.

This particular conference was called Native Americans and First Nations: A Transnational Challenge, and there were people in attendance from fifteen different countries, all eager and willing to talk about Native people behind their backs. Even though it was stuffed with academics, I still found the experience interesting. The presentations these people spend weeks writing and then travel to foreign countries to expound upon never fail to amaze me.

For instance, there was one workshop called "Moby Dick in the Strait of Juan de Fuca: The Multicultural Construction of the Nootkan Body Politic." What the hell does that mean? "The Cultural and Political Work of the American Indian in Nineteenth-Century Czech National Discourse." I shall, of course, wait for the movie of that one. My personal favourite was a workshop on Kateri Tekakwitha, the seventeenth-century Mohawk who is well on her way to becoming our first Catholic Native saint. As part of the presentation, she was referred to as the "First Iroquois Virgin." That was news to me. This does not say a lot for the rest of Iroquois womanhood. Maybe it's an academic term used to theorize sort of a postmodern, post-colonial type of virginity.

One bizarre side effect of these conferences is that I meet all the great and notable American Indian writers there. In Helsinki, I had dinner with N. Scott Momaday, and we both turned up our noses at the mustard herring. The man has the most amazing speaking voice ... something like if James Earl Jones had been born a Kiowa. In Vienna, I drank beers with Gerald Viznor and made him laugh when about a dozen of us were at dinner talking away as the waitress brought our food. He said, "You ever notice that when a bunch of people go out for dinner, order, then get lost in conversation, you forget what you ordered when it comes out?"

"The same thing can happen in a brothel." Or so I've heard. Really.

But the most unusual thing I came across on this trip concerned dream-catchers. I had been lucky enough to arrive in Austria just as they were setting up their Christmas markets in various parks, those marvelous little arts and craft booths with all sorts of interesting knick-knacks for sale. At least two stands were selling examples of the familiar and ubiquitous dreamcatcher, including a stand that was run by what appeared to be a Native guy from Surinam in South America, but who assured me he regularly visits a Shuswap medicine man in British Columbia.

Anyway, it's no secret that Germans have a unique preoccupation with North American Native people, even people who look more German than Native—like me. One of the presenters from Germany told me of a company in Düsseldorf that actually cleans dreamcatchers for you. That's right, cleans them, both physically and spiritually. They vacuum the dream-catchers, dust them off, or god knows what, and, of course, after prolonged periods of the webbing catching and dissolving all those bad dreams in the morning sunlight, there's also bound to be some bad psychic residue left on them, so this company will perform a ceremony to cleanse them and make them as good as new. Man, I'm in the wrong business.

Oh well, all in all I had a fabulous time, primarily because Austria is what could be called a Native man's paradise. Look at it this way; I spent a week doing nothing but talking, eating schnitzel (fried meat) and apple strudel (for all us latent diabetics), and drinking beer, all served by big buxom blondes. You know, any three of these activities would make for a great weekend. Any four, and it's Christmas and your birthday all rolled into one. But all five ... check your pulse and see if you're still alive.

CAN I STILL WEAR A BEADED BELT?

If there is a line between what I once was and what I now am, I may have to turn around to see it, because it is now behind me. The line of which I speak is that boundary most of us transgress in our lives—the boundary over which we cross into uncharted territory, a land where we never expected to be, and are frightened by what we have done to get there. If there is such a line, I may have crossed it. I suspect I have officially gone from being a Rez Indian, to being an Urban Indian—even to, and I say this with great trepidation, an Urbane Indian.

This startling and curious revelation came to me, in of all places, the town of Stonnington, Connecticut, where I was staying for a couple days with some friends. We had all returned from a Native theatre festival in Providence, Rhode Island. Betsy Theobald Richards, a Cherokee with a degree from the Yale School of Drama, had, over the years, directed many of my plays. Sheila Tousey, the talented and well-known Menominee actress (*Thunderheart, Medicine River*) and New York University drama graduate, had performed in the workshop of my play *The Buz'Gem Blues*, an Elder's love story.

After the festival, we had some time to kill and had retired to Betsy's house in Connecticut on the shores of the Atlantic Ocean, surrounded by some hard-core New England atmosphere. Sheila and I were scheduled to grab a train to New York and go our separate ways soon, so we were reminiscing about our past theatrical adventures with Betsy, out on her deck, chatting away. Betsy's husband was making margaritas, and we were sipping them casually as we watched the moon rise over the ocean. I think we were on our third margarita when the conversation slowly turned to rumours we had heard about somebody writing a musical about the life of Crazy Horse.

That's when it struck me. I was discussing the possibility of a musical about Crazy Horse. I was no longer the little kid who used to carry the Eaton's catalogue to the outhouse. I was an Urbane Indian—a YUPNI (Young Urban Professional Native Indian) ... Yale graduates, margaritas, Connecticut coastlines, Crazy Horse musicals ... this was not the life I had expected to be living when I was growing up back home. My life had somehow transported me into a foreign land with foreign ideals. Had I wandered too far from my humble Rez roots? Was I no longer part of the larger Aboriginal collective? The Crazy Horse musical discussion was horrifying enough, but what truly scared me was the simple fact that the conversation *did not take place in the kitchen!* Yes, I'm not joking. With that realization, all my claims to any Aboriginal roots went out the window.

I started assessing my current life for further signs of cultural erosion, and there were plenty. For instance, I don't eat as much baloney as I used to ... instead I now prefer the gourmet version, mortadella, a type of Italian baloney. And since I had never, ever, had a fondness for fried baloney (which embarrasses my mother to no end), I've never tried fried mortadella. When shopping for Kraft Dinner, I still pick the Original recipe, but now simply because it actually has 0.1 grams less fat than the White Cheddar or the Extra Creamy varieties. That's sad, I know. I am also on time, nine-tenths of the time, and my house is surprisingly dreamcatcher-free. In terms of Native cuisine, I no longer consider lard a spice, and I do not accept the old Rez adage, "When in doubt, deep fry." The last time I paddled a canoe was to impress a White chick, but that was a waste of time. Six months later she married somebody else.

Connecticut is a long way from home. The shores of Curve Lake are a lot less salty, and the margaritas aren't nearly as good. And I've actually checked—there is no mortadella to be seen on local store shelves back home. They don't know what they're missing.

But perhaps there's hope for my heritage yet—I do have a Johnny Cash CD, and everybody knows you can't be Native without a healthy appreciation of both country and western music. The Band Office could and would take away your Status Card, or at the very least your gas tax exempt card, as your first warning if you didn't know the difference.

Now I do know a lot of Native people who have vacationed in the Carribean ... and I've heard margaritas are plentiful down there. And of course, take a moment to consider the life of Crazy Horse ... that would indeed make for a very interesting musical, you'd have to agree. Maybe being Native is not what you do, but how you feel. Now, that's almost Zen ...

Okay, never mind. I take it all back.

HOPEFULLY THEY WON'T TAKE MY STATUS CARD AWAY

There is a good chance that I will be going to the Aboriginal equivalent of Hell, for I have argued with an Elder. Quite forcefully too. And for that, if I have fully understood traditional teachings, the Creator will banish me to some mid-level civil service position with the Department of Indian Affairs. Probably ordering stationery and shredding the minister's speeches. I am truly damned.

It all happened in Edmonton, hardly one's image of the portal to First Nations damnation. I was at the Dreamspeakers Film Festival, a yearly celebration of Aboriginal film and the video arts. This year, a made-for-TV movie I wrote, called *In a World Created by a Drunken God*, was opening the festival. I was honoured, flattered, and delighted. It's based on a play I wrote of the same name, that was nominated for a Governor General's Award. Basically, it's about a Native guy (actually half Native, of a single parent), who is surprised to find a half brother from the USA, entirely Caucasian, knocking at his door announcing that their father is dying and needs a kidney. Essentially, the stuff of your standard drama.

At the opening night party, I was summoned quite briskly to a table where I sat chatting with several women of varying ages. It was a pleasant enough conversation, until the very end. As I got up to leave, the woman sitting beside me, an older woman, wouldn't let me leave. She told me to sit down, and then she proceeded to chew me out, quite animatedly, for the film. There is a section in the film where a Native woman enters into a sexual relationship with a White guy (thus the reason for the central character being of mixed blood—standard biology, I believe) on a camping trip.

This Elder took great umbrage with that portrayal. She said, and I am admittedly paraphrasing her, that she has dedicated her life to presenting positive and constructive portrayals of Native women, and trying to instil a sense of pride and confidence in them, and how dare I show these two people getting personal under an overturned boat. I should be ashamed of myself and she strongly urged me to do what I could to destroy, erase, or bury the film. During most of the diatribe, she literally glared at me.

I was extremely shocked. Not necessarily by her comments—all writers, artists, and performers are used to being assessed and critiqued. It comes with the job, and everybody has an opinion. But not necessarily so intense or personal. I tried to explain, very respectfully, that in my experience, sex between Native people and White people did occasionally happen. I have it on reasonably good authority that it's not unknown. (I should mention I have blue eyes.) And most importantly, it was loosely based on a true story. "Then keep it to yourself. Don't inflict it on other people," she said.

By now, I was beginning to get a little angry, and I said to her, literally, "Are you trying to censor me and what I write?" Without hesitation and staring me straight in the eye, she said, "Yes." To most writers, that's like waving a red flag in front of a bull.

I feel it should be pointed out that most people familiar with my work know I do not make a regular habit of writing negative portrayals of women. In fact, I have publicly stated many times that I refuse to write work that shows women as hookers or victims of sexual abuse. Too many Native writers revel in that kind of writing. I've always preferred the more positive approach—witness my *Someday/Only Drunks and Children Tell the Truth/ 400 Kilometres* trilogy.

The conversation/argument went on for about twenty minutes. It went back and forth, with me—again respectfully, not raising my voice or using nasty words—asking her how she would respond if I asked her to do something ... such as stop telling other people what she thought they should do. Eventually the Elder's ride was leaving and I was spared any further writer-bashing. She left, giving me a stern look and returning an unconvincing handshake that I initiated. On one hand, I felt justified in standing up for my rights as a writer—the scene I wrote wasn't exploitive or over the top, and as an individual, my agenda has never been to trash Native women— just the opposite. Plus, I always thought Elders were supposed to have a softer, more supportive and constructive approach. But I had argued with an Elder and worse, sent her away angry.

I could feel the ground trembling beneath my feet, threatening to open up beneath me. I wonder what kind of cubicle the Department of Indian Affairs will give me. And I must remember to buy a tie.

IF ONLY WE WERE SO POPULAR OVER HERE

I have written frequently about the interest that exists overseas regarding Canada's Native people. I have just returned from my ninth lecture tour of Germany, and my second to the Czech Republic, extolling and spreading the Gospel of Native literature and culture. Once again, I have to say it— Native people, however we are perceived at home, are sure popular over there. In many ways we are romanticized, exoticized, and adorized. Confidentially, I kind of like it. In the environment that created residential schools and Saskatchewan's infamous "Starlight Tours," it's nice to be in a place where saying you are Native Canadian will get you an eager smile and a handshake, instead of a breathalyzer or a federal apology. Living up to the image is, however, a little harder.

For instance, in my Prague hotel, I found brochures near the front door advertising many interesting things for bored tourists of any culture to do while in town. Chief amongst them is a place called Club K 5. It's a unique establishment that offers many diversions, including a restaurant, sauna, steam bath, a solarium, and massage, pedicure, and manicure services, for starts. But those are just the appetizers. Club K 5 has more unique offerings, including strip shows and escort services. What's of particular interest— Aboriginally speaking—is on the fourth floor. It offers what could be called theme rooms for the romantic. You can find yourselves as a knight and a maiden in the medieval room, an emperor and a slave in the Roman room, astronauts in the cosmic room, or—I'm dyin' if I'm lyin'—as Aboriginals in a cave. Yes, a cave. As Aboriginals.

Coincidently enough, a cave is where my Indigenous date and I went after our Native high school prom. There's nothing like rock, moss, insects, and dampness to set that First Nations libido on fire. How did the Czech people know? You ain't been properly loved by an Indian until your head has been bruised by a stalactite. Headboards are for wimps. Unfortunately I didn't have enough per diem to do further research.

Germany however was just as, if not more, interesting. I was scheduled to lecture and perform a reading at Theatre Bonn. The first two things of interest occurred on the walk from the hotel to the theatre, where I passed by a large storefront, broadly proclaiming: "THE EU [European Union] LOVES CANADA." Inside the store were all kinds of representations of Canada, almost all of them Native, specifically West Coast Native—blankets, totem poles, sculptures, etc. Incidentally, in Prague I also attended the opening of an exhibit of Native art at a local museum. Again, all West Coast art. I began to notice a theme here. It seems most Central Europeans equate Native people only with the West Coast. And I happen to know for a fact that there are caves all along the West Coast. In these dark economic times, I wonder if the Kwakwaka'wakw, Salish, and Tshimshian know what potential tourism possibilities exist in their back yards.

The other interesting thing that happened while I was in Bonn was having the assistant dramaturge of the theatre company, a young and intelligent woman, ask me quite seriously and innocently, what my name, Drew Hayden Taylor, meant in English. She assumed it was my Ojibway name. For a brief moment a number of phrases danced across my mind: He Whose Eyes are Blue but Heart Is Red, or Spread Eagle, or, just simply, Cave Dweller. But that would be like shooting fish in a barrel and I confessed it was the only name I had, other than "occupant."

But perhaps the most interesting revelation that I had came to me in Würzburg. At a dinner, a local academic told me that when she was young, in fact when most Germans were young kids and they scraped their knees or stubbed their toes or banged their elbows, their parents would frequently tell them, as a way of psychologically dealing with the pain, "An Indian knows no pain." Supposedly the little kids would then develop a stiff upper lip and stop crying, wanting to be like Indians.

An Indian knows no pain.

Obviously I don't think we know the same Indians.

I know pain ... you should see some of the relatives and ex-girlfriends I have. On one hand, I suppose this kind of aphorism could be construed as some sort of a compliment, but obviously whoever came up with it has never met a residential school survivor. Or someone who was forcibly taken away for adoption. Or made to fill out forms for the Department of Indian Affairs. There's a world of pain in the Native community.

An Indian knows no pain.

Maybe that's why they think we have sex in caves. That's gotta be painful.

I SHOULD HAVE TAKEN THAT LEFT TURN AT ALBUQUERQUE

Prague, Czech Republic, is an awfully long way from my Reserve; in distance, mentality, and culture. Yet there I was, on yet another one of my many attempts to spread the Gospel of Native literature to the world, like an apostle of the Aboriginal. Already this year I'd been to such exotic places as Germany (twice), Los Angeles, Sante Fe, Austria, New York, and La Ronge, Saskatchewan—exoticism I guess being in the eye of the beholder.

Prague is a stunningly beautiful city, with architecture unrivalled anywhere in the world. Gothic, cubist, baroque, and a dozen other styles, all standing side by side, like different species of trees fighting for sunlight in the forest. Personally, I know the difference between a teepee, a wigwam, and a longhouse. That's about it. However, it is the age of these buildings that was truly awe-inspiring. Don't forget, Canada being a country that was "discovered" in 1497 by John Cabot (born Giovanni Caboto in Venice), our perception of time and man-made objects differs substantially from those across the ocean. I heard one woman pointing out a certain building, saying, "It was built sometime in the mid-nineteenth century, so it's relatively new."

A friend who was showing me around Prague told me that when she was in St. John's, Newfoundland, doing some research, a local tour guide told her excitedly that she was walking on a cobblestone road that was laid down probably 250 years ago! Unimpressed, she was tempted to respond that when she gets her morning coffee in Prague, she walks along a six-hundred-year-old cobblestone street. Again, it's that cultural time thing. Among my friends in this country, anybody who can remember drinking from beer stubbies and watching first-run *Beachcombers* episodes is considered ancient, or from an era known as BC—Before Computers.

During my time in that Eastern European country, I was invited to a wine-tasting event in a fourteenth-century wine cellar that was located seven metres below the streets. That was so cool. Literally. Now, visit anything fourteenth-century in Canada and you'd be tripping over archaeologists.

Because of its age and history, museums of every make and model abound everywhere in the city, and in unique locations—for instance, the Museum of Communism sits atop a McDonald's. Would you like a side of fries with your Marx? Would you like your Lenin supersized? When I was getting out of a taxi, the Museum of Medieval Torture caught my eye, but I didn't have enough money to get in. For a moment I thought about sneaking in but then, I thought, because of the nature of the museum, that might not be advisable. I didn't want them to get medieval on me. The gift shop, however, was eye-opening and scary.

According to my friend, Prague also has one of the oldest established Jewish cemeteries in the world, dating back to the twelfth century. She asked me if I'd ever been to a Jewish cemetery—evidently it's a tourist attraction there—and I had to confess there weren't a lot of Jews on my Reserve.

The other most obvious thing I noticed during my trip to Prague, was that it could be considered a place in Hell for most vegetarians. I, myself, proudly enjoy a lifestyle prone to the consumption of meat. You know the old joke: What's another word for a Native vegetarian? A very bad hunter. We live by that credo in Curve Lake. That being said, in the Czech Republic, I'd have to say they love meat more than most Native people do. And though I may be exaggerating a tiny bit, I think I may have actually seen a vegetable for the first time on my third day there.

Most meals, I discovered, consist of two or three servings of meat. Various menu options at a restaurant that opened in 1499 (I think the original cook still worked there) consisted of pork medallions with a side of duck, and bread dumplings. Or pork shoulder, sausage, and bacon, with potato pancakes. Or beef goulash layered with strips of bacon, with potato dumplings. You get the idea.

To wash this all down, there was plenty of Czech beer. Evidently, the Czech Republic has the highest per-capita consumption of beer in the world. Something like 168 litres per person, per year. Canadians are obviously not putting enough effort into "being Canadian."

YET ANOTHER MINISTER TO TRAIN

A couple of weeks ago, Ontario Premier Dalton McGuinty shuffled his cabinet, moving the very capable Michael Bryant, minister of Aboriginal affairs, up the food chain to economic development. The former attorney general of the province had been appointed the first ever minister of the newly created Aboriginal portfolio in October of 2007. Less than a year! Since nature (and politics) hates a vacuum, Brad Duguid, former labour minister, rushed in and is now thumbing through paint swatches for his new office. As with both our provincial and federal governments, the Aboriginal affairs portfolio's theme song is that classic Trooper tune "We're Here for a Good Time (Not a Long Time)."

Several Native leaders are upset with the shuffle, saying that they will have to go back and start training the new guy all over again. Sometimes it just seems these White boys can't hold down a job for very long. Two to three years is the average life span for such ministers. Most appointees spend their time accepting gifts of tanned, smoked moose-hide beaded gloves, traditional Native carvings and paintings, and cool leather fringe jackets from Aboriginal bigwigs before being hustled out. If you're looking for cheap Native arts and crafts, check eBay after each cabinet shuffle.

Still, I want to be fair to Brad Duguid. He's got a bit of a roller coaster coming up—good luck with that Bryant leftover, Caledonia. Still, with such frequent and rapid turnover, it concerns me that these new ministers might not be fully informed about the complex and varied cultures and characteristics of Ontario's, and Canada's, Aboriginal people, beginning with the fact that we are not all one people. It's true. I have it on good authority.

So I would like to suggest to Premier McGuinty that he prepare some sort of exam for people in Duguid's situation. One that would inform us of his overall knowledge of the people he will be responsible for negotiating with and about. Below are twenty-four suggested questions dealing with Ontario Native arts and culture, and also several exploring a much broader national perspective, since, no doubt, Duguid will occasionally find himself talking to First Nations people in other provinces. No province or minister is an island (except Prince Edward Island and Newfoundland of course).

If Minister Duguid scores twenty or higher, start sending him the birchbark-bitten wall hangings. Fifteen or higher should get him a dreamcatcher. Ten or higher, offer him a seagull feather. Anything less, a bus ticket out of the province might be appropriate. Here are the questions in order of difficulty:

Easy

1. What language is spoken in Kashechewan?
2. What does Nunavut mean in English?
3. What does Canada mean in English?
4. George Ryga wrote the play *The Ecstasy of Rita Joe*. Was he Native or not?
5. What's the Indigenous name for the Queen Charlotte Islands?
6. What year did Native people get the right to vote in federal elections?
7. What was the name of Nick's Native best friend in the television series *The Beachcombers*?
8. What is the name of the Dene' community in *North of 60*?

Moderate

9. Who coined the phrase "My heart soars like an eagle"?
10. Who is the only First Nations person to ever win an Academy Award?
11. What town does Tom King's *Dead Dog Café* take place in?
12. From what Ontario community was Jay Silverheels, the actor who played Tonto?
13. Which of the following crops were not originally cultivated by Ontario Native people: wild rice, barley, or squash?
14. In the movie *Dances with Wolves*, what is the name of the character played by Ontario's own Graham Greene?
15. What language do the Métis speak?
16. What Ontario First Nations community has laid claim to a portion of Caledonia for the past two years?

Difficult

17. In the classic *Star Trek* episode "The Paradise Syndrome," in which Captain Kirk lost his memory and was adopted by a Native tribe, what name did they call him?
18. What is Tommy Prince best known for?
19. What year did the Red River Rebellion take place?
20. Name the two members of Kashtin.
21. Name Ontario's only Native lieutenant governor.
22. What is the name of the Cleveland Indians baseball team's mascot?
23. What did the Vikings call the Indigenous people of the newly discovered Vinland?
24. What American tribe's language bears a substantial similarity to that of the Dene'?

Answers

1. Cree; 2. our land; 3. a village or group of houses; 4. no; 5. Haida Gwaii 6. 1960; 7. Jesse Jim; 8. Lynx River; 9. Chief Dan George; 10. Buffy Sainte-Marie; 11. Blossom, Alberta; 12. Six Nations, Ontario; 13. barley; 14. Kicking Bird; 15. Michif; 16. Six Nations, Ontario; 17. Kirock; 18. Canada's most-decorated soldier; 19. 1869; 20. Florent Vollant and Claude McKenzie; 21. James Bartleman; 22. Chief Wahoo; 23. Skraelings; 24. the Navajo.

HOME AND ABROAD

Just from the smell of sea air, smog, and silicone I could immediately tell I was back in the city of Los Angeles—Beverly Hills to be exact. I was there to accept an award from the First Americans in the Arts, an organization set up to help foster, develop, and promote Native participation in the arts, for my book on Native humour, *Me Funny*. Luckily for me that included Canadian writers. I always love coming to Los Angeles, but I will withhold judgment on whether I could live there or not. So many pros and cons. But Beverly Hills, let me tell you, if there was ever a place I wanted to stake a land claim ...

I knew I was living the cliché when a woman in a Saab convertible picked me up at the airport and drove me to my hotel by the ocean. Things were off to a good start, I thought. I could get used to this. The awards were fun and fabulous, though a bit long. Of course, they could have been even longer—unfortunately, two-thirds of the winners weren't there.

The event was held at the Beverly Hilton, an amazing hotel—the kind of place that convinces you your shoes would and could never be shiny enough to walk its marble halls. It was a pretty special evening, with the cream of the artistic Aboriginal crop wandering among the tables, exchanging cards and daily rates. Gary Farmer was there in the thick of things. Adam Beach was also supposed to be there, because he was receiving an award for his work on *Law & Order: SVU*. I tell you, I never saw so many young ladies' heads swivel every time a young Native man walked through the door. And a few men's heads too. But alas, he was a no-show. So they had to settle for Gary and me.

The whole evening was quite the experience for this little lad from Curve Lake First Nation, population approximately 1,200—depending on what's playing at the Cineplex. Imagine the scene: 400 of the best-dressed Native people in the country making small talk. There were tuxedos, bolo ties, shined cowboy boots, immaculate Stetsons, black dresses, and, surprisingly, plenty of plunging necklines (on the women, not the men). That's what really caught my attention for several reasons. The first is obvious. Second, that's not something Native people are particularly well-known for. In my travels I've noticed Native women are usually more reserved (no pun intended) about the wonders that exist in the valley between the mountains.

But not here. There were gorgeous dresses on a multitude of lovely Native women, showing off their multiple copper-coloured assets. I guess I shouldn't have been so shocked—after all, this is Beverly Hills—and most of the people here worked in show business. When in Rome ... Still, it was unexpected and admittedly breathtaking. I kept thinking two things: that maybe this could catch on in Curve Lake; and, for some reason, that I must remember to bake more bread.

Unfortunately, there was one challenge to the gala: trying to figure out what to bring back for my cousin Laurie. I always make it a point to bring her a gift that is culturally unique to whatever area of the world I'm visiting. When I went to Milan, I brought her back some authentic Parmesan from a local cheese shop. From Germany I brought her some cider. From the Czech Republic, beer. From China, green tea. I do this because she doesn't get the opportunity to travel like I do—what with having a job, a husband, and kids (I'm told they can interfere quite substantially with a person having fun). So, I try and bring the world to her. In small increments.

Being the sweetheart she is, she's often offered to reciprocate as best she can. In a few weeks she's off to Nashville for some country music festival, and she's offered to bring me back a souvenir or something unique to the area. From the state of Tennessee. All that comes to my mind is moonshine. And *The Beverly Hillbillies*.

Still, I know it's the thought that counts.

So there I was, at the Beverly Hilton, circulating amidst the beautiful Indigenous people, holding my stomach in, wondering what to get my cousin back home. What says LA? What says Beverly Hills? Oranges? Kelp? Cocaine? Then, from all around me, the answer came with a flash of lightning. I was blinded by the solution.

On my return, I brought her back a set of fake boobs from a nearby clinic. I guess you could say they were more for her husband, Danny, but he can thank me later. Maybe she can use them in Nashville.

There is a possibility that I might get a chance to go to Russia in the near future. I wonder how hard it is to get an AK-47?

A FUNNY THING HAPPENED TO ME ON
THE WAY TO BINGO

Native people are funny people in many different ways. Some are funny-looking. Some just smell kinda funny. Others are "kinda funny ... if you know what I mean." A few are funny in the head, while others walk kinda funny. Some dress funny. A select few Aboriginal politicians have had their hands in some funny business, but should have been on a funny farm instead. I've even known a few who were more fun than a barrel of monkeys (though I've never had the opportunity or inclination to investigate that phenomenon from a more clinical or objective perspective).

Native people have a long history of humour, telling jokes, having a good time, and tickling the proverbial funny bone in many delightful and culturally specific ways, despite many centuries of oppression, colonization, and ill-mannered or lost explorers. For example, the supposed "settling" of this land by "pioneers" has always reminded me of that children's song about the ten little bears lying in a bed. The bear on one end says, "Roll over," and they all do, making the little bear on the opposite end of the bed fall off. This is done till there's only one little bear left on the bed. A European bear.

I've spent quite a few years researching the true nature of Aboriginal humour, and like I always theorized, there's more out there than we tend to think. Centuries of being portrayed as the tragic or vanishing Indian tends to blunt the dominant culture's belief that we have anything worthwhile to laugh about. In my NFB documentary, *Redskins, Tricksters and Puppy Stew*, I explored the pudgy underbelly of what makes us Native/Aboriginal/First Nations/Indigenous/Indians chortle, snicker, and guffaw. And based on the success of that film, I compiled a book further exploring that genre, called *Me Funny*. It investigates the different forms of humour that we all grew up with. Hopefully it's everything you wanted to know about what makes an Aboriginal laugh, but were afraid to appear culturally insensitive in asking (that's chapter three, "How to Tell an Indian Joke without Using the Three 'B's: Beer, Bingo, and Bannock").

That being said, comedy is really a very serious business. I know, I've been in the business for two decades, with an occasional foray into what could be referred to as serious drama—like living on Italian food but ordering in Chinese occasionally. I was once told by an Elder from Alberta's Blood Reserve that "humour is the WD-40 of healing." Intriguing. Messy, but intriguing. Humour is also, in my humble opinion, the best way to deliver a message—the proverbial spoonful of sugar that makes the medicine go down. And who doesn't like a good laugh?

But lately there seems to be (and I could be paranoid) this sort of subversive plot to turn me towards I guess what can be called "the Dark Side of the Farce"—I've been getting more and more requests to write ... dare I say the words ... "serious stuff"—material that rings with Aboriginal angst, First Nations anguish, and Indigenous agony. And it's beginning to scare me. Oppression, depression, and suppression of cultures have been known to give me hives.

Often the seduction of "the dark side" starts with a seemingly innocent question like, "Do you ever write stuff that isn't funny?" or a statement like, "I prefer your more serious stuff." It is assumed by these innocents that humour and comedy are the illegitimate cousins of writing. Look how rarely comedies are nominated for, or actually win, any of the major movie awards.

In 2007, my first novel came out. Just your average Ojibway vampire story (write your own joke) called The Night Wanderer. Not a comedy per se but lots of funny bits scattered throughout the book. Just telling people it's a First Nations vampire novel will often make them smile. For my next book, the publisher kindly hinted that she would love me to write a residential school novel, from a Native student's perspective. Now there's proof positive that you should be careful what you ask for. As we say in funny business, "And the jokes just write themselves." And I don't think the world's ready for a residential-school comedy, any more than it is for a musical about the Holocaust. So I turned down the request, hinting that perhaps I wasn't the right person for the job.

A few years back, I was writer-in-residence for Native Earth Performing Arts in Toronto, and was about to start work on a new play for them. It was there that the artistic director told me directly, and rather strongly, that she would prefer something of a more serious nature from me. Paraphrasing, she wanted me to write something depressing that celebrated the dysfunctional Aboriginal: "We know you can be funny, Drew. Let's see you be serious."

I've been serious. But the novelty wears off after a while. And being funny is more ... fun. And who's to say the two cannot go hand in hand? Some of the best humour I've seen resonates with pain, reality, and darkness. And there are already so many people out there who excel at presenting the darker side of First Nations existence. Why should I eat from their plate?

I've just had my second novel published—no, not the residential school story—instead it's a tale about a contemporary rural legend, titled Motorcycles and Sweetgrass. My agent, upon reading it, said: "it's a lot more comedic than literary." Again, why can't the two be intertwined? Ever read Green Grass, Running Water or Catch 22? Still, my agent wants that serious novel from me sometime. Maybe, in a fit of depression, I'll write one, just to get these people off my back.

Eventually, I did give in to the artistic director's challenge—I did write that serious play for the theatre company that had hired me. After much soul-searching, I wrote about a residential school survivor seeing his abuser on the street and following him to work. It was difficult to write. Unsettling. Not my usual material. I did manage to slip in some black humour, because in my experience, that's the Native way. Even when facing tragedy, we still laugh. I'd hoped those would slide by the AD's notice.

Alas, it wasn't serious or depressing enough—it wasn't produced. And should it ever see the light of day, people might not want to see it because, after all, I'm known for my humour. In the USA I have been called "the Native Neil Simon" many times—which is both a good and bad thing. It's still hard to envision him doing that Holocaust musical I mentioned earlier.

Still, I'm glad I wrote that play, because I always wanted to see if I could. Now that I know I can, I can get back to my first love—the kind of humour that spreads the laughter of recognition, and not the kind that spreads the stigma of shame: "What do you call sixty-four Métis in one room? One full-blood."

In my research on the topic, I came across many other Native writers across Turtle Island, most of them far more respectable than myself, who have postulated and pondered the existence and essence of the Indigenous funny bone. Most of them have been to university so they must know what they're talking about. So please accept their ruminations about the nature of Aboriginal humour below. You may agree or you may not. That's your business. What you read may shock you. It may scare you. It might even make you think or laugh. But always remember ... smile when you say that, whatever that is.

"Humour is the mainstay of Indian life."   —Jaune Quick-To-See Smith

"Humour is really where the language lives, you know. It's very close to the centre and very important."   —N. Scott Momaday

"The Oglala were, and perhaps still are, the meanest group of Indians ever assembled. They would take after a cavalry troop just to see if their bow strings were taut enough."   —Vine Deloria Jr.

"Why is semen white and urine yellow? So the Chippewas can tell whether they're coming or going"   —Vine Deloria Jr.

"Not to make too much of it, but humour is the best and sharpest weapon we've always had against the ravages of conquest and assimilation. And while it is a tiny projectile point, it's often sharp, true and finely crafted."
                    —Paula Gunn Allen

"What's three feet high and a mile long? A Pueblo Grand Entry."
                    —Paula Gunn Allen

"A smile is sacred."   —Hopi proverb

"Everything is funny as long as it is happening to somebody else."

—Will Rogers

"When a people can laugh at themselves and laugh at others and hold all aspects of life together without letting anybody drive them to extremes, then it seems to me that people can survive."   —Vine Deloria Jr.

"One of the best ways to understand a people is to know what makes them laugh."   —Vine Deloria Jr.

"Wipe your Indian hands on your Levi jeans, get into your Toyota pickup. Throw in a tape of Mozart, Led Zepplin, or ceremonial Sioux songs; then throw your head back and laugh—you are a survivor of a colonized people. Paint what you see, sculpt what you feel, and stay amused."

—George Longfish

"My father was one-eighth Cherokee Indian and my mother was a quarterblood Cherokee. I never got far enough in arithmetic to figure out just how much 'Injun' that makes me, but there's nothing of which I am more proud than my Cherokee blood."   —Will Rogers

"For a people who are as poor as us, who have lost everything, who had to endure so much death and sadness, laughter is a precious gift ... We Indians like to laugh."   —John (Fire) Lame Deer

"Children, the insane, and primitive peoples all still have—or have rediscovered—the power to see."   —Paul Klee

"For Hopis, making fun is a way of making sense."   —Clyde Kluckhohn

"We have brought the earth. Now, it is time to play. As old as I am, I still have the feeling of play."   —N. Scott Momaday

"Humour has an important role through the Indian world in general. It is a tie that binds tribe to tribe to tribe. Humour has been a panacea for what ails. The woman tend to express their humour in a more subtle way than the men (who are often more blatant and slapstick) ... Indian humour is known to be sardonic, sometimes sinister, and it always appears in unlikely places. Humour is considered to have a role alongside the art forms, the landscapes, storytelling, and religion. Humour is a mainstay of Indian life."

—Jaune Quick-To-See Smith

"Traditional people talk about the importance of laughter and joy because when one is happy, it is easier to accept and learn new things."

—Frank La Pena

"I see the Indian capacity for humour as a blessing. And I see it as one of the fundamental miracles of our lives. It's a miraculous thing that's pulled us through so much. It's a force that's part of religion ... I truly believe that the older Indians laughed and laughed and laughed."

—Hanay Geiogamah

"Humour is widely used by Indians to deal with life. Indian gatherings are marked by laugher and jokes, many directed at the horrors of history, at the continuing impact of colonizations, and at the biting knowledge that living as an exile in one's own land necessitates."   —Paula Gunn Allen

"He's half Creek, half Plains. I'm part Creek and White. 'Which part do you want tonight?' I ask him."   —Joy Harjo

"Humour is a primary means of reconciling the tradition of continuance, bonding, and celebration with the stark facts of racial destruction."
                    —Paula Gunn Allen

"Indian humour draws the people together tribally, drives out an enthocentric aggressor, and redirects expectations towards a more collaborative future."   —Kenneth Lincoln

"It may be the one universal thing about Native Americans from tribe to tribe, the survival humour."   —Louise Erdrich

"... and Chippewas have the best sense of humour of any group of people I've ever known."   —Louise Erdrich

"I like to warp reality a little."   —James Welch

"When we reverse the 'contrary' twice, we're back where we started."
                    —Kenneth Lincoln

"You have noticed that the truth comes into this world with two faces, One is sad with suffering, the other laughs: but it is the same face, laughing or weeping."   —Black Elk

"Humour is a wild thing, quick on its wings."   —Max Eastman

"How do you keep White women in South Dakota from chewing their toenails? Make them wear shoes."   —Ward Churchill

"Cross-tribal humour tends to be 'inside,' and might be viewed as sexist, racist and all that ... but is really designed to keep folks with ample reason to do so from going off the deep end; hence it is in its way anti-racist."
                    —Ward Churchill

"There are two kinds of people in this world: Indians and those who want to be. There are two kinds of Indians in this world: the Sioux and those who want to be. And there are two kinds of Sioux in this world; the Oglalas and the rest who know better."   —Vine Deloria Jr.

"Humour is the WD-40 of healing."   —Blood Elder

FEAR CAN BE A SPOKEN WORD

Just a few weeks ago I attended the Calgary Spoken Word Festival where several dozen poets and other such spoken word artists had gathered together to extol the virtues of speaking out loud to entertain an audience—just them and their words. So the immediate question you might rightly ask is: what the hell was I doing there?! I am not a spoken word artist. I am not a spoken word anything. Well, I once ran a theatre company for three years, but never once did I feel the need to get on stage and actually speak words of emotion and knowledge, to dazzle and enthrall a paying audience with literary somersaults. In my younger days, the only performing I used to allow myself to do consisted of rattling off a few well-worn routines in singles bars. But even back then I rarely got a round of applause.

While it's true I've also delivered quite a few lectures to people in my day, that is hardly performing. That is … lecturing. So there I was, sandwiched between hip-hop artists and others who manged to make lines like "I saw a frozen coffee cup float by, half-filled with regret," sound intelligent and touching.

To try and prepare myself for this event, I actually did manage to write a poem—the first one since my angst-ridden teenage years. It went something like:

For I am old and bittersweet,
'Cause I refuse to twitter and tweet.

At first, I thought this might be my official submission to the Governor General's Award for Poetry, but I later thought better of it. It had come a little too easy, so I became concerned I may have unconsciously stolen it from Homer or Shakespeare or something, I wasn't sure. Still, it was an honest attempt at the genre and the audience seemed to appreciate it, but then two lines do not a poem make.

Still, I must have been invited there for some reason, so I asked. The powers-that-be at the festival claimed to have heard me speak and told me not to worry. Everything would be fine, don't worry, said the White woman to the Indian. Worse yet, I was performing on an evening featuring all male poets—at an event called Sexy Words, Hot Men—"the Chippendales of poetry," they advertised. That's all I needed, more pressure. I was worried I might not be able to … perform. I had visions of embarrassing myself at a literary version of The Full Monty—The Full Metaphor.

Over the years I have been to innumerable authors' festivals across Canada, and a few other countries to boot, promoting my novels, plays, creative non-fiction, and other books. So, as I said, I am not afraid of reading to a crowd. But you'll notice this wasn't a reading festival. The poster said "spoken word." For a few days after agreeing to show up, I desperately thought of perhaps trying to change the direction of my career and diversifying into Aboriginal hip-hop. After all, several years ago I had MC'd the opening festival for the Museum of the American Indian in Washington, and there was a hot young group from Alberta performing there, called War Party. They sounded pretty cool. Maybe I could do that.

Unfortunately, in the Native community, I guess I am viewed as being the white bread or cracker of the literary movement—or I guess in keeping with the proper literary metaphor, the brown or whole-wheat part. Not a cutting-edge kind of guy. I should mention here that I happen to like to wear my pants up about around my waist, where they don't show my underwear to the world. Call me old-fashioned, but a guy's gotta have some rules. Also, that I am blingless, unless belt buckles count as bling ... and while we're on the subject, who do you consult on sartorial issues like that?

As I was pondering these thoughts, I heard someone call my name. Rising from my seat, gritting my teeth, and making sure my pants were properly positioned, I went up to the mike. And talked. That's all. I had not really deconstructed the term "spoken word" properly. It means just that. Speaking words. I started to talk about things I knew, some of my books, humour, and Native sexuality. I just talked and told stories and jokes. Storytelling is spoken word. I and a lot of other people had just assumed it was poetry and related methods of vocalization. In the end, everybody applauded and I felt good about what I'd accomplished. In this new field of expression that had initially terrified me, I had just gone back to the basics, and come across just fine. I like it when that happens.

However, it has inspired me—I think I'll take a weekend off this summer and write a book of poetry.

East

East is typically represented by the colour red. Many of its teachings (and the substance of these articles) deal with culture and identity. Other attributes include the season of spring, the body, and all things of a physical nature, including the Earth (one of the four elements). Since it is the direction of the rising sun, a beginning, if you will, it also represents childhood, and therefore a path of guidance, leadership, and the spiritual. This is the place from where change can come. Tobacco and the eagle also come from the East, as do fishes and the turtle.

FLUFF AND FEATHERS/BEADS AND BLANKETS

Marketing Native North America Conference

There are two ways to go to London, England. One is to pay your own way. The other is to have your way paid. Luckily I ended up in the latter category when I was asked to give a keynote address at a conference being held at the British Museum—Marketing Native North America—where the promotion and sale of art and design of things Native North American was the theme. I guess I should say I am not a marketer. I am however a Native, and a North American involved in the arts, but not in design. And as a freelance playwright and writer, I always have more than enough words to share, especially since I usually get paid by the word. It's amazing how many adjectives you can stuff into a sentence when you get paid by the word. Really. Honestly. I'm not kidding. It's true. Uh-huh. And now that I think about it, that's a clever marketing idea.

I guess on a personal level, I first became aware of people's interest in buying practically anything Native when I was in college, a very long time ago. I had recently left the Curve Lake Reserve in Central Ontario in search of higher education and cable television, and was nervously but eagerly trying to make my way in Toronto, a city of three million people, the vast majority of them non-Native. So I concocted an entrepreneurial plan with a cousin of mine. He liked to fiddle around with odds and ends and make clever things, and he had started making some rather simplistic walking staffs—basically three-foot painted sticks with a few feathers and paint slapped on them: nothing awe-inspiring, but functionally pseudo-Ojibway.

I would then take them to the city and peddle them to some of my fellow students at the college, netting a decent 40-percent cut. It was then that I discovered two very important facts about the marketing and merchandising of Native "art"—and I'm using the term "art" quite loosely here. The first: a lot of people will buy anything as long as it looks exotic or, at the very least, seemingly steeped in another people's culture. One woman asked me to say a brief Ojibway prayer over the walking stick she was buying. Not being completely fluent in Ojibway, I obliged her by counting from one to ten. Hey, she was happy, I was happy. Welcome to the world of effective promotion and sales. The second thing I learned was that the marketplace can be quite fickle. Having saturated the market, my cousin's walking staffs quickly joined the ranks of other such dubious fads as pet rocks, bell-bottoms, and the mullet.

Making Native art, in its various forms, is a very popular pastime, and as luck would have it, from a very early age I was steeped in it. There is a building on our Reserve called the Whetung's Ojibway Centre, and it includes what we call the Art Gallery—I believe it's the largest privately owned Native art gallery in Canada. In years gone by, my mother used to work for the Whetungs, and as a kid, I used to work there too, doing odd jobs—practically everybody on the Reserve has worked there in some capacity or other. Surrounding me in that building was a plethora of art forms, ranging from soapstone carvings from the Arctic, to paintings by Norval Morrisseau, Daphne Odjig, and Roy Thomas, to various other works from a host of other up-and-coming Native artists. I was barely into my teens when it became obvious to me that people were coming from all over the world to our small community of maybe 800 people, two hours by car from anything very interesting to us. In those formative years I met Germans, Italians, Japanese, and a veritable cornucopia of international identities, all having travelled to our community to look at the art and buy some t-shirts, cheap tomahawks, and maybe even some turquoise jewellery.

Now this was back in the 1970s, when only a small fraction of the world knew of Canada's fabulous Native artistic traditions. We were the proverbial well-kept secret that was slowly leaking out like air from a worn-out tire. In the intervening years, Native art has become a major international growth industry in both good and bad terms. I have travelled the world and attended, among other things, an opening of a West Coast art exhibit in, of all places, Cologne, Germany. You wouldn't normally that think beer, schnitzel, and totem poles go together, but they sure did there. I have also had the dubious fortune of attending the launch of a "classic" book in Turin—again I use quotation marks in defining the term "classic"—translated into Italian: it was a little anthology called (and some of you may be familiar with it) *Tales from the Smoke House*, a thirty-year-old collection of erotic Native legends of questionable provenance. Well, as you know, nothing is quite as international, or sells as well, as sex.

More recently, I was in Australia. And in some discount store in a suburb of Brisbane, while looking for, of all things, a spatula—yes it's a little-known fact that Ojibways are masters of the spatula and I try to collect exotic and culturally based kitchen utensils whenever I travel—I came across, tucked in a dusty corner, a rack of one of the most internationally marketed symbols of Aboriginal culture ... the ubiquitous dreamcatcher. Ah yes, the mighty dreamcatcher—perhaps the best example of Aboriginal marketing gone mad. I have seen these things ... these supposed symbols of our culture, from Germany, to South Africa, to Italy, to Australia. They have become so universally prevalent that there are several of us in the Native community who wonder if they actually are of Native origin, or whether they are the product of some anonymous non-Native marketing genius. Several years back Stephen King even wrote a novel with *Dreamcatcher* as the title, and it was turned into a mediocre film. The dreamcatchers that I saw in Australia were made in China ... now there's a cultural headspin if there ever was one. Dreamcatchers are everywhere! As a result, there's a belief amongst our people that if you cut a dreamcatcher into five different pieces, when you wake up in the morning there will be five whole, complete dreamcatchers in your house. That's the only way to explain the sheer volume of them.

Historically, trade in artifacts amongst the First Nations of North America is as ancient as its people. The famous wampum belts of the Iroquois Confederacy and the Algonquin Nation were made from quahog shells, salt-water clams found along the eastern shores of the continent several hundreds of miles from the Ontario/Quebec border. That was a substantial distance back in those days. It would be like finding evidence of salt-water shrimp in Switzerland several thousand years ago. The shrimp wouldn't have migrated there naturally. But back before the days of FedEx and UPS, more than just things were traded amongst the First North Americans. The Iroquois have a social dance called the "Alligator Dance," and trust me, the Great Lakes are noticeably lacking in alligators. The dance had been traded and adopted from their Tuscarora cousins farther down the American continent, where alligators are more common.

Whether what I write is art or not has been debated for years. But perhaps this is as good a place as any to talk about what I am familiar with, the somewhat related world of theatre—Native theatre to be exact. And its plans of worldwide conquest. Back in the 1990s, I used to be the artistic director of Native Earth Performing Arts, Canada's premiere Native theatre company. My mother affectionately refers to those years as the last time I had a "real" job. Be that as it may, it was during this time that I became increasingly aware of the growing influence, internationally, of Canada's Native theatre.

Tomson Highway, an immensely talented Cree man from Brochet, Manitoba, is one of Canada's leading Native playwrights, but more than that, he is simply one of Canada's leading playwrights. In 1986, Native Earth premiered a play he wrote called *The Rez Sisters* that took Toronto, then Canada, by storm. In 1988, he was invited to take it to the internationally famous Edinburgh Fringe Festival where it, to use the Canadian vernacular, "kicked ass." Since then, it has been produced in many countries, including—I hear—a very interesting production in Japan. Occasionally, when I feel like my world has become a little too intense and I need a surreal break, I try to picture this production and its cast of seven Japanese actresses attempting to speak Cree. And I bet you that somewhere on that set there was probably a dreamcatcher.

One of my plays, *Toronto at Dreamer's Rock*, has been translated into German. That's why I've learned to say, "Ich bin ein Ojibway." And perhaps most amusing or interesting from my own personal perspective was a production of a play of mine called *The Baby Blues*. It's a pow wow comedy that takes place on a fictional Reserve in Central Ontario. So picture this: I got a call one day from a gentleman with an unusual accent who said he'd just read my play and loved it. He said he would be very interested in producing it. I said, "Great. Fabulous. Send me the cheque." He then said, "But first you'll have to help me translate it."

"Translate it into what?" I asked.

"Oh, I'm sorry. I'm phoning from the University of Venice."

My first thought was: "That's the place with all the water for streets." So, my humble little comedy about pow wow politics had caught the eye of the head of a university theatre department half a world away. "Why?" I couldn't help thinking! It's a play about an aging fancy dancer. Let me give you some context. Basically, pow wows back home break down into two types—traditional and competitive (I think the differences are pretty self-evident just from the titles). And at the competitive pow wows, there are three types of competition dancers among the men: "traditional," the slowest; grass dancers, the next up the chain; and fancy dancers, at the top. They are often the most spectacular, adorned with the brightest and most extravagant plumage and costuming—and this form of dancing is the most energetic and spectacular. And as is often the case with any athletic sport or form of dancing, it is the sport of the young. Because it is so aerobically oriented and physically exhausting, it begins to wear and tear on the knees and the lungs. As the dancer gets older, he may go back to the less stressful, but just as culturally important, traditional or grass dancing.

So, now that you're armed with that background information, my play is about a thirty-nine-year-old fancy dancer who refuses to acknowledge the passing years. He still dances fancy, but he isn't winning at the pow wow competitions anymore; he's getting too old. Up until now, he has spent most of his life believing in three things: dancing, partying, and chasing girls. He's not a very deep fellow, and getting a bit moth-eaten around the edges. He also hates responsibility. He isn't married, has no kids, and doesn't want any. He just wants to party and have as much fun as possible, for as long as possible. Basically, he has refused to grow up. I don't know if you have men like that in your culture?

So the play deals with Noble—that's his name—driving to this Reserve that he hasn't been to in a number of years for the annual pow wow. Hungover, he starts setting up his tent when he spots this beautiful young girl. His interest is piqued, and he approaches her, trying to sweet-talk her using all his tried and tested moves. Through the conversation, both he and the audience discover the girl is his long-lost daughter, conceived during his last trip here eighteen years ago. Don't you hate it when that happens? So, typically, he tries to run away, but is stopped by the mother of the girl, who sabotages his truck and refuses to let him leave until he can come up with, on that weekend, seventeen years of back-payments for child support. All in all, a typical story of life in the community.

So I'm asking, "Why do you want to produce my play that's basically about a man who hates responsibility? Who just travels around chasing women, knocking them up, and refusing to deal with his actions—a very shallow and selfish man?"

"I think it's something Italians can relate to," he says.

So eventually he ended up producing the play, god bless him. I was scheduled to go over and see it, but for a number of reasons I missed the actual production. But the man sent me a videotape of it, and the Italian version of the play was quite surreal. Picture it if you can: A theatre, or more accurately I believe it's called a *teatro*, on the canals of Venice. The set was quite probably designed by somebody who's never been to Canada, let alone a First Nations Reserve. The actors are in costumes no doubt designed by a designer who probably has never seen a Native person, let alone been to a pow wow. And the actors are all Italian for obvious reasons—not a lot of Native people speak Italian. The video shows a bunch of Italian actors running back and forth across the stage yelling out, "Ill pow wowa!" Now, if that's not a case of successful international Aboriginal marketing, I don't know what is. Indigenous theatre in Italy. Who'd have thunk it? The play did get laughs. Which doesn't surprise me.

In my own career as one-time artistic director of Native Earth, I've had to deal with issues of a marketing nature—specifically, marketing a particularly Native product, our plays, to a primarily non-Native consumer, the audience. Let me explain. Toronto, which by the way, is the third largest English-speaking theatre community in the world after London and New York, is a city of three million people in the downtown core (or five million taking into consideration the Greater Toronto Area). Of that three to five million, approximately 70,000 are of Native ancestry. Toronto is often referred to as the largest Reserve in Canada. And of those 70,000, maybe three or four hundred at best are regular theatre-goers. As with most companies, we usually produced plays for a three-week run in a space that sat roughly 100 to 120 people, depending on the configuration of the set. Now, if you do the math, you can immediately see the difficulty if we were to produce plays primarily for the Toronto Native community. We could close down after three days, because our entire target market would have seen the play. We could extend that run to four days if they had relatives coming in from out of town.

So, as a production company, we had to be conscious of the fact we had to market our Native plays to non-Native audiences as well. After all, we had two and a half weeks of seats to fill, which meant marketing primarily to non-Native audiences. Keep in mind our company's mandate was to produce plays by and about the Native experience. While it was important for us to be contemporary storytellers and chronicle our place in Canadian society, it was also important for us as a business to put bums in seats (to use a theatrical term). I'm sure all the businesspeople out there will understand this concept. And to tell you the truth, we didn't care what colour those bums were. In a dark theatre, all bums look alike. Luckily, the very essence of theatre itself provided for those non-Native bums. In terms of comedies, if it usually makes us laugh, generally it will make them/you laugh too. We're funny that way. For example, we watch *Friends* and *The Simpsons* and frequently wonder, with considerable amusement, if this is how White people really live.

In terms of drama, the emotions a play generates in members of a non-Native audience, believe it or not, are usually the same emotions generated in us. We all cried during *E.T.* and *Old Yeller*, right? So while the theatre we at Native Earth produced was Native in content and voice—thus the name Native Earth—in essence it was still about people who laughed, who cried, and who watched bad television. Native people are not from another planet. As I like to say, there is no particularly Native way to boil an egg. Non-Native audiences would come and see our plays if they were good. Quality theatre does not require cultural baggage, and can be appreciated by all, regardless of origin.

However, I retain the right to assert the caveat that there are exceptions to every rule. Some things are very Native in content and style. There have been many performances or exhibits I have attended that have appealed specifically to my Aboriginal heritage, and I'm sure some of their aspects were lost on the larger population. One of my plays, a comedy, that had a normal running time of one hour and forty-five minutes, swelled to almost two full hours when we held a special fundraising performance whose audience was composed entirely of Native people. This special audience suddenly got all the "in" jokes, and their laughter added a surprising extra fifteen minutes to the performance, which is unusual in professional theatre. In fact, there was so much laughter that it actually threw the timing of the actors off. While the play was still enjoyed immensely by the predominantly non-Native audiences that attended on other nights, it's just that there were special nuances within the text and performances that were appreciated by the Aboriginal crowd. So don't misunderstand me when I say cultural and artistic barriers are not as limiting as they may seem. There are differences. I would love to see an episode of the television cooking show *Iron Chef* featuring muktuk, an Inuit delicacy of whale skin and fat. Yumm! Or the fast-food version—McMuktuk.

When people think about things having a universal appeal, they tend to forget even the universe has finite borders. As a result, there are just as many cultural trapdoors and pits of moral quicksand that permeate the Aboriginal marketing landscape as any other niche market. The roads to Swiss bank accounts are littered with the bodies of misjudged commercial ideas— from all fronts. Recently, a situation arose during the Junos—the Canadian music awards—that created a very interesting dilemma about what is Aboriginal music. A few years back, the Junos had instituted, for the first time, a best Aboriginal music category. Everybody commented, "What a fabulous breakthrough." But as with anything that's being tried out for the first time, it was discovered over time that the rules needed some ... adjustments.

During that first year, a young non-Native woman whose name escapes me was nominated for the award. She had recorded a traditional song that belonged to a prominent West Coast Native family, the Georges. In her liner notes she acknowledged the copyright of the George family, so that passed muster with the award's screening jury. But after she was nominated for the Juno, the George family reported that she hadn't received permission to record the song. She claims she did, and the ensuing controversy created quite an uproar. A non-Native woman being nominated for a Native music award was legally permissible at the time because the Aboriginal Recording of the Year Award rules had stated: "Eligible music styles include all traditional Aboriginal music: Iroquois social, pow wow drum, all hand drums, Inuit throat singing, traditional flutes, Métis, Cree, and Micmac fiddling. In addition, fusions of all genres of contemporary music that incorporate the above and/or reflect the unique Aboriginal experience in Canada, by virtue of words or music." Nothing in the rules said anything about the artist having to be Native.

That same year, a talented Cree country singer named Vern Cheechoo was not even nominated for his album *Lonesome & Hurting*, a collection of country tunes and ballads he wrote and recorded. Even though Vern was a Cree from the very Cree community of Moose Factory, the selection committee felt his songs were generic country music, with nothing vaguely Native about their content, words, or music. So technically the singer/songwriter was Native but his music wasn't, according to the jury, so he didn't qualify—an interesting conundrum. The next year the rules were changed to prevent such controversial situations from happening again.

But this does bring up an interesting point: is there a clear delineation between what is or isn't Native art; or more simply put, how does anybody define Native art? I remember having many discussions over the years with visual artists of all types who during the last couple of decades had been discussing whether Native art was art by Natives, or about Natives, or a combination of both. And who has the right to control this debate? Back in the 1980s there was an artist in Central Ontario who would do pseudo-Inuit sculptures and sell them under the pseudo-Inuit name of Dimu. Dimu was short for his real name, Dieter Muckenheim. "Ich bin ein Inuit." And yet on the other hand, there's a wonderful visual artist in Ottawa named Leo Yerxa, an Ojibway from the Fort Frances area of Western Ontario, who had a very traditional Ojibway upbringing. Yet, if you look at some of his paintings, they have an almost Japanese watercolour texture to them—not a style usually associated with Native visual artists.

Because these boundaries are so loose and varied, there has been some concern among Native artists over the appropriation of Native designs or cultural artifacts by profit-oriented non-Native organizations. For example, such culturally specific Aboriginal designs as the inukshuk—the stone men erected by the Inuit to mark trails or food caches—have been wholly appropriated by various non-Native businesses, including, among many others, the International Olympic Committee.

Another recent example is the case of a British Columbia winery that commissioned a local artist named Ken Kirby, a non-Native, to design the label for a new bottle of wine. The design he came up with prominently featured an inukshuk, raising some concerns in the Inuit and Native communities regarding cultural theft and, of course, the inappropriateness of such an image on a bottle of wine, given the effect alcohol has had on many Indigenous communities. Historically, generic symbols like the inukshuk were not owned by any particular Nation and the idea of private property was a foreign concept to many Nations. But because of a proliferation of such obvious and controversial appropriations, conferences and seminars have popped up in many Canadian cities in recent years dealing with the concept of "TK"—Traditional Knowledge. In fact, the Department of Canadian Heritage is planning gatherings in six Canadian cities this April to discuss the issue. They will ponder and discuss what is fair and unfair in the world of Traditional Knowledge, arts and culture, and marketing and merchandising. Both Natives and non-Natives are invited to participate and, needless to say, the discussions are bound to get a bit heated.

And it's not just an issue in Canada. Traditional Knowledge has been discussed in nine United Nations Forums, and twice a year in Geneva there is a meeting of the Intergovernmental Committee on Traditional Knowledge, Genetic Resources, and Folklore. Its aim is to develop international standards regarding the use of TK. So, if you want some words of advice, never ask a North American Native about such issues as sports teams like the Atlanta Braves, Cleveland Indians, or Washington Redskins ... I've been to Washington; their skin isn't any more red than any other football team's. In fact, most of them are Black. Same with the Indians and Braves ... so their naming logic is lost on me.

But I digress. The world of Native art and design has expanded past the "traditional"—and again that word is in quotation marks—forms of expression. Paintings, sculpture, pottery, and various other conventional artworks usually associated with Native artists are now only the tip of the artistic iceberg. The sky is the limit in these art forms. Music, theatre, film, video, dance ... the list is as long as a pow wow grand entry. Several years ago, David Wolfman, a Native chef, competed in the Culinary Olympics held in Paris, France. He and his team walked away with seven gold medals for his creative fusion of traditional Native foods and contemporary cooking methods.

The shirt I am wearing today is by Dorothy Grant. She is a talented Haida designer located in Vancouver, who uses and honours her traditional heritage in the design of shirts, suits, dresses, jackets, and even cummerbunds. She is at the top of her game in Canada, and trust me, the price I paid for this shirt proves it. The jacket I walked into this building wearing is a Pat Piche, a talented Cree designer located just outside Edmonton. She's famous for her fabulous and distinctive jackets and ribbon shirts. I could give you the emails and phone numbers of half a dozen other designers I have come across in the last year. One of the more exciting events at what some consider the largest pow wow held in Canada, the SkyDome pow wow held every year in Toronto, is the fashion show. And this will tell you how far Native designers have come in that department. Last spring I was at an art gala in Saskatoon—yes they do have art galas in Saskatoon—and this reporter came up to me and asked me who I was, what I did, and who I was wearing. That's a true story, and I was so proud to answer her.

But perhaps the most exciting thing about the growth in the promotion of Native art and design is the fact that, in many cases, it is in the hands of the Native artists themselves or their representatives. Many of the artists of various disciplines I've mentioned are masters of their own artistic and entrepreneurial worlds. The trading-post days are hopefully over. Either that or we have taken over the trading posts. For a while I had a Native agent, an Indian agent if you will, who handled my career.

I remember hearing a bizarre story once. It could be the Arctic equivalent of an urban legend, but several decades ago when Inuit settlements in the Far North were beginning to appreciate the lucrative possibilities of soapstone carvings, they threw themselves into the business wholeheartedly. Many communities set up co-ops that helped foster the development of this fast-growing industry. So lots and lots of top-quality carvings were coming out of the North. But Canada's North can be a very hard and distant place to get to, or more importantly, a very hard and distant place to get lots and lots of heavy stone carvings out of. So much of it was being made and flown out by airplanes, Inuit soapstone carvings became the only art you could buy by the ton. Whether it's true or not, I don't know. Ask one of the experts here in Inuit art. I'm an Ojibway—all I know is that beaded gloves don't weigh a lot.

I will leave you with one final First Nations tale about the changing face of commerce. I heard this story in Halifax. Back several hundred years ago when settlers were first arriving, they made a deal or treaty with the local Micmacs. For a set fee, they got a couple of miles of land to build their houses on. So a small community was built and a trading relationship was set up with the local Native population, who learned the way things were bought and sold in the Caucasian community. But as is often the case, before you knew it these settlers began to multiply, and more and more of them began to show up on the beaches. It wasn't long before more and more land was needed. So, a meeting was quickly established with the local Micmacs. "We need more land," the settlers said.

The Micmacs heard the words of their White neighbours and went off to discuss and argue the request. They came back a few days later. The mighty Micmac chief approached the leader of the Caucasian community and said, "We have talked long and hard about this. Some did not want to sell you any more land. Others did. Finally, after much discussion, we came to a consensus. We will sell you more land. But we will sell it to you the same way you sell us things—by the pound." I'll leave the moral of that story up to you.

Personally, I think conferences like this one are a great opportunity to explore what is out there in the Native artistic community. I also think such a conference is a great opportunity to see what happens when you marry art with commerce. The bastard child of this union will emerge on Sunday. And you get to change its diapers. So have fun, learn a lot, pay attention, and please remember, art starts with imagination—as do marketing and promotion.

Oh yes, and my final word on the promotion and sale of Native art and design ... feel free to order and buy any of my fourteen books. Christmas is less than eleven months away.

A HORSE OF A DIFFERENT COLOUR

One of the questions I am asked frequently by non-Natives when I'm off travelling the world spreading the Gospel of Native literature and humour is: "In referring to Canada's original inhabitants, I've heard the terms Aboriginal, Native, First Nations, and Indigenous tossed about a lot, even the term Indian sometimes. It's so complicated in these politically correct times ... but what is the technically accurate term I should use when talking about your people?" My first response is usually "tolerant," but then I start to seriously ponder the issue.

This is a good question because it can indeed get quite complicated for those inside and outside our communities from time to time. As William Shakespeare wrote, "A rose, by any other name, would smell as sweet." It's the same with Natives/First Nations/Aboriginals ... "an Ojibway, by any other name (Saulteaux, Chippawa, Algonquin, etc.), would smell as sweet." That is so true. Feel free to test the hypothesis. I'd like to see that phrase on a pow wow t-shirt someday.

Sometimes, even within our community, it tends to be a little difficult making such a decision—coming up with that all-inclusive, generic, one-size-fits-all term. Most people would say First Nations is a safe bet, but a lot are more comfortable with Native or Aboriginal. And even if you are part of that same Native community, and frequently of an older generation, the term Indian can indeed still be heard quite often.

I, myself, in order to live a more politically correct life (not that I try real hard, but it sounds good) sometimes urge people to adopt a term I came up with several years ago: NAFNIP. We are NAFNIPs, stand proud and tall! In case you're curious as to the acronym's origins, it stands for Native, Aboriginal, First Nations, Indigenous People. NAFNIP. It's one word that covers just about everything. Once more, I see a world of t-shirts bearing this name.

However, I recently came across another single word that describes who we are in a new and original way. I had been unfamiliar with this word. It was in a newspaper article about a spelling bee of all things. It was the final award-winning word, so I knew it had good karma attached to it. It is a relatively new word I believe, one born in English, yet it seems to be all-encompassing and accurate. So, for those of you out there who happen to care, I would like to suggest to the Assembly of First Nations that we consider adopting this homogeneous name that will bond us all together. I humbly submit that we call ourselves "autochthonous." It's a word, I've read, that means "native" or "indigenous." Hey, that's us. Autochthonous. Nobody else out there seems to use it. I think we should adopt it. I do believe it is the technically correct term for our dilemma ... "Hey, dude, I'm autochthonous. Pass the lard."

Of course the Assembly of First Nations would have to change their name to the Assembly of the Autochthonous. Then instead of being the AFN, it would simply be ... AA. Now how's that for irony? Their meetings would take on a whole new meaning.

Think of our national anthem: "Our home and autochthonous land." Or a community of people walking into a lawyer's office, wanting to establish their autochthonous land claim. Doesn't that sound so natural, almost rolling, as it does, off the tongue? You can picture yourself waiting around to fill out all those damn forms at the government's Department of Autochthonous Affairs, after seeing your local autochthonous agent. See, it gets easier after a while. Try it.

You know, you blow into town, you're thirsty and want to find some of your people to hang out with, so you hunt down the local autochthonous bar to throw back a few beers with your fellow autochthonous brothers and sisters. You are Proud to be Autochthonous! The militant American Indian Movement would become the American Autochthonous Movement, otherwise known as AAM.

The new First Nations University in Saskatchewan, whose initials always make me laugh—FNU, or more graphically put, Effin' You! (to resolve this, they added the letter C to the acronym, for Canada; it became FNUC, as in Fnuc Off!)—would now be known as Autochthonous University, or AU: Hey, you! People would be telling autochthonous jokes, eating autochthonous tacos, spending all their money at the autochthonous casinos, driving their autochthonous cars, filling up on their cheap autochthonous gas, and smoking their discount autochthonous cigarettes ... well, you get the point. No point in beating a dead horse (too late, right?)

I know change is a frightful thing, and not all might be willing to adopt such a radical shift in title. But keep in mind, it might just be the way you're saying it. Autochthonous ... Maybe if they can't understand, it's because your accent is too thick.

NATIONAL ABORIGINAL DAY

For those of you not aware of the significance of June 21, it is National Aboriginal Day. It is a day of First Nations celebration, of Indigenous reflection, of Aboriginal commemoration, and of Native pride. All in one day. We affectionately call it by its acronym—NAD. Traditionally (and that's a loaded word in the Native community) this is the day most Native organizations give their employees a day off, or if they're Métis, half the day off. So, in keeping with that spirit, today is the day you should take an Indian to lunch—remember, they like a lot of carbs, most of them simple, not complex. Or let that Cree go first at the dry cleaners. Hug an Innu. If you see a Salish person on the highway, let him or her have the right of way with a happy wave of your hand. Settle a local land claim even. It's all good karma stuff.

Personally, however, I must confess to a certain amount of mixed emotions with respect to this particular holiday. Like people who celebrate or criticize pow wows, such an event has its pros and cons. I guess you could say, culturally speaking, it's like our own St. Patrick's Day ... but I don't think we need another holiday that celebrates massive amounts of drinking and puking. Too much baggage and bad press. And that Christian connection hasn't exactly worked for a lot of Native people either, in case it isn't apparent.

By the way, to all the Irish out there, we invented the potato. Just want to get that straight. I once got into a half-hour argument with an Irish woman over that. It led to tragic results that for legal reasons I can't elaborate on.

And while I suppose it's good that June 21 is the longest day of the year—we can use those couple of extra hours of sunlight to enjoy our buffalo wings—I have to point out that Afro-Canadians get four friggin' weeks for Black History Month. Granted they could have picked a better month, it being the gloomy and frosty month of February—which is also the shortest month of the year. Still, they have a month. So, does that mean we're only one-twenty-eighth as good or important as them? And let's not forget, National Aboriginal Day is jammed right in the middle of Gay Pride Week in Toronto. So what does that infer, over all? I'm not sure, but all this does make you pause for thought.

After all the recent awkward happenings in Caledonia and other places across the country, maybe such a holiday is a good thing—we could sure use a break. It's been a hard year, what with debates over how much residential school survivors should get, and let's not forget the constant chaos and anarchy regarding the administration of Regina's First Nations University of Canada, affectionately known as FNUC, my second favourite acronym. And who could forget all the fun things that happened up in Kashechewan, Ontario, last fall, where drinking water became more dangerous than serving David Ahenakew gefilte fish.

So hopefully, a holiday like National Aboriginal Day will massage our wounded and sore cultural muscles. It will allow us to stand tall and proud, or short and proud, generally depending on what Nation we come from. It will also remind Canadians that there is more to Native culture than blockades, protests, and tobacco shacks. Believe it or not, none of those three things is included in most treaties. Across Canada, different cities and communities will be doing their own thing to celebrate this holiday, and everybody is usually welcome. National Aboriginal Day, not to be confused with the lesser-known Regional Aboriginal Day, is not just for Native people, any more than most of the people drinking green beer on March 17 are actually Irish. Christmas these days is no longer just for Christians, and Groundhog Day is celebrated by more than just groundhogs in these enlightened times. So, be hip and bring a Caucasian friend. As I frequently confess, some of my best friends are White.

So to all you people out there, every June 21 I want you to think of all the Native people you know and have met in your lives. And high-five them. This is their/our day. After all, 500 years of colonization, residential schools, forced adoption, ignored treaty obligations, the Reserve system ... come to think of it, maybe we do only need twenty-four hours to acknowledge all the good things that have happened in the past year or so. And, on second thought, maybe there should be massive amounts of drinking involved.

So on behalf of all the Native people of Canada, I hope your NADs are great. If not, see a doctor.

IT'S NOT EASY BEING RED

You know, it's not easy being Native in Canada, and I'm not talking about residential schools, land claims, racism, and all the other stuff you hear about in the media. I'm talking about the issues you don't normally hear about, quagmires of decision that our own moral conscience make difficult. Sometimes even driving an automobile can be a political statement for us— heaven forbid any self-righteous Aboriginal person be caught driving a Cherokee, Winnebago, or Pontiac—they could revoke your Treaty Card for that, although the jury is still out on the Aztek.

Even choosing a baseball team presents its own set of difficulties ... no Cleveland Indians or Atlanta Braves for us. That Indian chick on the Land O'Lakes margarine container makes me uncomfortable, and don't even talk to me about eating any Oka cheese. There's a danger of flashbacks, you know.

My own personal moral dilemma got its start last year when a theatre company on the northern shore of Lake Erie offered to produce a play I wrote called *400 Kilometres*. It's a touching yet humorous story about Native adoption and identity—so far, so good. Then, several months ago, this little incident called Caledonia happened in Southern Ontario, where Iroquois members from the Six Nations Reserve blockaded a housing development and a road to protest inactivity on a long-neglected land claim and the building of a subdivision on disputed land. That's the Coles Notes version of a more complex story.

My problem began right around then. You see, Caledonia turned into a long, often antagonistic siege which turned non-Natives against their Native neighbours, and though it's been nominally settled, tensions and anger still run pretty deep in the area. There's still name-calling and everything. Here's where things get complicated. Lighthouse Festival Theatre, the non-Native theatre company that was producing my play, is about twenty minutes down the same highway that was blockaded. Though the road has now been open for a while, memories are still slowing down the traffic. Ticket sales for my play are way down because there's a sense in the area among the non-Natives: "Why should we support Native theatre after the hell they've put us through?" Thus the problem.

I think the technical term for what's happening to my theatrical child is called collateral damage. Or fallout. This is my fourth play at the theatre in a dozen years, and all have done exceedingly well. Until now. And the frustrating thing is that these two incidents/issues, whatever you want to call them, are completely unrelated.

First of all, the characters in my play are Ojibway, not Iroquoian. In the Native community that makes a huge difference—like the Maple Leafs and the Canadiens. You do NOT mix up the two. But evidently for some sports fans, we all supposedly look alike and share the same land claims. While I support the aims of the Six Nations people for the most part, I have to ask … what did I do? I had absolutely nothing to do with the goings on at Caledonia. Honest. I have an alibi. I was playing cards. And my play was written a good six years or so before anything happened there. I don't even live in the area. I like White people. Really! Some of my best friends are non-Native, honest! I even have one that cleans my house twice a month. She's a good worker with excellent references.

The theatre company is worried that the play might lose money. Understandably they are reluctant to address the whole Caledonia issue directly in their publicity for the show. It might do more damage than good. But do you ignore the elephant in the middle of the living room or address it? It's important to note that nine-tenths of this theatre company's audience is non-Native, though it is just twenty minutes from Six Nations, the most populous Native community in Canada. Native people are not big theatre-goers, unfortunately.

So what does a humble Ojibway playwright do in a situation like this? Tell people, "Just ignore what happened at Caledonia and come enjoy the play?" That might alienate me from all my friends in Six Nations and I can't have that. "My play is 100-percent land-claims-free?" Again, might be some alienation involved. Post signs saying, "No blockading allowed!" or "White people welcome!" or "Leave your lawsuits at the door!" or "I had a great-great-grandmother who was part Native and she never blockaded any-thing!" Hard to say.

I recognize that there are larger issues in the world than just my ability to pay my landlord. But in the end, I'm just a playwright looking for an audience. Some say art imitates life … I hope not. I don't want my play to become a victim of collateral damage.

THE SUMMER OF OUR DISCONTENT

On June 29, the Natives were restless. It was to be a day of protest, the Assembly of First Nations urged. Time for Aboriginals of Canada to unite. Raise your fists to the sky and yell out, "We're mad as hell and we're not going to take it anymore." Nobody really knew what was going to happen—there could be road blocks, train routes compromised, taxes hiked way up on Native cigarettes, anything and everything was possible.

With things still percolating in Caledonia, and that little flare-up a few months ago in Tyendinaga, the AFN thought the time was right for Aboriginal people to band together collectively and let the citizens of Canada and their various governments (in particular, a blind Prime Minister Harper and his myopic Conservatives) know that ... well ... it's not easy being red.

This October will mark the 515th anniversary of the introduction of illegal immigration into North America. Five hundred and ten years in Canada alone. And in that time, the First Nations of Canada have, through no fault of their own, managed to accrue a substantial plethora of grievances. Here are but a few that were discussed in private*:

WE DEMAND that Indian and Northern Affairs Canada (INAC) hire a public relations firm to initiate a campaign informing the Canadian public that the majority of Native people do indeed pay taxes. Only those who live and work directly on the Reserve are exempt—just a percentage of the overall Native population. Trust me; my bookkeeper, my accountant, and I have done the research. Four times. If you ever hear someone say, "You Native people don't pay any taxes" again, ask where their cottage is, and a land claim form will be issued.

WE DEMAND, on a similar note, something be done in general about the belief that Canada's First Nations get everything for free. This is true only if you count the bad water in Kashechewan, illnesses from black mould in inadequate housing, linguistic genocide, diabetes, and rampant physical and sexual abuse. Trust me, we've paid for all this. In many ways. I've heard the phrase "Give until it hurts," but this is ridiculous.

WE DEMAND that the federal government embrace the radical concept of actually appointing a Native person as the minister of Indian affairs. We humbly ask: Isn't the attorney general usually a lawyer? Isn't the minister for the status of women usually a woman? Doesn't the minister of transportation have a driver's licence? Isn't the minister of defence usually defensive?

WE DEMAND that filmmakers of any nationality be stopped from using flute music on the soundtrack of any and all documentaries about Native people. And no more feathers either. And dreamcatchers. On TV too.

WE DEMAND that White people (or more politically correctly known as People of Pallor) stop angrily saying, "They shouldn't do that!" in regards to Native protests and blockades, and exchange it for the more understanding, "They shouldn't HAVE to do that." It's technically more correct.

WE DEMAND that somebody do something about the persistent, offensive, and inaccurate stereotype that all Native people have drinking problems. Personally, it's been about three years since I had my last mimosa.

WE DEMAND that Lorne Cardinal be given his own spin-off series from *Corner Gas*.

WE DEMAND there be educational classes for warriors on how to dress for protests and court. Somebody should explain to them the true function of camouflage, and the simple fact that in a court of law, camouflage's intended effect is somewhat limited, due to a lack of substantial vegetation. If you want to disappear into the background in a court house, I'm told a suit is far more effective and less noticeable.

WE DEMAND all commercials advertising Lakota pain medicine be pulled. Immediately.

WE DEMAND the Assembly of First Nations explain what it is it actually does. Other than call for days of protest.

WE DEMAND the police forces in this country stop shooting, assaulting, and otherwise abusing the civil rights of Native people. It's for their own benefit. There are substantially more Native people in this country than police. And per capita, Native people have more guns than the police.

WE DEMAND the federal government apologize to survivors for over half a century of abuse at the hands (and other parts of the body) of residential schools. There are just some things children should not learn in school.

WE DEMAND that instead of being forced to recognize the passage of time by the dominant culture's BCE (before Common Era) and AD (*Anno Domini*), we use the more culturally sensitive TI (Time Immemorial) and PC (post-Contact).

* None of these demands was discussed, much less authorized by the Assembly of First Nations, Lakotas, warriors, or Lorne Cardinal.

GLOBALIZATION AND POSTMODERNISM COME TO TURTLE ISLAND

Just a little while ago I was invited to speak at a conference in Regina dealing with international human rights and globalization—not my normal areas of expertise, but since my career as a First Nations writer began, I have been asked to speak or write on a multitude of topics not usually associated with the Native community: subjects like crystal meth (while a problem in some Native communities, there are no labs in my laundry room), Leonard Cohen (he's a singer or something, right?), or Jane Jacobs (a guy who lives on a Reserve was requested to write about a leading urban planner?)

But it was trying to see the topic of globalization from an Aboriginal perspective that did get me thinking—about this and a whole bunch of other fashionably popular technical terms to describe elements of modern Canadian society. How many of them are mistakenly believed to be shiny and new, but in fact have been around since the first Caucasian boot set foot on Indigenous soil? It's all a matter of perception.

Most people think globalization is a current topic, but some of us actually believe it's been an issue around here for over five hundred years. When two lost Italians, Christopher Columbus, working for the Spanish, and John Cabot (born Giovanni Caboto), sent by the English, came knocking on the door of Turtle Island, Europeans first recognized what countless other civilizations and cultures knew before them—that the world is a globe. Ever since then, First Nations people have been dealing with the threats (and dubious benefits) of "globalization." It was, after all, 1492 and 1497 respectively that the first North American restaurants opened, offering shepherd's pie, tapas, and some decent pasta primavera. Economies changed. Our people's methods of existence on the planet had to be modified and restructured to meet the oncoming flux of European capitalization and trade. Our entire continent became a source of raw materials for them; global economies shifted and shivered as our gold, fur, lumber, and other goods were redistributed around the world. The work force available on Turtle Island (and to a certain extent in Africa) had to radically adapt to the needs of this new world economy. It was laissez-faire at its worst. The original name for NAFTA was the TICADWYWA (Turtle Island—Come And Do What You Want Agreement).

However, it's not all one-sided. I have seen evidence of a conspiracy to take over the world, perpetrated in its own way by the Native people of this continent. Two years ago, on a month-long visit to Australia, I found myself in a dollar store in the fine city of Brisbane hunting for, of all things, a spatula. In a dusty old corner near the salt and pepper shakers stood a rack of several dozen cheap but familiar dreamcatchers of various sizes—all made in China. Several months ago, in Vienna, I saw two stalls in an outdoor Christmas market that were selling dreamcatchers, medicine wheels, mandalas, and a whole assortment of pseudo-Native paraphernalia to an eager Teutonic audience.

Italy and Chile have their fine wine. Germany has its fine cars. India has its fine tea and telemarketing services. Colombia has its fine coffee and cocaine. Native North America has its fine—dreamcatchers? I believe the technical term for this kind of situation is a "trade imbalance."

Globalization—thy name is Turtle Island.

And let's not forget the concept of postmodernism, a popular school of thought in contemporary western literature that began early last century. If memory serves me correctly, one key aspect of postmodernism refers to a new way of storytelling. Simply put, allegiance to the traditional narrative form of storytelling, A leads to B leads to C leads to D, is being re-examined. Time is re-evaluated. Alternative narrative sequencing becomes the new method of telling a story—start off with C which leads to B which leads to A and then to D—the movie *Pulp Fiction* being the most often cited example, along with the writings of Michael Ondaatje. Most academics assume the European way of storytelling to be the baseline, the norm by which all others should be evaluated. In terms of the importance of a linear storyline, Shakespeare, Cervantes, even the Bible are considered to be ... well I guess, the Gospel. Most traditional Aboriginal storytellers, however, took great delight in shuffling and rearranging cause and effect in their narratives, foregrounding the holistic nature of creation, and the notion of "what goes around, comes around." But the residential school system drummed that kind of Indigenous postmodernism out of the "new world" in pretty short order. I submit that there should be a different definition of postmodernism. For us, the very word itself is problematic. Who is to say what "modern" is? From the Aboriginal perspective, our encounter with the word began, along with "globalization," back at the end of the fifteenth century, when Turtle Island became a truck stop on the way to China.

Eurocentrism—thy name is Turtle Island.

To use a cliché borrowed from our Italian friends Columbus and Caboto, "when in Rome, do as the Romans do." Since a lot of this discussion is talking place on Turtle Island, and can and often is used in deconstructing Native literature, shouldn't the standard for storytelling start here? And if so, the way Native people used to tell their stories should be the standard, and everything that happened afterwards should be considered postmodern (not to be confused with postcolonial). If that is the case, the very act of telling stories in English could be considered a postmodern act. In our Indigenous eyes, the written language itself is a postmodern creation. Publishing and printing alone could also be considered postmodern cultural and technological phenomena. The very fact that you are reading an article about postmodernism and globalization written by an Aboriginal educated in English (rather than in Mayan, Aztec, or Incan, civilizations that also had forms of writing) could be considered postmodern. Or maybe that should be "post-postmodern." Or maybe it's so postmodern a thought, its positively "pre-postmodern." But wouldn't that make it just ... modern? I've really got to stop going to these conferences.

CARDS AND CENTS

I admit it. I don't get White people (or as we call them in the 'hood, the colour-challenged). More specifically, I don't get White businesspeople. They and their ways confuse me. I'm sure they make sense, as much sense as do Canadian politics, the war in Iraq, or the popularity of *Canadian Idol*.

For instance, Reserves all over Saskatchewan have suddenly been flooded with sheets and sheets and sheets of faxes from local car dealers advertising their vehicular wares. This is because in the next few months, over a billion dollars will be paid out to survivors of the residential schools. Some former students will get over $30,000 in compensation for what they had to endure in those institutions of debased learning. In total, we are talking about tens of thousands of Native people across Canada. Like good entrepreneurs, most car dealerships know that low-income people who suddenly get a large influx of cash tend to go on shopping sprees, like those who win the lottery or beat the odds at casinos. Thus the need to fax every faxable number in these Saskatchewan First Nations communities. This I understand. Capitalism. A little sleazy in this case, but understandable. Why just Saskatchewan though—who knows. One Saskatchewan car dealer claims he was completely unaware of the compensation packages. He just decided that late June is a hell of a good time to paper the electronic Native world advertising his rock-bottom price for a 2007 Kia Sportage. His prices just can't be beat.

So, what a coinkydink.

Yet here in Peterborough, a different battle of commerce and Aboriginalism occasionally takes place. In the Curve Lake newsletter a few weeks ago, it was reported that a certain bath and bedroom store in town refused to honour Aboriginal Status Cards. That is to say, despite what is mandated by the Indian Act of Canada, the merchant refused to deduct provincial sales tax from Status Indian customers' purchases being taken back to the Reserve. The same thing has happened, I've heard, at other local shops and stores, including a well-known international perfume and bath company. I, myself, when visiting a store specializing in repairing and replacing glass, was told when whipping out my Status Card, "Oh we don't do that here. If you want to do that, you'll have to apply to the government yourself."

Needless to say, I and a lot of fellow Natives were and are disappointed by this attitude. When you consider the bigger picture, these companies could be losing a heck of a lot of money from irate and annoyed First Nations customers. Granted we may not be an overwhelming tidal wave of consumer force, but we can still give a good consumer kick in the shins when we want to.

Especially when you consider the other side of the coin. I am speaking of the flood of White people who storm the smoke shacks searching for low-cost cigarettes in this and other Native communities, looking to save those precious few cents they will need as they toboggan towards a promising future of lung cancer and emphysema. I've been in some of those stores buying less health-inhibiting products, and been absolutely amazed by non-Native people staggering out the door carrying cartons of cigarettes in their arms. Thanks to these people for supporting our Aboriginal businesses, really, but there is such a thing as overkill. Literally.

There is no better way of illustrating this point than mentioning Highway 21. That is the highway that runs along the eastern shore of Lake Huron. Somewhere south of Grand Bend is a place that is forever emblazoned in the Aboriginal psyche. To many, it is a name no different than Oka or Gustafsen Lake or Caledonia. I am talking about Ipperwash. Once a Native community, then an army base, now once again a Native community. Since its return to Native hands several years ago, it has been Indigenized very quickly. You can tell this because as you drive by, you will notice at least two smoke shacks set up amid the deserted army barracks. The most obvious and immediate examples of Native occupation. And I thought to myself, "Not exactly the proud manifestations of Aboriginal culture I was expecting to see there." This is what Dudley George died for? Discount cigarettes.

Obviously I am of mixed feelings on the topic. I don't smoke, never have, but everybody picks their own poison, as the old saying goes. Who am I to pass judgment? However, it is becoming an increasingly politicized issue because, for many, the selling of tax-free cigarettes on Reserve to White people is highly illegal.

One side of the discussion would argue that, good or bad, smoke shacks are rapidly becoming one of the leading images of contemporary Native life and existence in Canada. Practically every Native community has at least one, and more than likely a lot more. My First Nation has at least six. The reason: simple economics. These smokes are substantially cheaper than those bought at most corner stores in non-Native communities. They are at the forefront of a limited economic revival. If you sell it cheaply, they will come.

So here's the irony—very few people I know personally in my community still smoke. A few do, but clearly the vast majority of the people patronizing these places belong to those people First Nations citizens like to call in these politically correct times the colour-challenged or pigmentally denied. By far. I know. I've seen and watched them, much as a biologist might study a cat looking for catnip. I remember standing in line at one particular store, wanting only to buy a tub of ice cream, and there was a Person of Pallor standing in front of me, buying thirty-seven bags of cigarettes. I counted them as I stood there waiting. Two thoughts came immediately into my head: 1. melatonin-deprived people sure like to spend an awful lot of money to save a little; 2. the person who owns this particular store is wasting his time selling a single tub of ice cream to me.

The flip side of this whole issue is that it's all a symptom of this thing called sovereignty. And as most students of political science and history can tell you, sovereignty—like tobacco—can be quite addictive. Once you start going down that path, you ain't never getting that monkey off your back. What's that old saying, something about the world will end not with a bang, but with a whimper. Well, the same could be said about Native sovereignty, it won't be achieved with a big gun battle or with elections or first minister's conferences. Smoke shacks. I bet you Karl Marx never thought of that. Add to that the fact we invented tobacco a thousand years or so ago, it all has a certain completion or resolution to the journey, doesn't it?

Of course, many people might disagree with this philosophy. Unfortunately, the end result of this branch of sovereignty is usually cancer, emphysema, heart disease, and a host of other lovely maladies. Hospital wards will be awash with unknowing supporters of Aboriginal autonomy. I think we should have oxygen tank shacks ready for the next wave. And the Aboriginal tobacco industry is unregulated, meaning nobody really knows what is going into those Indigenous cigarettes. They are manufactured completely independently, with little or no safeguards. I heard one rumour that little kittens are somehow used in the process. As I said, people tend to pick their own poison.

And as usual, Native people are being blamed for White people's weaknesses. We usually are. We sign treaties and expect what's in them to be honoured. In the end, it isn't, we complain about it, and then we're considered whiners. Because the federal and provincial governments are losing lots of money, the support of this kind of Aboriginal enterprise is somewhat limited. Recently, police forces are treating this complex issue like another complex issue—prostitition. They're going after the Johns, not the ladies. Just outside Six Nations where there are approximately 100 smoke shacks, the police have been catching and releasing smoke shack patrons, after confiscating their booty. Smoking can be an expensive habit.

So, do you see my dilemma? Some stores give us attitude for requesting something that we are allowed as an inducement towards achieving a certain amount of economic success. Yet average Canadians are so willing to take advantage of a particular loophole regarding the sales of carcinogens on Reserve. Next week one of the smoke shacks is having a sale on Agent Orange and some home-grown nuclear waste.

As for applying for reimbursement of the PST ourselves, I've read the Indian Act. Nowhere in it could I find any mention of us doing the paperwork to get money back that we shouldn't have had tagged on the bill in the first place. Hey, you guys invented paperwork. So you do it.

Or how about this—in order to keep a certain amount of commercial parity happening, everybody who has ever bought a cigarette on a Reserve, boycott a store that charges Native people PST. Let's see what happens then. This might work, because rumour has it that bath and bedroom place recently back-tracked on its policy after receiving some irate responses and feared a potential blockade of its pots and pans section.

Q: WHEN IS AN INDIAN NOT AN INDIAN?
A: WHEN HE'S FIRST NATIONS

There is a magazine published in Toronto called *This Magazine,* in which I recently read how "everything is political." I've been wondering about that phrase ever since—is everything indeed political? Is the reason you passed over those kosher dills for those generic gherkins anti-Semitism? That bottle of Australian shiraz you bought this weekend—was that in celebration. of the Australian election that threw out John Howard, who had been the right wing prime minister for the last eleven years? Have you been avoiding going for dim sum until the Chinese get out of Tibet? Is it finally okay to have English muffins again, since some sort of accord has been worked out between Ireland and England ... you mean breakfast no longer means choosing sides in the Troubles? Sometimes you just have to wonder.

Being Native is presumably no different in this regard—if anything, it's even more highly political. Some of us have identity cards issued by the federal government that say who and what we are. And a lot of Native people don't have those cards, but ironically that makes them even more political. It has even been said that being born Native in Canada is a political statement in itself—a strong one. And soon after that birth, the very act of dirtying your diaper is a comment on the effectiveness and authority of the Department of Indian Affairs and the Indian Act. I bet you didn't know that.

When most Canadians think of Native people and politics, images of Oka and other land claims come to mind. Or Elijah Harper lifting his feather in the Manitoba Legislature and putting a stop to the Meech Lake Accord ... or was that the Charlottetown Accord ... or was that the Treaty of Versailles? I forget. Other common images of Native people include Chief Phil Fontaine urging a less confrontational approach for the Assembly of First Nations in Canada than that of Crazy Horse at Little Bighorn.

Those are the big-picture questions. But I also want to talk about the small-picture ones. Whether I'm in Canada or traipsing across the rest of the world, I invariably get asked for the Native view on things—like there is only one. I was once asked to appear on a radio talk show at the University of Alberta, hosted by a Native woman. I had just gotten off the plane, rushed quickly to the studio before the program began. Tired, my luggage still with me, and dying for a coffee, I was ushered into the studio, given a coffee, and just as I was about to take my first sip she popped her opening question:

"Why is it Native men, when they reach a certain level of success and affluence, end up dating and marrying White women?" She assumed an air of anticipatory silence as my cup hovered near my mouth, the coffee suddenly going cold in the dead air. I became immediately aware that this was a live broadcast, and for reasons completely unbeknownst to me, I had suddenly been trapped into becoming the spokesperson for all Native men in Canada. As I struggled to come up with a coherent answer she continued to wait expectantly.

I began a verbal tap dance as I continued to grope for an answer. "Um ... um ... well, you know. There are more successful White people than Native people. And ... and ... those Native people that are successful, there tend to be more men than women in the, uh ... political and business worlds. So ... um ... you tend to date and marry those within your socio-economic group." I had no idea if this were true but it sounded good enough to at least postpone the crisis. Towards the end of my verbal tap dancing exercise I began to get annoyed with the host's sneak attack, and ended my answer with: "Or, it just could be White women are easier to find in the dark. And remember, never, ever date a White person after Labour Day. It's just not done, socially." Now the host of the show didn't quite know how to respond. It had all begun, and ended, rather badly for all concerned.

But now at least we all know that who you date is political in the Native community, as is where you live—on the Reserve or in the city—or even in a foreign country. I've talked with relocated Native people in Germany, Australia, Switzerland, and a few other such nations. It turns out that whether you speak English or your grandparent's tongue says a lot about your politics.

I also am beginning to wonder about people's vehicular preferences, dietary choices, reading habits, and sexual proclivities. Does the fact you drive an Explorer or a Cherokee reflect merely your personal tastes, or does it telegraph your political views to those with whom you share the road? See, it never ends. Do you read Tony Hillerman and W.P. Kinsella, or Sherman Alexie and Thomas King? Eat white rice or wild brown rice? Buffalo/deer/moose, or beef/pork/chicken? Pemmican or baloney? Even porn film preferences could constitute a public disclosure of your political positions: choosing *Debbie Does Dallas* over *Pok-a-Hot-Ass* begins to have dire social consequences. If we are looking for it, there's a political slant to everything.

It's gotten to the point where I'm beginning to tell people I am not political by nature, but by birth. When I climb onto a plane to go somewhere in Canada, I make sure to show them my Native Status Card instead of my birth certificate. I used to do the same thing when heading for America, but an appreciation of the North American Aboriginal right to be citizens of the continent, and therefore to cross the Canada/USA border at will using that card, seems to have been forgotten since 9/11. I've tried a few times since then, but they just shake their heads and demand to see my passport.

So now I'm a Canadian, not an Ojibway, when I cross the border, which, I have to admit, beats by a slight margin the puzzled responses I often got from customs officers in both countries when I presented my Status Card in response to their question about my nation of origin: "What the hell is that?"

POW WOW PRIDE

On my wall is a photograph of a man at a pow wow. He is dressed in traditional Ojibway regalia, including an impressive feathered bustle on his back, a leather vest and breechcloth, and a multicoloured roach adorning his head. He looks quite magnificent, proud, and utterly Aboriginal. In his hand is a can of Pepsi and he's also wearing some pretty cool sunglasses. I bet his stomach is full of an Indian taco that he chewed with the non-Native fillings in his teeth. He is a contemporary pow wow dancer, with his moccasined feet planted firmly in two worlds.

Fantastic, fabulous, and fattening, every weekend in the spring, summer, and fall, somewhere on this continent, there are a couple of pow wows happening. In my ceaseless travels, I've been privileged to see pow wows from the Okanagan to the Ottawa valleys; from the fields of Oklahoma to the halls of Yale University. Every one is different, yet each is familiar. That is the nature of pow wows. Some might argue it's a state of mind. When I was growing up on Curve Lake First Nations Reserve, two hours northeast of Toronto, the highlight of every boring summer was the pow wow. And the highlight of every pow wow was the challenge of sneaking into the grounds without paying the entrance fee.

Once inside, we would eat ourselves silly—all the fried foods an eight-year-old tummy could hold. There was nothing more exciting than comparing the hamburgers from three different tribal nations and, of course, watching all the strangers flood into our community. The population of our Reserve practically doubled during the pow wow—visitors from all over, checking out the arts and crafts and asking, "What kind of dance is that?" Different Native people from across the land appeared in bright, gorgeous outfits. (Please do not call them costumes!) That was back in the days of bottled pop, and all of us kids would scour the grounds looking for the precious empty returnable bottles that were as good as cash. Today they're plastic, only "returnable where eligible," and many Native people are predisposed to diabetes. The times, they certainly have changed.

On the pow wow trail, I've heard many stories and rumours about the origins of this cultural phenomenon. One has it that Oklahoma was the birthplace of the modern pow wow where, during the Depression, hungry and poor Indians managed to scrape up a few meagre dollars by putting on a show for the few tourists who wandered by. Others have suggested the pow wow traditionally began before the arrival of the White man, when family groups would meet in spring after the harsh winter. There they would trade, arrange marriages, celebrate their survival, and sing and dance in the warm rays of the sun. I think I like that story better.

Today, the reasons why First Nations people go to pow wows haven't changed all that much. For most of those not involved in the actual planning and running of the gatherings, it's essentially a chance to hang out, meet some old friends, maybe make some new ones, and revitalize their t-shirt collections. And where else can you get a buffalo burger, some corn soup, and maybe some deer stew in today's fast-food world? Contrary to popular belief, the vast majority of Native people, especially those who live in urban areas, do not stock their refrigerators with wild meat. It is a delicacy for many of us, as it is for most people of European ancestry.

Oddly enough, the majority of pow wow-goers are non-Native. Sometimes half to two-thirds of the audience is White, with a sprinkling of African-American, Asian, and other bits of humanity. Why they come to pow wows is a mystery to me. Is it to look at all the exotic Native people? I hope not. To tell you the truth, we're not that exotic. Whenever I'm on the Reserve, I watch *Friends* and *Star Trek* while eating potato chips. Maybe they go to watch the dancing and listen to the drumming. I sometimes go for that. Yet, I'm fairly sure that many of the non-Native people who are interested in Native dance seldom go out to see some of their own unique cultural dance performances, such as ballet, for instance. Granted, pow wow tickets are cheaper, but, at the risk of being accused of cultural bias, I would rather see some jingle-dress dancing than a production of *Swan Lake* (and I work in theatre). But that's because I grew up with this kind of dancing. It's home. It's comforting.

Most pow wows in Canada call it a day around 6:00 P.M. That's what we call "Dinner Time," an ancient Aboriginal tradition, mired in mystery and ancient teachings. But in Oklahoma, the party doesn't start until 5:00 P.M. and goes on till the wee hours of the morning. I wondered why these people chose to pow wow in the dark, until I actually stood in an Oklahoma field at one o'clock in the afternoon. You do not want to be jumping up and down clad in leather and feathers in that hot sun. It would be an awfully short and hazardous pow wow.

Whatever pow wow you may attend, you can be guaranteed some universal observations. Even if you're at the Gathering of Nations in New Mexico, chances are you'll bump in to someone you know—maybe even a relative. This is not idle boasting—it is Gospel in the Native community. You could conceivably see some of your old girlfriends (or boyfriends), and definitely some potential new ones. You will eat too much. You will browse through the vendors' booths and comment on all the different kinds of dreamcatchers that are made in the world. You will giggle at all the sunburned white people until you realize that your arms are beginning to sting. And you will hold your head high because you are celebrating the culture and spirit of your people.

So regardless of the pow wow's origins, or its nature, you can expect that practically every Friday and Sunday on this continent we call Turtle Island,

Indigenous caravans will be making their way from Aboriginal community to Aboriginal community in search of summer pow wow freedom. The days of the buffalo hunts are long gone, replaced by minivan sojourns, but the spirit lives on, as do the power and memory of the dances and drum songs.

As the pow wow MC might say, "Ho, that's a good one."

A KID AT HEART

Somebody once asked me, after I told them many Native Reserves look like a lot of small non-Native towns except people are a lot darker, how they can then tell if they are in a First Nations community. All the standard jokes went through my head: when you hit your first three-legged dogs, when you notice all the vast dreamcatcher factories, when you spot more cigarette shops than convenience stores; and then there are the much older versions—abandoned cars on lawns or passed-out Indians used as speed bumps. I thought for a moment before answering, and then it came to me: when you see a lot of kids, that's usually when you're on Native territory.

First Nations people love kids, and love having kids, which can be a good combination. It's no secret that the birth rate among Canada's Indigenous people is practically the highest in the land, and it's been that way for a while. I know—my mother is the oldest of fourteen, so as a result I have about twenty-five first cousins, at least. It's part of that ancient old Aboriginal custom that insists when you know how to do something well, keep doing it. I'm not sure, however, that this custom accounts for why building canoes and skinning muskrats got so boring after a while.

We've all met those people from down in the States who are "part Cherokee," or had a great-great-great-great grandmother who was a Cherokee princess. I've always wondered whether it was just this one lone and tired Cherokee woman who kept pumping out these kids, and all the other Cherokee women pretty much kept to themselves. No one seems to know.

With all these Native kids running around the country, and all the kids from other cultures who currently inhabit these Four Directions, I have found myself—through no fault of my own—becoming one of the leading writers of Native theatre for young audiences. In one single year, I had three plays written by me, specifically for kids, touring various parts of the country. They might have been at a school near you. My very first play, *Toronto at Dreamer's Rock*, written in the late 1980s, started me driving that metaphorical school bus. And last year, my novel *The Night Wanderer* was published, and that was written specifically for teenagers. Vampires and Indians ... I've been told adolescents can't get enough of either.

But rest assured, I'm not complaining. Writing has provided me with a good and rewarding living. In addition, during the last several years I have lectured frequently for several Aboriginal and non-Aboriginal youth, education, and librarians' organizations across the country, and already have several talks on writing booked for the coming year, specifically on Native youth and literature. Next month I'm off to Adelaide, Australia, to lecture at a huge TYA (theatre for young audiences) conference being held there, on Native TYA in Canada, and if it all works out, hopefully I'll be spending time and working with an Australian Aboriginal company that does similar work in Perth.

The trouble is, I feel I'm getting kind of old to be working in this field. There are people older than me who write for "young audiences" (YA), but they are usually parents of some sort. My worry is that some people may come to believe I could possibly be an imaginative writer of youth literature for reasons slightly more creepy than a desire to entertain and/or make a living. You see, I have no kids of my own (that I know of—though 1993 is kind of murky), yet I still seem to be in touch with their imagination, which may or may not be a good thing. Hopefully people won't think I'm entering Michael Jackson territory with my career. I say this now because I have a new book coming out this month that explores and deconstructs the world of Native sexuality. It's called Me Sexy. Sex and kids—not something you as a parent might be comfortable with.

Now at one time, both Me Sexy and my vampire novel, The Night Wanderer, were supposed to be released in the same month (because they have two different publishers), but as my agent pointed out, that might not have been such a good idea. What if I were being interviewed for both books at the same time, and for some reason, forgot which interview I was doing? That could be disastrous.

I keep telling myself I shouldn't be so paranoid. After all, the one does lead to the other. In theory, there would be no kids without sex, unless we all were lab technicians with turkey basters.

I remember that Ian Fleming wrote the James Bond novels as well as Chitty Chitty Bang Bang, and that Roald Dahl wrote all those cool horror stories, but also James and the Giant Peach. The one thing that makes me believe that maybe I am getting paranoid is something my girlfriend told me when I brought this subject up.

"Drew," she said, "I wouldn't worry about it. Speaking as a woman, most men are big kids anyway. You've just found a way to make a living at it." I was relieved for about ten seconds—then I couldn't shake the feeling that I'd just been insulted.

PUT THAT IN YOUR PIPE AND SMOKE IT

I swear, it happened just this way: I was at the Toronto airport on my way to the USA to give yet another lecture, standing in the line-up about to go through airport security. My shoes were off and I was just removing my buffalo horn belt when I felt a tap on my shoulder. Attached to the intrusive finger was what appeared to be a non-Native woman about forty years old, looking me over. She said, "I noticed your jacket [a Pat Piche original, complete with a buffalo on the back] and your shirt [from Haida designer Dorthy Grant]." What, me wear something off the rack? I don't think so. Evidently I was looking particularly Indigenous that day, if you ignored the blue eyes. So I wondered where she was going with this assessment of my clothing.

"Do you do ceremonies?" She asked breathlessly, as people waited impatiently behind us. On my way through the metal detector, I was trying to find the correlation between supporting contemporary Indigenous designers and performing sacred ceremonies—not including the traditional waving of my turquoise watchband to the Four Directons, of course. That woman's train of thought seemed somewhat puzzling. Still, it's not the first time I'd encountered it. Once in college I was asked to bless a walking stick by a fellow classmate who was a member of the colour-challenged people.

To make a long story short, I took the stick, happy to indulge her, and counted to ten in Anishnaabe. She didn't know the difference and everybody was happy.

Obviously, ceremonies and sacred objects hold a unique place in Native culture. For instance, the pipe has often been perceived as one of the most sacred and cherished implements of Native spirituality. Pipe ceremonies are used as a method of opening or closing many spiritual gatherings in First Nations cultures—the practice is found all across North America in many Aboriginal cultures. Nothing makes an archaeologist salivate more than finding a pre-contact pipe in a 600-year-old garbage dump.

I've often heard Elder William Commanda, a wampum belt holder from the Algonquin community of Kitigan Zibi in Quebec, referred to as a pipe carrier, a very revered position. But he himself says that he does not carry the pipe—it carries him. The pipe is often seen as a direct connection to the Creator. Tobacco is the most highly regarded of the four sacred herbs—the other three being cedar, sweetgrass, and sage. This is how Doug Williams, an Elder from the Curve Lake First Nations in Central Ontario and a member of the Native studies faculty at Trent University put it: "The pipe is basically a helper. The helper that will take your tobacco that you smoke and transport your prayers to the Creator, or [the object of] your desires." Basically it is a gesture of respect and honour to be invited to participate in a pipe ceremony. It means the participants are all of the same mind and spirit.

But in this modern day, what once was a reverent practice might now be considered by some to be a health hazard. It was in that very community of Kitigan Zibi where I was directing a documentary on Mr. Commanda that I met a man who was there to listen to Mr. Commanda's teachings. He told me that as honoured as he was, he no longer participated in pipe ceremonies. "I'm afraid of what sharing the pipe could result in." He was concerned about possible infections arising from the communal sharing of the pipe. He told me, "In today's world, there are a lot more diseases out there that our Elders didn't know about when the pipe ceremony came into effect."

Ironically, later that same day I was asked to participate in such a ceremony held by Mr. Commanda. As I stood there, one of about eight people, watching the pipe being passed from person to person, each drawing the tobacco into their lungs, it eventually made its way to me. I took the pipe and noticed the mouth-piece of the pipe was wet with saliva.

I should point out here that as a Native person, I have great respect and support for traditional teachings. They are essential to us as a people. I have attended and participated in many pipe ceremonies, as well as a variety of other ceremonies across North America. So I too hold the teachings of the pipe in honour. And admittedly I experience a certain amount of reluctance in writing about anything critical about such matters. But I will admit, smoking that pipe was a little more difficult that day.

First Nations people are no strangers to the possibility that even necessary and beneficial objects may have a more sinister viral nature. In the nineteenth century, it was common practice for governments to magnanimously give Native people blankets purposefully infected with small pox and measles as gifts, or as payment for treaty obligations—one of the first and most effective cases of viral and bacterial warfare. Small pox may have been eradicated in today's society, but a host of new diseases from around the world have once again come calling at the Aboriginal door.

Upon investigation, Trish Warner, a registered nurse practitioner told me that diseases such as mononucleosis, hepatitis, strep, meningitis, the common cold, and possibly influenza could be found in the average person's saliva. Now there's an icky prospect. So what exactly does this mean regarding the continued practice of sharing the pipe? I asked Doug Williams, an Elder in my community, if this issue has ever come up.

"We've had discussions amongst ourselves about some of the health issues surrounding the passing of water and the pipe. They both involve touching with the mouth. It's a discussion that's been around for some time now. I've worried about the pipe and I'll tell you why. There are a lot of viruses around, and I'm now almost at the point of refusing to take the pipe at a big event because of it. And there are a lot of people refusing the pipe because they don't want to have their lips on a pipe. I think there we have to, somehow or other, protect the pipe. We have to smoke it the way we always have, but what are the compromises? So my compromise at the moment is … like if they said to me, 'Hey, come and do a pipe ceremony at the community centre tonight,' I'd go, but I think I'd only smoke it with a small group. Or maybe they should say, 'we're gonna bring the pipe around and you touch it with your hand and pass it on.'"

Something as sacred and central to Aboriginal spirituality as the pipe ceremony is bound to have people with a much more fundamentalist approach have very strong opinions on the issue. I've discussed my observations over the past few years with several of them, trying to find out what other First Nations people feel about this controversy. And on more than one occasion it's been suggested that I drop the topic. One young lady, who was adopted by a non-Native family and has re-embraced the Native way, told me that it was her belief that the pipe protected itself. That it was so strong, it would protect everybody that believes in it. Some time later, a prominent Native actor/activist told me that I shouldn't bother writing about such a topic. "There should never be any criticism of the pipe. It's too important to our people."

Doug Williams disagrees. "I think what these people are concerned about is the pipe is a sacred thing. So one has to be careful. But nothing is above reproach. I'm almost tempted to go to a paper cup company to come up with something to put over it."

In researching this article, I contacted Anishnawbe Health, an Aboriginal health services organization located on Queen Street East in Toronto, which is integrated with Toronto's vast urban Native population. I wanted to talk with their Elder-in-Residence and with the resident doctor to get their perspectives, and was asked to submit a formal request by email. I did so, and then followed up with several calls over a two-month period. I never heard back from them. It's a controversial issue.

A while after I originally researched and published this article, somebody posted a comment on my website's guest book, expressing a strong opinion on the subject. Essentially, he or she said: "The pipe protects the people and the people who are smoking it. Regardless of the illness, saliva passed on, or cuts in the lips or not. If you have no faith in the ways, then there's much to learn … the pipe is safe, to be shared with anyone who wishes to smoke it. Cut lips, flu, TB, HIV, anything, the spirits protect us. Hope you have found this useful … Merci, never question that again." Pretty strong words. Then came the assumed name of the person who left the message … simply, The Legend. No esteem problems there.

I noticed The Legend didn't mention small pox, measles, or the plethora of other illnesses that have decimated our population for the last 500 years. I guess all those old-time Indians didn't believe in the pipe enough. I know that probably sounds harsh, but over the years I've asked a few people in health services for their opinion on the topic and they seem to disagree with The Legend, all the while sounding very respectful of the question, the situation, and the pipe. The whole controversy sounds a bit like faith healing to me. I was always taught the pipe was more for spiritual and cultural healing than for spreading massive viral and bacterial infections. But that's probably an interesting ecumenical discussion for a later column.

Still, ceremonies can be big business. We've all heard of those less-than-reputable individuals who run sweat lodges on a profit margin. Writing a cheque for such an experience just turns it into an expensive sauna. You are supposed to leave your clothes and wallet at the door. Anybody who tells you anything different probably has a mortgage somewhere they really have to pay off.

The Internet isn't making things spiritual much easier. Online you can find anything, including ceremonies and wise Elders for sale. There are two ways of approaching this: with anger or with amusement. Amusement is definitely the healthier alternative. If you choose anger, then you'll have to see an Elder or medicine man for anger management and ulcer therapy. So it becomes kind of counterproductive.

Like anything else—say Internet dating, or discovering that somebody from some impoverished African country has specifically selected you amongst six billion people to share their several million dollars with—you have to take it all with a grain of salt. But watch out for high blood pressure. The salt, you know ...

I AM ABORIGINAL

At a pow wow recently, I saw a Native person walking the grounds wearing one of those "I AM CANADIAN" t-shirts that are so popular these days, several years after the similarly popular television commercial from the same Molson campaign. On the shirt were a series of pithy and semi-humorous observations about the Canadian lifestyle, as opposed to the American way of life.

Yet, most First Nations people would argue that they are first and foremost (insert own First Nations here) before they are Canadian as a matter of Indigenous pride. Except of course, when travelling abroad. In places like China and Cuba, when I say I'm Ojibway, I get blank stares. "Canadian" cuts down the need for explanations quite considerably.

So, in order to achieve a kind of cultural pride parity, I would like to substitute the following humble alternative for the "I AM CANADIAN" t-shirt campaign:

I have a dreamcatcher, but it was given to me by a White person.

I do not own a canoe, but I know somebody who does.

I have lived here forever, but, have only been a citizen since 1960.

I've never rubbed noses as a sign of affection, but I'd be more than willing to try.

I do not personally have a land claim, but I have not ruled out the possibility.

I have enjoyed watching Graham Greene on television and reading the other Graham Greene's novels.

I have lived on the Reserve and in the city.

I watch APTN and CNN.

I am Ojibway/Cree/Iroquois/Haida/Inuit/etc., but I am also Canadian.

I personally have never worn buckskin, but I support the Indigenous right to do so.

I am not from India, but I do like their food.

I am better with a video game than a bow and arrow.

Contrary to popular belief, I do pay taxes and, like you, also find it annoying.

I was at Oka, if not in body, than in spirit.

I have ridden a horse, if not in body than in spirit.

My great-great-grandmother was part White, but that doesn't change anything.

I have never hunted buffalo, but I've had their wings.

Contrary to popular belief, I prefer my baloney raw, not fried.

I love going to a pow wow as much as I love going to a hockey game.

I am glad you had a Native friend once, but I'm sorry, I do not know all of the approximately one million people of Aboriginal heritage in Canada.
Yes, I have seen *Dances with Wolves*, but it's not my favourite movie.
I drive a Chevy pick-up, a Ford Escort, a Kia Sportage, a Hyundai Tucson, and a Kawasaki.
I listen to country music, rock, rap, blues, and opera.
I have blonde/brown/black/red/grey hair.
I have a university degree.
I own my own house, and it is not a teepee.
I AM ABORIGINAL.

A WHITER SHADE OF PALE

Well, it happened again. The location was new, the faces were new, but not the issue or the question. This time I was in Winnipeg lecturing at a Native education conference. On a panel with maybe eight or ten Native teachers, I was waxing on poetically about the basic structure of what I call the Native Narrative, and how it differs from that of mainstream Western drama or storytelling, when I stupidly asked if there were any related questions. A man to my left immediately asked, "Is your mother treaty?" It was not a question I was expecting, nor did I really understand what it had to do with the fundamental structure of playwrighting, but being the amiable sort of chap I am, I answered in the affirmative.

Then came the next question: "Are you treaty? Do you have a card?" Even more puzzled, I answered in the affirmative. "Can I see it?" he asked, and when I showed it to him, he seemed completely amazed. "You are Native?! When I first saw you, I didn't think you were at all." To a chorus of gasps around the table, he mumbled something to the effect of, "I didn't mean to be rude, it's just you don't look it." I thought I was used to this, but after forty-two years of a very public life as an author, playwright, and screenwriter, and, specifically, with four books titled Funny, You Don't Look Like One: Observations of a Blue-Eyed Ojibwa, I was amazed at how very little has changed in my social life.

He later added that the woman beside him, who evidently shared the same observations about my appearance, had suggested that maybe I had been adopted by a Native family, which might explain my familiarity with the subject matter under discussion. Now there's a new one—the reverse scoop-up, or what we might call the Shania Twain Syndrome. I am not saying that to be cruel or even funny; she has always acknowledged the fact she is indeed White but really loved her Native step-foster father, who was very supportive of her early career. Both parents died in a car accident. Alas, no, I was and still am Native or at least consider myself so, born on the Curve Lake First Nations Reserve ... though admittedly, the 50 percent of my blood that's Caucasian still seems to be of far more interest to most people than the Indigenous half. Not that I have anything against White people. They are a fascinating and industrious race, with customs and beliefs that are unique and should be respected by all the people of the world. I honestly believe that. A White person comes in and cleans my house once a month. She has a key and everything. That's how much I trust her.

In order to put my liberalism on public display, I've even been known to date the odd White woman (and some of them have been very odd indeed), though usually, I must admit, the relationship has not gone much beyond primarily a fashion statement. Everybody knows White goes with practically every colour.

However, due to these ongoing private and public confusions regarding my obvious lack of brown eyes and skin, I have thought of doing some research into my genetic origins. That's why it seemed to be a sign of providence when I saw this ad in a Native newspaper—it was as if God were talking to me. It read ... and I'm being absolutely honest here:

> Are you curious about your Aboriginal origins?! Recent advances in genetic testing give us the ability to measure your ancestral origins. If you are curious to know whether you have Aboriginal ancestors or want to know what percentage of your ancestry is Aboriginal, our Ancestry DNA test is the only method available for this purpose today. Our Ancestry DNA test will provide you with a simple and objective description of your ancestral origins. The test gives you an estimated percentage of ancestry for [Aboriginal groups]. Start unravelling the mystery of your DNA and heritage today.

It's from a company called Genelex. Darn clever, these people.

Genelex has been located in Seattle, Washington, since 1987. The company's website boasts: "Our ethnicity DNA Test provides a global overview of your genetic makeup telling you what percentage of your DNA is shared with [Native Americans]. Our Native American verification testing can confirm if you are of Native American Ancestry." Oh, god, another Status Card to carry. Using the same methods, they can also check into your Indo-European, East Asian, or African background, should you be curious. How comforting.

DNA testing—how *Star Trek*: "Damn it, Jim, he's not a Klingon, he's a Mohawk!" Unfortunately I'm not exactly well-informed on DNA technology, so I'm not too sure how to read this kind of ad. It all seems a little far-fetched to me, but what do I know? I guess anything is possible. I think it might be fun to try though ... all it would take is just a little drop of blood: people in white coats staring through microscopes, counting genes and chromosomes and whatever, a big chalk board behind them with Caucasian written on one side, and Ojibway on the other. Every once in a while, I imagine one would look up from his microscope, saying, "Got one," and put a check mark under either Ojibway, or Caucasian, until they were all out of DNA to count. In the end, would that change anything? Probably not. I, and others in my community (well, hopefully most of them), know who I am, and that's what "counts," it seems to me.

I guess the real solution to dilemmas like mine is to simply ignore those nosey people. I've been called worse and a lot stranger things than White. Last Christmas, I went to a house party in Toronto. As I walked in the door, this guy looks up at me and says quite clearly: "Hey, you remind me of the Angel of Death." I think he may have been referring to the actor playing the character on a show called *Touched by an Angel*, but still ...

YOU ARE WHAT YOU EAT

Let me know if this makes sense to you. Recently, in Finland, I was talking to this woman from France, who now lives in Canada. That in itself may make sense, but the rest of it is difficult for me to understand . She was lamenting what she called Canada's bizarre preoccupation with all meals chicken. She was sick of being served chicken all the time. It was putting her in a fowl mood. Then she began to tap dance down the nostalgia highway a bit, reminiscing about how much she missed eating rabbit. Evidently rabbit meat is quite popular in France. She found it much preferable to the poultry feasts she is now forced to consume so frequently in Canada. But alas, rabbit is far more expensive in Canada than in her home country of France. It's at least $16 a serving, she said.

Now, a price that high surprised her, and me even more. Sixteen dollars for rabbit! That's a lot of money. Do you know how much Spam that could buy!? I grew up in the country with rabbits running everywhere, eating my mother's flowers, and it's from those furry creatures I learned the tragic term "collateral damage." I remember a cousin of mine shooting at a rabbit that happened to be running out back, dangerously near our propane tank. It's hard to forget something like that.

For those of us who live in rural Canada, rabbits are the equivalent of squirrels in the city. More importantly, rabbits were once also thought of as a poor man's food. That's what Indians who couldn't afford baloney had to eat. Could you ever imagine yourself paying $16 for some freshly prepared squirrel, perhaps with some delicately flavoured scalloped potatoes? What kind of wine goes with squirrel anyway? Probably something with a hint of nuttiness. It was then my French friend told me that in her country, escargot, commonly referred to as snails, had once been eaten only by the poor. Luckily, my family has never been that poor. Now it's an international delicacy. I've often heard, too, that out east, lobsters were originally consumed largely by the lower classes. Maritime kids were ashamed to take lobster sandwiches to school. The Atlantic Canada version of the potato for the Irish. I've even heard lobster was frequently used as fertilizer.

What has happened to the world? Lobster, I'm told, can now cost $20 for just a piece of tail (insert own joke here). For some reason, the foods of the under-class have now become the fare of the patrician class. Now, poor people can no longer afford to enjoy their culinary legacies.

As a Native person, I'm no stranger to food for the poor. But you won't see any Cree or Ojibway slamming down sixteen hard-earned dollars for a serving of rabbit, not when there are much more economical pet stores— also known as Aboriginal take-out—in the area. I make a parrot penne you would die for. But back to my original concern: what about some of the other local cuisines that all us First Nations grew up with? Someday, will they be the delicacies of only the rich and influential? Now there's a scary thought—our beloved fried baloney just might one day be advertised as free-range, organic, brandy-seared *Bal Onné*. Only $22, but that will come with a side order of *Le Dîner de Kraft*. Instead of the Anishnaabe, we'll be the Ani-snobs.

And of course, there is always the meal that has allowed Native families to survive for untold decades. It provides complex carbohydrates for energy, the vitamin C necessary for good health, and protein for muscle mainte-nance. It's been consumed for generations. I distinctly remember enjoying it in my baby bottle. It's known affectionately as "hangover soup," or simply macaroni and tomatoes. I get a lump in my throat just writing about it. It's a motley mixture of hamburger, elbow macaroni, and tomatoes. Cultural variances may include salt, pepper, onion, tomato soup, and for the truly daring, a dash of garlic salt.

When I travel in Europe, Asia, or wherever, it is the memory of a warm bowl of hangover soup that my mother used to bring me still steaming, that makes me want to come home—the ultimate comfort food. It's just not the same in China, India, or Sweden, and god knows I've looked. I'm afraid someday I'll come home, and I'll see it advertised in some high-end restaurant, for some ungodly amount of money. That's when I'll know the end of the world is coming.

Actually, you know, that squirrel idea might not be so stupid. It's all in the presentation. *Chittimo* is squirrel in Ojibway. Chittimo Chowder—natural, free range, hormone free—I like it ...

WHAT A WAY TO BEGIN THE YEAR

In America, the beginning of this New Year was bright with promise. All the Americans are going nuts over their brand-spanking new president, all fresh and shiny. Even our Native neighbours to the south are waxing on poetically about Barack Obama and his promise. During the campaign, he was even adopted into the Crow Nation. It's so rare to see such enthusiasm in politics, anywhere. Since the inauguration, Obama has named six American Indians to his transition team.

Hopefully, some of that enthusiasm will be smuggled across the border, because I sure can't picture our beloved prime minister doing anything similar. I don't suppose anybody's willing to adopt him. Stephen Harper prefers to keep company with the likes of Tom Flanagan, a Conservative advisor whose opinions on citizens of Canada's First Nations are controversial and subject to severe Aboriginal annoyance. His book *First Nations? Second Thoughts*, which thoughtlessly questions Aboriginal Canada's alleged "dependence on federal money" is required reading in many Native outhouses across the country.

Up here in Canada, I couldn't help wondering what wonders the new year will bring for us, and specifically for me. Last year we had the famous apology for residential school abuse, the promise of financial compensation to its victims, the establishment of the Truth and Reconciliation Commission (they're still working on that one), and the awarding of the Giller Prize to Joseph Boyden for his novel *Through Black Spruce*, to name just a few. Definitely a banner Aboriginal year for sure.

Unfortunately, so far 2009 is proving to be a not-so-positive and encouraging year. Currently we are all wallowing in the ubiquitous financial crisis that has gripped the world, and it keeps getting bleaker. As somebody who works in the world of Native theatre and publishing, let's just say my anticipation for a prosperous and happy New Year keep waving like a flag blowing in the Arctic wind. What I do for a living is not exactly a magnet for disposable income. People do not naturally envision surviving on food, water, warmth, and a theatre performance. I'm beginning to have visions of soup lines for Native playwrights, novelists, and columnists wrapping around Friendship Centres, and First Nations artists on each street corner, displaying signs saying: "Will write a play for food," or "Spare change for a metaphor." These visions, more than the current cold snap, are making me shiver.

Alas, this winter has become a lot darker and colder than I anticipated. A few weeks into January, my mother passed away from a stroke, and the end of an era suddenly appeared. I am an only child of a single parent, and I always credited her with giving birth not only to me, but also to my sense of humour and perspective on life. The time I told my mother I had been presented with the opportunity to open for and MC a night of Aboriginal comedy at the grand opening of the Smithsonian National Museum of the American Indian in Washington, DC, she paused for a moment, then said: "Well, you'd better learn to be funny." Wise words indeed. And I have tried.

Though we are very different, she is somebody I always tried to emulate. She was strong, independent, trustworthy, fun, and always made the room she was in at that moment definitely a better place to be. I shall miss her, but I will continue to draw strength from knowing she will, in my mind, never be gone.

It's been said that every time an Elder passes away, a library disappears. One time while driving somewhere, my mother and I heard a commercial on the radio advertising classes in French. Wistfully, she said, "I wish I was bilingual." I had to remind her she was. And after thinking about it for a moment she said, quite proudly, "I guess I am." Fully fluent in Anishnaabe as she was, that circle of speakers has just grown a little smaller, and the world is definitely worse off for it.

My mother, Fritzie Taylor, always had time to listen to all my bad jokes, my unusual perspective on society, and my reflections on Native life. It will be a different world without her for sure. I admit, there's a galaxy of difference between the election of African-American President Barack Obama and my Ojibway mother passing away ... but each is monumentally significant on so many different levels—and they both mark the passing of an era.

Fascinated as she was with all things American, my mother watched Obama's rise to success with an almost incredulous pride. She once told me about when she was working in "the States" as a domestic during the fifties. She felt guilty about being told to only let the Black people who worked for her boss drink water outside the house. My, how things have changed, both there and here. Obama never met my mother, but I think they would have understood one another.

I guess, in that light, 2009 can only get better for all of us.

AN ACT OF OLYMPIC PROPORTIONS

This should brighten up next winter's blues around here. Olympic Winter Games fever has officially come to my Rez. A couple of weeks ago my community got word that on December 16, the Olympic torch will wind its way through our sleepy little First Nation on its journey west. Somehow, on its way from Greece, the original home of the Olympics, to Vancouver for the February 2010 Games, it is to pass through Curve Lake. The International Olympic Committee may want to get a new travel agent. Still, it's caused quite a bit of stir at the local coffee shops ... as if we have coffee shops.

It will be an interesting event for sure. There are pros and cons to the idea of welcoming the torch. First, the cons: it wasn't that long ago when the idea of some person, more than likely a person of non-Native heritage, running through our village waving a flaming torch might not have been so universally welcomed. Then there's also the issue of Curve Lake being a peninsula. There is only one road in and one road out. The flame might have to be waterproofed. In theory, the Band Office has said, if the lake has frozen sufficiently, the runner could possibly run across the frozen water, along with all of his or her support vehicles. I'm not sure how much he or she will like that idea. Around here, December is still a little early to be out on the ice—with or without a flaming object. Local legends talk about the bottom of our lakes being piled high with abandoned snowmobiles, evidence of White cottagers eager to take their new Christmas presents out onto the lake a little too early. Or too late. But I suppose one little torch wouldn't hurt.

Of course there is talk about the possibility of taking the torch across the lake in a boat. It would give the runner a chance to catch his/her breath, I suppose, though it would surely be an odd sight. I doubt the Greeks could have foreseen the torch, a symbol of the Games started in 776 BC, being carried across the lake in an aluminium boat powered by a ten-horsepower Evinrude motor, steered by an Ojibway. I think it would kind of take the romance out of it for them, but it would be very authentically Canadian.

The pros to such a visit are more interesting. It might get people thinking more about the benefits of sports. I have thought for many years about joining the world of professional sports, but alas, my opportunities for such a career are severely limited. The official motto of the Olympic Games is "Citius, Altius, Fortius," which translates as "Faster, Higher, Stronger." Unfortunately, my "faster" days are long gone. In fact, there's talk about them actually never having existed. I just prefer to think of them as being lost in the mists of time. "Higher" what? Blood pressure? Blood-sugar level? Weight? Many of us already have achieved all those highs, so it's not as if we have to start training for it now. "Stronger" … that's a possibility. I have been working out … pushing my car out of the snow. Pushing myself off the couch. Lifting the turkey during the holidays. Wrestling with moral dilemmas. Lifting my spirits. Fighting temptation. I do those all the time, but I don't think they are considered Olympic sports.

Actually I have been contemplating what sport would be good for me to take up, should I ever work up the nerve. It would have to be a winter sport of course, in honour of the Winter Olympics in Vancouver. I can't ski. I'm not that good of a skater. The only thing that I can think of is that event I think is called the luge. That's the sport where you go sledding by yourself. I always thought that sounded like fun, and I've done it before—non-professionally of course. And the best part of it is you get to lie down while doing it. In fact, you can't win unless you are lying down. Of course those incredibly tight costumes look a bit … revealing. And I don't think all the Spandex in the world could make me aerodynamically desirable. I may have to rethink that option.

Still, the torch will be stopping at many Native communities across Canada as it journeys to the actual Olympic Games. I believe it will be coming from the Mohawk community of Tyendinaga before it hits our shores, which adds an added element of concern. Whoever will be carrying the torch will have to survive on a diet of corn soup, bannock/fry bread, and Indian tacos.

Good luck with all that running, buddy. You're going to need it.

BLOWING SMOKE OUT YOUR ...

In the sleepy Band Office of Curve Lake, people are still talking about two things around the water cooler, one great, one not so great. The first was the arrival, a few weeks ago, of the Olympic torch in our fair community, as it made its way across Canada. A whole day's festivities were planned in its honour. The second thing was the comments made on his show by Wolf Radio 101.5 morning man T.J. Connors, on the morning of November 25, regarding that same anticipated visit by the Olympic torch. In what can only be described as a rather tasteless attempt at humour, he made reference to the convoy stopping in Curve Lake to "buy smokes." Perhaps he speaks of this practice from personal experience?

Now, one can take this questionable comment several different ways, all of them less than flattering. He could be referring to the handful of smoke shacks that do exist in Curve Lake. Or possibly, he might be referring to the few members of our village with the last name Smoke. But firstly, it should be noted strenuously that while there are smoke shacks located here, ironically, they are patronized primarily by White people, not Native people. So Mr. Connors' issues should be directed more toward People of Pallor than towards us. And besides, illegal cigarettes can be found in any non-Native community. Secondly, Curve Lake does not endorse, practise, or permit human slavery, so it is exceedingly difficult to buy people named Smoke here. Thirdly, Mr. Connors should have a little more respect for this representation of the Olympics—it's probably as close as he's ever going to get to them.

I realize this is a stale issue, what with this having occurred quite some time ago, but I have just become aware of this incident since my recent return from Germany, where I was on a lecture tour about Canadian and Native humour. Being aware of the top-notch, sophisticated, and erudite humour available on early-morning DJ radio in mid-sized Ontario cities, I usually don't comment on the work of amateurs, but I thought, "What the hell."

First things first: humour should amuse, not abuse. I've seen this on t-shirts, so it must be true. T.J. Connors basically reduced the hundreds and thousands of years of history, culture, and existence of Curve Lake—the real reason the Olympic torch is coming here—to a questionable retail business involving cigarettes and tax evasion—a pretty lean socio-economic endeavour and essentially not very accurate. The best humour is usually rooted in reality—though again, maybe Mr. Connors speaks from personal experience. Granted, many of us have issues with the smoke shack practice, but not in such a dismissive manner. Still I'm sure he thought it was very funny.

All of us in the humour business have heard the phrase: "Geez, it's just a joke—can't you take a joke?" Yes we can, but usually only when it's funny. It's in the comedians' union rule book. Look it up. Granted, humour is subjective, but we don't have to be subjected to all that represents itself as "humour." And I understand that when Keith Knott, Chief of Curve Lake First Nations, expressed the community's concerns to the powers that be at the station, the management was less than receptive. Fred Patterson, program director, conveyed Wolf 101.5's attitude towards its listening public by responding: "What, are you embarrassed?"

I am a regular listener to the Wolf, where I enjoy all the geezer rock, being a borderline geezer myself. And I will continue to listen. No need, as they say, to cut off my leg to spite my foot. So I urge you to think of Mr. Connors metaphorically as a White person who likes cheap Native cigarettes; and of me as a Native person who can tolerate cheap White humour.

So everybody's happy.

SWEATING FOR MONEY

My goodness, how times have changed. Up until the 1950s, it was highly illegal for Native people to practise any form of their religious beliefs, whether it was participating in a sundance, a potlatch, or a sweat lodge—bingo excluded, of course. Nowadays, those same rituals have become exceedingly popular, especially amongst the dominant culture.

About ten years ago, I directed a documentary about Algonquin Elder William Commanda and the Circle of Nations, a gathering of people from all around the world, in Kitigan Zibi (formally known as Maniwaki), Quebec. During a long weekend in the summer, over 2,000 people now regularly camped on Commanda's front doorstep for a series of workshops, lectures, and seminars on a variety of subjects ranging from teachings of the wampum belt to the running of sweat lodges. It was an interesting place to be.

Of course, three-quarters of the people there were non-Native. Not that there's anything wrong with that, as Seinfeld would say. Knowledge and spirituality need no Status Card. Some of my best friends are White and looking for direction. Some of my best friends are also Native and looking for direction too. Anyway, I remember interviewing these three people who had made the journey up from New York City. Two were White women and one was a Black guy. All three said they practised the Lakota path of spirituality in the Big Apple. Another guy said he used to hang out with the Hells Angels at one time, till a conversation with the Dalai Lama convinced him that Hell didn't need angels, and so he now found himself tending the fires at sweat lodges. Obviously, there was an eclectic group of people gathered there, all being welcomed, fed, and taught.

But then you find out things that happen in places like Sedona, Arizona. In October, three people died from participating in a poorly run sweat lodge ceremony. Twenty-one additional people were taken to hospitals in the area with illnesses ranging from dehydration to respiratory and kidney failure. This is a lesson in what can go wrong. Here's an advance tip on how to avoid tragedies like this—*don't pay for it!* If the guy running these kinds of ceremonies presents you with a bill or tells you the path to spiritual strength requires a credit card, chances are it's not for you.

The guy who ran this enterprise, James Arthur Ray, charged these people $9,695 a pop to sit in a big round artifice and sweat their brains out, literally. It was part of a five-day "Spiritual Warrior" event that culminated in a ceremony where a reported sixty-four people crowded into a single sweat lodge. That's almost $640,000 dollars for less than a week's activities. Excellent work if you can get it, I suppose. I don't mean to sound snarky, but after all, this is a true tragedy.

However, after getting his guests to sign a liability release, Mr. Ray did promise the retreat would absolutely "change your life." It most certainly did for at least three people. He told participants they might experience "physical, emotional, financial, or other injuries" during the five-day spiritual quest in the wilderness. Note the term "financial." In case I didn't mention this earlier—don't pay for it. That must be stressed; 99.9 percent of the people I've met who have run or held sweat lodges don't charge—it kind of negates the point. At the risk of sounding racist, most Native people know this. It's mentioned rather extensively in the operator's manual we get with our Status Cards.

Alvin Manitopyes, a Cree healer, says it all: "Our Elders conduct sweat lodge ceremonies out of love for their people to help them in their healing and spiritual growth. When someone attaches a price tag to the ceremony, then the sacredness is gone and it comes down to them playing around with our sacred ceremonies."

Then again, $640,000—that's an awful lot of money. For five days. Obviously if people are willing to throw it away on something like this, it's money they don't want or need. That gave me an idea. Just come over to my place, we'll sit around my living room wearing only towels, I'll jack the thermometer up as high as it will get, and I'll read aloud from some Tom King or Tomson Highway book. We'll sing a few Native songs by Kashtin or Buffy Sainte-Marie, and then I'll give you all traditional Indian names. After the five days of traditional Native foods (baloney and Kraft Dinner), we'll roll around outside in the leaves and call it a day. I do take cheques, as long as you have two pieces of ID. The price does not include GST.

I'm half White, I should know how to do this. .

VOICES FROM THE DARKNESS

I lecture a lot. I am somewhere in the world giving at least two lectures a month, sometimes more. In May I'm scheduled for my sixth lecture tour of Germany where I will extol the virtues of Native literature in at least five German cities. Sometimes I feel like a prophet, going forth into the wilderness, spreading the Gospel of contemporary Aboriginal storytelling. This month alone I've been to La Ronge, Chatham, Vancouver, and Saugeen. I know what you're thinking—after visiting La Ronge and Saugeen, what could Germany possibly have to offer?

The trips themselves are quite enjoyable—the places I've been, the things I've seen, the people I've met, the food I've eaten, the plane and train seats I've sat in. Ninety-nine times out of a hundred, the response is wonderful, interesting, and worth the hours I spend fearing the loss of my luggage. Seriously, LaRonge was a blast, and how often does somebody get the chance to say that? But then there's that other one percent. Occasionally, and I do mean quite rarely, some of the responses I get from audiences make me wonder why I bother to pack my best underwear for these trips. I am not referring to people who don't necessarily agree with what I am writing or talking about—that is expected, and often leads to great discussions—it makes for an interesting debate. I am instead referring to people who suggest you change not what you are talking about, but how you say it—a far more insidious proposition.

About two years ago I was in Ottawa giving a lecture on the nature of Aboriginal humour. Actually, I was an opening act for Buffy Sainte-Marie at a big conference, so there were a lot of people there, eager for a good time. And the audience response was lovely. However, I was invited to the bar for some post-celebration discussion and it was there that this lady from the conference provided me with an alternative way of handling my career. Instead of lecturing to the audience, telling jokes, and celebrating the Native sense of humour in its many different forms, as my contract required, she suggested I hire some students to go up and read selections from some of my plays. She was very adamant. Spread the wealth, she said. Violate my contract I responded.

I understood what she was suggesting and, in the right circumstances, I've done just that. But that was not what I'd been hired for. I know doing what the person on the other end of the phone is hiring and paying me for might make me some sort of rebel, but I'll have to live with that. This lady spent a good chunk of time trying to tell me I was being selfish for hogging the spotlight and I should give back to the community by locating, hiring, rehearsing, directing, and training two or three young students in the ways of Native theatre and my work, in the three hours between landing at the airport and going on stage. Needless to say, the evening did not end well. All the good energy from the evening evaporated as, once more, I was told to change my manner of presentation.

More recently, in London, Ontario, to be exact, I was approached by a White woman (I wonder why women feel the need to correct me—no mother issues here) after a presentation at the university. This woman taught a unique course there on Franco-African literature. She immediately cornered me after my presentation and began to tell me that I should stop being funny and using one-liners when asked questions. It made me look superficial, she said. It cheapens what you're trying to say, she said. I tried to explain to her that the name of my most recent book was Me Funny, and that I'm usually hired to talk about Native humour, its structure, and usages. That usually requires using a little humour in my presentation, because there's nothing worse than a dry and boring lecture on humour. Except maybe one on erotica, but that's another article.

She wasn't interested in my logic, but things went from bad to worse when she told me she was a committed vegetarian and hated anything I mentioned about Native people eating meat. And when I joked about it, I was committing a double evil. She thought everybody should be vegetarian. "What about the Inuit?" I asked. Traditionally their diet was mostly meat— probably because you can't grow soybeans, or much of any other kind of vegetation in the high Arctic, I speculated. "Oh, I wouldn't worry about them," she responded. "With global warming, all the polar bears will die off and they'll have to become vegetarians." And did I mention that just prior to this exchange, she had also suggested I try to be more "traditional" in my presentation, whatever that means to a White professor of Franco-African literature. Methinks this woman needs a dictionary. And a cultural sensitivity course.

It's like back-seat lecturing. I think arguments like these should be reserved strictly for telling politicians how they should do their jobs properly.

I remember reading this sign at my local Rez store when I was young: "The only reason I hang around anymore is to find out what's going to happen next." I'm beginning to think that simple statement should sum up the second part of my career.

TIME IMMEMORIAL

During the opening ceremonies of the Vancouver Olympics, I noticed something interesting as the governor general was being escorted to the VIP seats. There seemed to be some confusion about the procedure, and people were milling around in the background as she was led in. Then the television announcer commented that the delegations from the four host First Nations hadn't arrived yet, and the governor general was supposed to have been the last seated. A bit of an etiquette faux pas, n'est-ce pas?

As luck would have it, I was watching the festivities on my Reserve with a room full of Native people. When we heard the explanation for the disruption, we instinctively looked at each other and all said in unison, and with a smirk, "Indian Time."

"Indian Time" is a term used when Native people are late. I've heard it used at grand entries, meetings, dinner parties, hockey tournaments, and even long-overdue births. In theory, it refers to a slower way of interacting in the world. Events happen at their own pace, and are not necessarily regulated by that thing on your wrist or wall or microwave. Things get done or happen when they need to get done or happen. It seems there's a larger cosmic sense of a starting time for events that only Native people are attuned to. Some First Nations people disagree with the concept of "Indian Time." When I ran a theatre company, I did. Late is late and rude is rude, regardless of the cultural baggage. You're being paid to show up on time. Still, for as long as I can remember, "Indian Time" has been an Aboriginal licence to add thirty minutes or so to getting out of bed in the morning.

Imagine my surprise when I discovered that we, the Aboriginal people of North America, don't have the market cornered on culturally determined lateness. Yes, there are other people in the world who, based on their geographic and ethno-cultural backgrounds, can and do show up for dinner forty minutes late, citing as an explanation (some would say "excuse"), their socio-political history. It seems we are not alone, and these pretenders to the tardy throne come from around the world. After doing a random sampling of friends and co-workers, it seems to be quite the worldwide phenomenon.

To start with, evidently there is something called "Caribbean Time." I understand it can include many of the different islands and people in those warm waters to the south, but one Haitian woman specifically wrote me that, "Haitian time is pretty much the same thing as Caribbean time. When my mother, my brother, and I were invited to an event organized by Haitians, we always had to clarify ... if we needed to follow our time or regular time, which really meant White people's time. Also, we were constantly amazed by the fact that people would be outrageously late, even to special events such as weddings, christenings, first communions, funerals, job interviews, the list goes on." That sounds pretty familiar.

Same with "South Asian Time," meaning that other "Indian Time"—not my Indian people, that other Indian people. A close South Asian friend told me, "I believe underlying this sense of time is the Hindu concept of 'yugas' or epochs. Time is calculated in epochs rather than by clock. For a people who count time by epochs rather than hours, minutes, and seconds, it stands to reason that temporal specificity has a somewhat different meaning than for a mechanical product of the industrial age. A South Asian seldom says, '10 o'clock sharp,' when making an appointment. She/he is more likely to say, 'around 10 o'clock.' And therein lies the clash between yugic time and clock time." That just seems like a fancy way of saying, "I'll get there when I get there."

When I was in California last month talking with a theatre company, they were telling me about a planned remount of Miss Saigon, the big musical about Vietnam during the war. The star, Leah Salonga, is Filipino, and the local joke in the Filipino community was that the curtain went up at 8:00, and at 7:30 for Filipinos (so they could be half an hour late). That explains a lot about that Newfoundland time they always announce on CBC.

Equally interesting, I mentioned this concept to a Korean producer who was interviewing me on "being Canadian," and she immediately told me there is a similar time in Korea, but that her people are split on the issue. Because of their desire to achieve success, much like the Japanese, most Koreans are on time in the business world. However, on a social level, it's a crap shoot.

It almost seems that White people are the only ones who see a need to be on time. Always bucking the trend.

RECONCILING DIFFERENCES

This has been an unusual month in the world of Aboriginal reconciliation. It's no secret that there's a lot out there in the First Nations community that remains to be reconciled and sometimes the process is fraught with sudden difficulties and unexpected surprises. It's been that way since 1492, or 1497, Newfoundland time. This week has had examples of both good and bad reconciliations. As legend has it, the Creator giveth, and the Creator taketh away.

A week ago Sunday was the twentieth anniversary of the beginning of what became known as the Oka Crisis. The little Mohawk community of Kanesatake, in a dispute with the town of Oka, the Province of Quebec, and the Government of Canada, blockaded an area of the town known as the Pines, severely inconveniencing several dozen potential middle-class White golfers who were anticipating an additional nine holes to be built over a traditional burial ground. These people should have spent less time on the golf course and more time watching movies like *Poltergeist*. Native burial grounds and White developers don't mix. Check the Indian Act.

The unfortunate outcome of this land dispute was a seventy-eight-day siege, the tragic death of Quebec provincial police officer Marcel Lemay, an army invasion, and an estimated bill to the taxpayers of somewhere around three to four hundred million dollars, once everything had been tallied. That's one hell of a green fee. Two decades later, though progress has been made, not all the wounds have healed completely. And then there's Francine Lemay, sister of Corporal Lemay. There's a lot of healing and reconciliation in that woman. By all rights, she should be the last person wanting to mend relations. Yet, she has done something fabulous. A translator by trade, she has personally translated the book *At the Wood's Edge* into French, which details the Mohawk community's history and struggle for justice.

Before the incidents at Oka, she knew very little about the Mohawk people or their history. The intervening twenty years provided less incentive to learn. But a chance meeting with some Mohawk women a year or so ago at a local church proved pivotal. Francine Lemay talked with those women, read the book seeking to understand their perspective, and afterwards offered to translate it so other French people could understand what had led up to those tragic events. Truly an amazing gesture by a woman, who by all reckoning, should be very angry. That sounds like true reconciliation. I am tempted to buy the book just on principle, even though I can't read French.

And then there are the newest revelations about the Truth and Reconciliation Commission on Indian Residential Schools. It seems the last thing on the commissioners' personal agenda is reconciliation, at least within their own group. Two more people have left the organization amidst bad publicity. Originally set up in 2009 to research and record the events and abuses that occurred at the dozens of residential schools once scattered across the country, the commission got off to a bad start almost immediately when the three original commissioners resigned due to internal squabbling. This set the commission back almost a year, endangering the completion of their five-year mandate.

Now two more individuals have decided, or been told, too much truth is not necessarily a good thing in their lives. Dr. John Milroy, the research director, has opted to seek other pastures. Only a few months into his job, he came under fire for making some controversial remarks over his frustration at the pace of document negotiations. He thought the Catholic Church was taking too long to release diaries, lest they reveal details about "buggering boys in the basement and that sort of thing." An apology by Commission Chair Mr. Justice Murry Sinclair to the Church soon followed. Though still an official adviser on research to the commission, Dr. Milroy's contribution to "reconciliation" has been downgraded. Both the commission and Dr. Milroy blame the unexpected amount of administrative work involved for his departure.

In addition to these troubling developments, Executive Director Tom McMahon has been replaced by Kim Murray, a lawyer from, ironically, the Kanesatake First Nation of Oka. However, like Dr. Milroy, Mr. McMahon will also stay on in an advisory capacity. Granted there is a fair amount of shuffling that goes on in any large organization, but all these exits and entrances seem a little too frequent and a little too high up the ladder to make any of us comfortable about the process. This can't be good for the commission.

All this changing of the guard takes the focus away from the important issues—detailing and recording the many unfortunate stories that come from the thousands of former students forcibly enrolled in the schools, where in many cases, they were physically, mentally, and sexually abused. There is a saying in the world of Native theatre: "before the healing can take place, the poison must be exposed." In other words: "Physician, heal thy self." As things stand now, a report the commission is scheduled to deliver at the end of its second year on its "historic findings" is looking less and less likely.

Maybe they should bring Francine Lemay in to have a good long talk with them. It wouldn't hurt.

West

West is typically represented by the colour black. It is also the element of water, including streams, rivers, and lakes. This direction represents adult life, including politics, academia, and the arts. With adulthood comes responsibility, parenting, and looking after children. The sun sets in the west, signifying the end of the day and the harvest—autumn, if you will. It is also the direction of mental processes and the development of thought. The Thunderbird, the buffalo, and grasses belong to the west.

WHO'S STEALING WHAT FROM WHOM, AND IS IT STEALING?

Appropriation in the arts has been a bee in many a cultural bonnet for the last fifteen years or so. The concept of somebody from one culture telling another culture's story has been discussed, argued, fought about, and a controversy frequently dug up again, only to be rehashed in dozens of different ways. Often the major sticking point deals with when enough is enough. When do respect and political correctness begin to infringe on the creative process, so much so, in fact, that they hamper, even compromise the art? The argument drifts between whether non-Native people should write Native stories, to whether men should write female characters, heterosexuals should write about the gay experience, dog owners should write about cat owners, and so on. The lines of demarcation become blurrier than promises in the bar at closing time.

More recently, there's been a new development in the cultural appropriation issue, specifically deep within the Native community. Renowned Cree playwright Tomson Highway is no stranger to the argument. For a long time he has been a proponent of colour-blind casting, and has often said art is colourless. This whole discussion annoys him to no end. In fact, several months ago at the Native Playwrights Summit in Toronto, he confessed that someday be plans to write a play, in French, with three White girls as the central characters.

This January, his first main-stage play in fourteen years opens at the Western Theatre Company in Kamloops, British Columbia. Titled *Ernestine Shuswap Gets Her Trout*, the play takes place in Kamloops, and all the major First Nations characters are Shuswap, Okanagan, or Thompson. The playwright is Cree. Is this an issue? Somebody familiar with the area recently asked that question. Tomson said no. He had had direct consultations with the local Aboriginal cultural centre to keep him honest.

Several months back, I was approached by a Toronto Native theatrical organization interested in doing something different. The artistic director asked me if I would be interested in adapting a Tlingit creation story, *How the Raven Stole the Sun*, into a dance theatre piece for her company. I am Ojibway from the wilds of Central Ontario. Truth be told, I know very little about the Tlingit culture, other than that they are located along the northern BC coast, as well as in the Yukon and Alaska. I also know there's probably some salmon involved somewhere. And I know very little about professional dance, but I thought, "What the hell."

Raven legends are ancient oral stories that vary from community to community, and the version I would be using was put down on paper by

Alaskan Tlingit Maria Williams, who was flown to Toronto as a consultant for the original discussions. I asked the AD if my being Ojibway (as was the AD, I should point out) would be an issue. Would we have hordes of politically correct Tlingit storming the production offices? The AD didn't think so. We were both Native, we were sensitive to the mistakes that could be made, and we had the blessing of Maria herself. But one Tlingit writer/actress/storyteller that I chatted with at some Native playwrights' Summit questioned, "Why not get a Tlingit writer to do it? Hire me. What's their number?"

In my own and Tomson's defence, there is a sense of collective understanding that seems to exist between the First Nations of Canada, regardless of what part of the country or Nation you're from. It's something akin to a sense of shared experiences, born of oppression, of survival, of disenfranchisement, of too much baloney (both in a literal and a metaphorical sense). I believe this allows us to relate to each other's existence, regardless of individual tribalism. We revel in our connectedness to this land.

My very first writing assignment, a thousand years ago, was for an episode of *The Beachcombers*. There I was, writing a story about Jesse Jim and his wife Laurel, two of the Native characters in the show. They were Salish, if I remember correctly. I was not. I had also never even been to British Columbia at that point. But in the end, the episode turned out pretty good and I managed not to culturally embarrass myself.

I was also once a writer on *North of 60*, a show about the Dene' of the Northwest Territories. Again, at the risk of sounding repetitious, I was not Dene', (unless there is something my Ojibway mother has not been telling me). One Dene' critic of the show was once quoted as saying: "It's a show about my people written by Jews and Crees." And, I guess, unbeknownst to him, one lone Ojibway.

It seems that when you're writing a script for television, or some form of the dominant cultural media, the specifics of your Nation become ir-relevant. Non-Native producers only seem to care that you can wave around a Status Card and can tell the difference between a bagel and bannock. Ojibways can write about the Dene' or whomever. The Haida can write about the Innu. I can even write about White people if I've got the inclination. Hey, I've been known to throw a few Caucasians into my scripts, just for lack of colour, and to find out if anybody would accuse me of culturally appropriating Oshawa culture. Hasn't happened yet.

But ears prick up in our own community when we Native writers start looking over the fence at other First Nations' stories. One woman on my Reserve was a little uncomfortable with the idea when I raised it, but then shook it off saying: "Well, at least you, being the writer, will be Native. That's something." Maybe it is something. Maybe it's nothing. It is certainly a question for those far more intelligent than me. In the meantime, I've got an idea for a story about a handicapped Black albino lesbian from South Africa … but it's okay, her car has a dreamcatcher hanging from her rear-view mirror.

HOW THE MIGHTY HAVE FALLEN

After nineteen months, it looks like David Ahenakew has lost his court case, his membership in the Order of Canada, and the respect of a good chunk of the population of Canada, both Native and non-Native. This seventy-one-year-old man from Saskatchewan that was once the pride of Aboriginal Canada now stands alone, supported only by his family, after having been convicted and fined a thousand dollars for promoting hatred against Jews.

The real shame here, apart from his toxic views, is the fact that at one time Ahenakew was at the forefront of the struggle for equal rights. A former head of the Assembly of First Nations and a decorated war veteran, he had long fought for Native rights and recognition in Canada, and much of where we stand today politically can be traced to efforts of Ahenakew and individuals like him. He was there pushing the envelope when the envelope didn't even exist. But alas, he reached a point in his life that all people in the political and public eye seem to do eventually. He began to believe his own press. After struggling for so long to have his voice heard by the various levels of government in this country for so many decades, he began to think his was the only voice worth hearing, and what he had to say was, by definition, Gospel. And that became his downfall.

All through this entire ordeal, you will have noticed a certain defiance or lack of contrition in his dealings with the press and the public. When he lost the first court case, he blamed the Jewish community, the Canadian court system, everybody but himself. It was the same when the allegations of racism first arose, in December 2002. Ahenakew blamed his medication, his health, even the media, and then went on to claim that he was taken out of context. He did later publicly apologize but many felt his apology was forced and insincere. I distinctly remember him in his first press conference after the incident, defiantly saying something to the effect, "Nobody tells David Ahenakew what to do," before resigning from all the political and business organizations he was affiliated with. Again, to him, the image of David Ahenakew was more important than that of the Jewish people.

Still, this should by no means diminish Ahenakew's contributions to the past. There is a sort of precedent for this situation. In 1885, during the trial of Louis Riel, most historians believe that Riel had long since lost his faculties—they seem to agree his bingo card was a few numbers short by that time. He was seeing images of the Virgin Mary and appeared to regularly suffer from other assorted reality lapses, they allege. Yet Riel is still venerated and respected today, particularly out west. In fact there's even talk in the Government of Canada of having his conviction overturned. Maybe the same might happen to Ahenakew's reputation, 120 years after his death.

More recently, Adolf Hitler, during his last days in the bunker before committing suicide, continuously cursed and blamed his generals, his soldiers, the German people, and of course the Jews for the loss of the war. He had given everything to the effort, and "they" hadn't given enough, he believed. Everybody was to blame for Germany's defeat except him.

I have never met David Ahenakew, and at one time I would have been delighted and honoured to sit at a table with him. As a Native person, I was always taught to respect and honour my Elders, and in situations like this, this instruction becomes a bit confusing. For instance, I have problems with Ahenakew blaming everything that's gone wrong with his life in the last year and a half on a court-inspired conspiracy: "My conviction says the power of this country lies with those who have the funds to back their lobbies and the corporate and financial influence to bend the Canadian judicial system and government to their will," to which he later added; "My case was as much about racism against First Nations as it was about alleged racism against the Jewish community."

No it wasn't. I may be somewhat naive on the subject, but one would hope that in a civilized country, when you call a race of people "a disease" and then justify the Holocaust, the courts should get involved. Perhaps the true irony here is that if somebody had made equally caustic and reprehensible comments about Canada's First Nations, or the Cree specifically, I have absolutely no doubt that Ahenakew would be there holding a press conference demanding a zealous investigation and legal action.

Yet in Canada, racism against Native people remains part of our ongoing social reality—try and find a Native person in this country who hasn't felt its sting. And yes, Canadian jails are disproportionately overcrowded with First Nations inmates, indicative of, among other things, some massive judicial malfunction. But some issues transcend our own little worlds, and I have yet to find the connection between the allegation that "Jewish people are a disease" and "Native people are rotting in jail." I know the Mormons believe Native people to be one of the lost tribes of Israel, but this is a little extreme on the other side of ridiculous notions based on race. Personally, I don't know that much about Jews, or Israel, for that matter. I do however know many fabulous people of mixed Jewish/First Nations heritage, affectionately known in the Native community as "schmohawks."

Some might argue that Ahenakew's remarks were not a case of racism. I once heard somebody of academic standing try to tell me that it is impossible for Native people, or any other marginalized people, to be racist. Only White people can be racist. Because, allegedly, racism works "from the top down." Only the privileged and those in control in any society can legitimately be called racist. I guess a case like this bucks the trend. Because David Ahenakew was always a groundbreaker, and most definitely someone who was "in control" within his society.

In the end, it was much ado about nothing. Ahenakew was retried in Saskatoon. In 2009, Saskatchewan Provincial Court Judge Wilfred Tucker acquitted Ahenakew because his statements, while "revolting, disgusting and untrue, did not show an intent to incite hatred."

It's a confusing issue and David Ahenakew is a confusing man.

But then again, he is Cree. And you know how they are.

EDEN MILLS—SOMETIMES YOU JUST DON'T KNOW WHAT'S RIGHT ANYMORE

Some time ago, I wrote about the Aboriginal Area at the Eden Mills Author's Festival, located in that tiny hamlet just outside of Guelph. For the last two years, the Aboriginal Area has been where Native authors have read their works in a small field to an appreciative audience. Prior to that, Native authors had been integrated with other non-Native writers in the September festival. This year, it looks like it will return to integration once more.

Three years ago a Cree man who happens to live in Eden Mills, approached the festival board of directors about wanting to host an area dedicated specifically to the literature and writing of First Nations authors. He had a big back yard that was perfect to accommodate such an event. The board thought this was a fabulous suggestion. Prior to this, an average of two Native authors would be invited each year. But with the newly created Aboriginal Area, three times as many, or approximately six First Nations authors, would be given the opportunity to dazzle the crowds with their literary talents. And these Aboriginal authors would range from nationally and internationally known writers, to local amateurs eager to mingle with their idols.

I was asked to help assist in programming last year's Aboriginal Area and set about it with great relish. But even back then, as I wrote about tackling this, I was aware that on a political level, there might be some criticisms—specifically about the apparent ghettoization of Native writers. God knows I had a few reservations of my own (no pun intended). Putting us off into a corner, like a sideshow, somehow felt a little regressive. Most of us wanted to play with the big boys/girls, and felt we had the talent and the track records to do so. The idea of going into an environment where automatically we were being marginalized felt odd.

However, on the logical side, we were getting paid the same amount, staying at the same hotels, and being treated just the same as all the other authors. And more importantly, the Aboriginal Area had been instituted by a Native host. It's hard to argue with those credentials. So I decided to leave it up to the audiences to decide. That afternoon, despite a vicious sun beating down on this little town, the Aboriginal Area was well populated with interested audience members. For the four hours of the programme, the field was awash with attentive and appreciative patrons.

I even asked a few of the people in the audience about what they thought of coming to the "Aboriginal Area." One Native woman said she preferred it—it was like "one-stop shopping." That begs an interesting question ... Is it better to play to a devoted and already interested audience, or try to find new converts, or, to use an old metaphor, were we just preaching to the converted? Quoting the movie *Jerry Maguire*, did we have them at "Ahneen?" Or are there, in truth, no colours in the Green Room (a waiting area traditionally set up for the talent with refreshments and munchies).

This year, things got a little difficult. Two of the invited Native authors felt the Aboriginal Area was fraught with more political and social intrigue than I had assumed. One, a popular novelist from British Columbia, the other an Ontario poet (I won't name them because I have high respect for both them and their work), sent letters to the board of directors complaining of being relegated to the Aboriginal Area. The novelist said she would never return to the festival, while the poet said that while she applauded the festival's giving increased visibility to Native authors, she felt we should be allowed to run free and wild with the other authors of non-Native heritage.

As a result of the two letters, the Aboriginal Area will not be seen this September at the Eden Mills Festival. The board of directors, concerned that their intention to highlight Native writing might be misinterpreted, have succumbed to pressure. There will again be two Native authors at this year's festival. They will be reading with the other authors. And somewhere in Eden Mills, there will be a Cree man's back yard, unused and unwanted at the festival.

ABORIGINAL SCIENCE FICTION

This has got to be one of my more unusual columns, but in this rapidly evolving world, you have to keep abreast of the changing times. It's no secret to most Canadians that the image and perception of Native people their parents grew up with has significantly changed of late. The spectrum of jobs open to First Nations people now includes doctors, lawyers, and Indian chiefs, as the old cliché goes. To quote the Ethel Merman song, "Anything you can do, I can do better," has now become our mantra.

It's the same with literature. Native writers, once considered as rare as a Conservative at a union meeting, are now flourishing in all genres of literary expression. Out there on the shelves of libraries and bookstores across the country are Aboriginal novels about love and broken hearts, detectives, politics, war, and even fantasy. If it can be imagined, it can be written. I think an Elder once told me that.

Yet oddly enough, there is one area of genre-fiction that Native people haven't yet completely embraced. I am talking about science fiction. You have to admit, there aren't a lot of First Nations sci-fi books out there. Oh sure, the few Aboriginal footprints wandering across the lunar landscape are but for the most part moccasins worn by White astronauts. How's that for a metaphor!

Perhaps the most well-known Aboriginal sci-fi character would be Chakotay from the *Star Trek: Voyager* series, though I don't know if it's the Canadian or Aboriginal in me that keeps wanting to call it *Voyageur*. Be that as it may, he is the second in command and sports a cool and funky tattoo on his face. They never actually say what nation he is from, but I do believe it's some Central American tribe. In one episode, they find a lost branch of his people living on a planet clear across the galaxy. They were no doubt sent there as displaced persons by some future non-Indigenous government intent on establishing their sovereignty on some other place far away from the dominant culture. It's been done before—just look at the Inuit of Grise Fiord.

My other favourite example of Native people making a token appearance in science fiction occurs in Aldous Huxley's *Brave New World*. Actually, it's more of a dystopian novel where John Savage, a severely displaced White dude, is born on a Reservation located in New Mexico, after his mother was marooned there on a sightseeing trip. It happens all the time, I hear. Needless to say, the representation of our people in this sub-genre of literature does not come off well. We are a backwards, drunken people who squabble and are very petty. (I'll avoid the obvious joke here.)

Other than that, the literary pickings are kind of lean. Certainly writers like Tom King and a few others have contributed bits and pieces to the genre, but essentially it is not a part of the forest we like to hunt or trap much in. I think this is because Native writers, like most Native people, are still dealing with what the past has taken away, and are somewhat preoccupied with reclaiming what our ancestors had. So we are more often than not pretty much looking to the past for our future.

Other Indigenous cultures around the world rank pretty much the same in the sci-fi sub-genre of fiction to my knowledge, with one notable exception. Oddly enough, the Maori of New Zealand seem to be living in the future quite comfortably already, particularly in sci-fi movies. Of course the sampling is small, but it is there. I first became aware of this anomaly when I saw Pete Smith playing the last living Maori (with a two or three White people) in the cult film *The Quiet Earth* back in 1985. Then there was Cliff Curtis fighting an extraterrestrial machine thing with just a Maori club (and a few guns) in the Jamie Lee Curtis movie *Virus*. He also, come to think of it, made an appearance in a cool horror film called *Deep Rising*, where he fought a sea monster with Cherokee actor Wes Studi.

But perhaps the best-known example would be Temuera Morrison, who made his first sci-fi debut in the Pamela Anderson film *Barb Wire*, as her ex-husband. It was a futuristic remake of *Casablanca* that few people saw. But he is perhaps better known for his role as Jango Fett in the second film of the *Star Wars* trilogy.

It's perhaps funny to mention here that George Lucas was soundly criticized for his casting decisions in the first *Star Wars*. If you were paying attention, you would have noticed that there were absolutely no people of colour anywhere in the cast. It seems in that galaxy far, far away, there were only aliens and White people. Again, I will refrain from making the obvious joke.

He attempted to correct his oversight in the second film, *The Empire Strikes Back*, by creating the character Lando Calrissian, and so on for the rest of the series. Here's hoping our literary future's going to be a little ... darker.

WHO THE HELL ARE THOSE PEOPLE AND WHY ARE THEY WEARING A HEADDRESS?

By now, everybody has probably seen those annoying Lakota Joint Care Arthritis Pain Relief Formula commercials on television. If you haven't, you're either blind or you don't own a television. They are so prevalent that you kinda get the impression that nobody quite knows pain like a Lakota. It's probably all that bareback riding they do (but if that were the case, it should probably be an ointment instead of a pill they reach for).

I think it was only last year that the ubiquitous face of Floyd "Red Crow" Westerman was on virtually every television screen urging you to try this herbal concoction named after his people, an American Plains Indian nation made popular by the *Dances with Wolves* movie. I once counted the identical commercial being broadcast on one single television channel four times in one half hour. One time, the same commercial ran twice in the same commercial block! No wonder Floyd's back hurts—it's from all the money he's carrying in his wallet from the residuals he makes every time the commercial is run. My heart soars like his bank account.

It wasn't long before I, a loyal and devoted Native Canadian (Ojibway, for those who like details), was sick of seeing Floyd's wise and handsome face. Nothing personal, I was Indianed out. I needed relief from the pain caused by the repeated viewing of the commercial. Then luckily, like a pain in my neck, they went away. For a while.

But like a migraine, those commercials are now back with a vengeance. Except this time, no sign of Floyd anymore. He mustn't be hurtin' anymore. Instead, we are presented with a cross section of Canadians going about their middle-class White lifestyle, all wearing what appears to be an eagle-feathered war bonnet, for some reason. There are scenes of people fishing, shopping, delivering mail, and engaging in all sorts of other Lakota-related activities. I'm not sure, but I think I saw an astronaut wearing one. Would those things be useful in space? One scene had a man playing with a dog. It wasn't long before I began to wonder why the dog wasn't wearing one. I call these commercials *Dances with War-Bonnets*.

This raises a number of difficult questions. First of all, how and why did the Lakota, and only the Lakota, corner the market on pain? I know several Ojibways, a couple Iroquois, and a handful of Crees that get headaches and joint pains too. Yet they aren't hawking some secret and special cure, other than Aspirin or Tylenol. We are obviously missing countless opportunities to widen our Aboriginal entrepreneurial possibilities here. For instance, we could get Gordon Tootoosis up there selling Cree herbal medicine. Imagine him saying, "Hi, I'm Gordon Tootoosis and I stubbed my toe the other day. Nothing helped me better than CREE! It's good for what ails you. But be careful, it's concentrated and powerful stuff. Just a little CREE will cure you. (Warning—keep away from children. May make you drowsy.)"

But to return to the Lakota commercials running now, I would like to point out that the actors in them are obviously White. Shouldn't they be showing the Lakotas in their arthritic natural habitat instead, going about their usual everyday pain-inducing lives, to promote the effectiveness of the product? I think there should be shots of Lakotas, all wearing war bonnets of course, making Kraft Dinner, hitchhiking into town, playing pool, peeing in urban stairwells ... you know—regular Native stuff like that.

What I find particularly amusing is trying to picture the ad man pitching the idea of the new commercial to the TV network. In these politically correct times, a non-Native guy is saying, "Hey, how about this? We show lots of White people running around wearing stereotypical war bonnets! Nothing sells pain relief like eagle feathers!" Seems highly unlikely. Even actionable. It seems more likely that the idea came directly from the manufacturers themselves, pushing the Native angle. The funny thing is, and I could be wrong, I heard a rumour that the people who own the company aren't even Lakota. It's a Canadian organization owned by a Métis out west.

So that begs the question—shouldn't this commercial have Métis running around, a fiddle in one hand, and a sash in the other, talking about their headaches and irritated bowels from too much jigging? That makes more sense. But instead it's the Lakota—again. Much like the Mohawks, Apaches, Cherokees, and Comanches, they have better press agents. It's true. They get all the publicity. Advertising is all a matter of brand recognition. You'll probably never hear of Shuswap or Haisla Joint Care Arthritic Pain Relief Formula. They haven't been branded yet.

DANCES WITH FILM

North America's Native population lives in lucky times. Today's film and video narratives abound with fairly accurate Aboriginal representations. Some days, it's like you can't turn on the television without seeing Gordon Tootoosis, Adam Beach, Tantoo Cardinal, Graham Greene, or Gary Farmer staring back at you. But it wasn't always that way. Not that many decades ago, almost all the Indians on screen were not in fact Indigenous people. They were ... colour enhanced.

I, like many Native people my generation and older, spent most of our youth looking for images of ourselves on both the big and the little screen. But what did we get? Rock Hudson as a square-jawed Chiricahua warrior. Or Jeff Chandler as a Jewish Cochise, in Broken Arrow. Chuck Connors gained fame as an actor cast in his role as Geronimo. It's more than mildly ironic to discover that in a film celebrating the life of a great Apache leader, there was not one actual Native person cast in the whole movie. What was also interesting was that a lot of these cinematic savages sported blue eyes, very similar to Grey Owl's. It was all very puzzling to us First Nations film fans. They say the camera adds ten pounds. In those days it seems it also anglicized the eyes.

As the years passed, what became even more bizarre was how the art of film didn't imitate life, it redesigned it. And then things got really confusing: our lives began to imitate the art that had redesigned life. I have memories of middle school, when us Native students would get a special hour of instruction in Native arts and crafts; we would sit around in the classroom, sewing cheap leather into headbands, and bead vaguely Aboriginal designs on the front. While some now think of this as an exercise in the postmodern, we thought of it as any excuse to get out of geography.

It should be noted that essentially, most Native people in the Americas never wore headbands. At least not the kind Western civilization associates with Native culture. They were actually a creation of Hollywood. It seems that when wardrobe departments dressed up Rock Hudson and Jeff Chandler as Indians, they gave them those ridiculously thick wigs with braided pigtails that were supposed to represent so many Native cultures. The wigs were uncomfortable and awkward to wear. They also tended to slip a lot as the actors wearing them gesticulated under those hot, sweaty lights. So some guy whose name is lost to fashion history came up with the cool idea of using headbands to keep the wigs on tight, even when the actors were riding their horses. Of such things are legends born.

Jay Silverheels, better known as the fictional Lone Ranger's fictional side-kick Tonto, is perhaps the best-known Canadian Native actor to ever have existed. Though he hadn't acted since the early 1970s and died in Los Angeles on March 5, 1980, his appeal has spanned more generations than Chief Dan George's, and had more of an effect on the dominant culture's perception of Native people (rightly or wrongly) than all the others combined. What is less known is that his real name was Harry Smith, and that he was from the Six Nations Reserve near Brantford, Ontario.

It seems only natural that Jay/Harry would finally make an appearance at the 2009 imagineNATIVE Film + Media Arts Festival, part of an exhibit at the Trinity Square Video called HOW: Engagements with the "Hollywood Indian." He is the focus of one of several media presentations, curated by Ryan Rice, that explores the contemporary Aboriginal's relationship with show business.

An icon of pop culture, Jay/Harry appears, in a voice-over only, in a modern video installation piece directed by artist Greg Staats, titled Harold J. Smith, Jay Silverheels, Tonto. Essentially, the short film is an unedited home video of a slow drive along the 7th Line River Road on the Six Nations Reserve, metaphorically the path that would take Jay/Harry home. Playing in the background is the soundtrack of an interview the actor did on The Jack Paar Show back in 1960.

I concede, installation art is not something with which I am overly familiar, so I may have missed something in that video installation piece. Now admittedly, Greg Staats is a talented man, and I have long admired his still photography, specifically a series he did about pow wow dancers. But I live on a Reserve and am already far too familiar with the wonders of dirt roads and pot holes to have learned much new from it, other than Jay/Harry's wife was Italian. And the audio left much to be desired. It was muffled and of poor quality, which is to be expected from a forty-eight-year-old talk show recording. In a later interview, he told Johnny Carson that he married an Italian woman to get back at Christopher Columbus.

For me, I found the two archival photographs of the man, both side by side, far more interesting: one featured the strikingly handsome Harry in a suite and tie; the other featured Jay dressed in his more familiar Tonto garb—the two sides of the Hollywood Indian.

There is a popular Rez story about Jay/Harry that I once heard. As a young man, he originally found success as a lacrosse player, touring the continent in the late 1930s. Reportedly, the nickname Silverheels was a reference to how fast he could run. Eventually he was discovered as a saleable commodity by a Hollywood scout because of his athleticism and good looks. So after he became practically the only working Indian actor in the 1940s, before he hit the big time as Tonto, he would always find himself a speaking part playing the generic Indian warrior or chief in a series of Westerns.

The story has it that more than a few times, the director would place him on a hill or bluff overlooking a vulnerable wagon train or cavalry troop, and direct him to address his numerous brave warriors in his own Native tongue, urging them to attack and kill. Even though he was Mohawk, Jay/Harry's grasp of his Indigenous language was somewhat tenuous. There he would sit, on his magnificent steed, urging his band of dangerous and lethal Indian warriors in "their own language" to descend upon the helpless White people and kill them all.

As the story continues, all his family and friends from Six Nations would go to Brantford to see his movies when they came out. They would sit in the audience enjoying Jay's success, and then, when this big scene came on, the theatre would erupt in laughter. There would be Indians killing themselves laughing, literally rolling in the aisles. The mystified White patrons would be wondering what the hell was going on.

Like many of us who are not as proficient in our ancestor's tongue as we would wish, most of us learn common words or short phrases from it first, rather than the whole lexicon of the language. So there on the screen was Crazy Horse/Sitting Bull/Geronimo, speaking in stilted Mohawk, extolling his warriors to: "Pass the salt! What time is it? It's raining! One two three four five six. Dog! Cat! I love you. Hello? Goodbye!" and so on.

I don't know if this story is true, but if it isn't, it should be. I should mention that Tonto wore a headband, though it was just a modest, simple, strip of leather. And he had no noticeable pigtails either. I guess those were reserved (no pun intended) for the White Indians. He got off easy.

READING, WRITING, AND REFUSING TO DO EITHER

It may be a generational thing but I really love reading—always have and more than likely always will. And I'm not talking about just emails or personal ads at the back of newspapers. I mean books and newspapers and magazines and practically everything I can get my ink-stained fingers on. I'm one of those people who will sit down to a meal and if I don't have any other text, I'll read the back of the cereal box, or the expiry date on the milk. Reading is one of the reasons I became a writer, and the side benefits include making me really good at Trivial Pursuit and television game shows.

I used to assume that the whole world shared my passion for reading. Each book is a doorway to another life, another place, a new adventure. To me, Hell is a long bus ride, with nothing to read (and a guy beside me who has a cold and a strange rash). In fact, I assume if you're reading this article right now, I must have found a sympathetic heart (or set of eyes). So, it came as a great surprise to learn that there are a lot of people out there who don't like reading. In fact, they will go out of their way to avoid it.

Many years ago, even before my theatre days, I picked up a copy of the play *Caesar and Cleopatra* by George Bernard Shaw. I'd heard about both the play and the writer and was curious to see what all the fuss was about. Add my modest interest in Egyptian and Roman history and I was hooked. The problem was, the lovely lady I was dating at the time wasn't as curious or intrigued as I was, either by Shaw or by history. She took one look at the book and said, if I remember correctly, "You're just reading that to impress people. Nobody reads those kinds of books for fun." Well, I did, so just call me Nobody. I should have known the relationship was in danger when I'd offered to teach her how to play chess and she had said, quite indignantly, "I don't want to have to think to have fun."

More recently, I visited with a young cousin of mine. I forget how we got on to the subject, but somehow I started talking about something I had read in the newspaper. I asked him if he'd seen it. He laughed and said, "I don't read newspapers. I don't read anything. It's all bad news anyways." The thing that sent a chill down my spine was the note, no, it was more like a symphony of notes, of pride in his voice. He was actually proud of the fact he didn't bother to read anything he didn't have to.

Then I thought ... in a way, it sort of made sense. My grandparents had told my mother not to let me read so much. "It's not normal." And trust me, this is no criticism of my grandparents, who I loved deeply. It was more reflective of the fact that we came from an oral tradition. The written word as we know it came over on those little boats, whereas our entire universe came down through the stories verbally told to us. We still honour that tradition. Nothing is as exciting or fun as watching a traditional storyteller in full glory. It's the ability to take the audience on a fabulous journey, using just the body and the voice, following a narrative that's been memorized. A good storyteller will send chills down your spine.

But so will a book. Keep in mind you can't always have access to a good storyteller twenty-four hours a day, seven days a week. How many of us have gone to the beach with a huge, sinful, summer book to wile away the hours? A Stephen King or Robert Ludlum novel is easier to carry in your tote bag than a traditional storyteller, who can also get kind of cranky telling stories on the beach while you bake like a potato. Storytellers are also hard to take on the subway. It's hard to hear them over the roar of the wheels and the babble of the multitudes of people—I've lost so many storytellers while changing subway lines during rush hour. See my point? And your average storyteller might not be up to date on what's happening in the Middle East or in Hollywood—thus, in my opinion, the need for newspapers and books to supplement all those traditional tales.

I always remind people, especially young writers, of the importance of reading. Even if you aren't interested in current events or science fiction, there are more subtle advantages to reading than you are probably aware of. The more you read, the better the understanding you have of the language. You develop an innate understanding of the meaning and place-ment of words—for instance, the importance of using the proper adverb. There's a world of difference between "playing by yourself" and "playing with yourself." I learned that the hard way. That's the kind of mistake you only make once in your life.

So, if nothing else convinces you about the importance of reading, let me impart upon you one last little snippet of wisdom from my high school days. Always remember, jocks get fat. Geeks get rich.

LIFE AS A STARVING ARTIST

Not that long ago I attended a conference in Montreal on Traditional Knowledge or, as it's affectionately known, "TK." As it drew to an end, we were all given a button to wear on our jackets. It said, "Mais avez-vous payé l'artiste?" Translated, it means: "But have you paid the artist?" Deep, meaningful, almost religious words for a freelance writer like myself. Looking back over the years, I figure the amount of money I have not been paid by organizations that approached me for work ... well, let's just say it could buy a hell of a lot of t-shirts on the pow wow trail this summer.

Granted, being a freelance writer is an existence fraught with potential liabilities—that is unfortunately the nature of the beast. Working with some Native newspapers and magazines, I have come to expect a certain amount of deadbeat-ism in my career. Sometimes it's like waitresses who return to a table with the bill only to discover the customers are long gone. It's par for the course. Kinda like treaties. You are promised one thing, but suddenly when it's convenient, the promises evaporate.

In some cases, you understand many of these papers are just starting up and have very limited finances, resulting in their having little to offer writers. The small magazine in this country is legitimately a labour of love, and that's fine, if they tell you that up front. As members of the community, it's expected that we put something back into that community. But there is a fine line between putting back into the community and being taken advantage of by that community. And it should be up to us, the writers, to decide what pro bono work we do.

I was once offered the opportunity to record some of my commentaries for a Native radio network for broadcast. I did it on faith and a hand-shake ... I know, I know—my first mistake. As I finished taping the second commentary, I asked when I was going to get paid for them. We had previously negotiated and worked out a fee. It was then I discovered, unbeknownst to me, the network had decided to slightly alter our agreement. The producer asked me if instead of receiving a fee, I would consider letting them advertise my website and books on air in lieu of payment. I thought about this for a moment, weighing the suggestion, considering the situation. In the end, I felt pretty sure my landlord wasn't interested in having my website publicized. Especially since I didn't have a website. And I didn't think the Loblaws on the corner would accept a promise to have my books advertised on radio as collateral for a loaf of bread and some baloney. There seemed to be a few missing equations there somewhere.

While bartering is a legitimate part of our culture, I don't think Revenue Canada would be interested in a free lecture or two on Native literature instead of my taxes. And what of my social commitments: "Mom, no birthday present this year, but my name is all over the place on the radio!"

In another situation, I wrote a lengthy article for a prominent Toronto Native magazine. It was published last fall. Looked fabulous and glossy. Haven't seen a cent from it since. I have called, pestered, emailed, and complained ... all for naught. Evidently I don't exist. Neither does my cheque. There is a gaping hole in my bank account with the name of this magazine on it. And I'm not alone.

Kim Ziervogel, founder of the Aboriginal Journalists' Association of Canada (AJAC), has contributed numerous photos to that same magazine, and has also not received credit or payment. She adds: "This rarely happens in mainstream journalism. You write an article. It is published. You submit an invoice. You receive a cheque. It's not that complicated. I've done it a lot. Unfortunately, some organizations feel that just because they're starting out, or are profiling the Native community, they can play with the rules a bit."

While this may sound like a personal diatribe or rant, keep in mind I've been lucky enough to survive in this financially volatile world. I do enough work for other, more reputable organizations that actually pay their invoices to take a hit every once in a while. It's other writers, those not quite so lucky as me, or those just starting out that have me concerned. Writing, like acting, is a tenuous profession at best, and so there's generally a whole philosophy behind running a professional magazine or newspaper—the operative word here being "professional."

If you want professionals to work or write for you, you have to treat them like professionals. It's not a difficult concept. It has to do with a little word called "respect." You may have heard of it. Aretha Franklin had a great song about it. It's also mentioned quite frequently in traditional teachings. In fact, going back to the beginning of my meditation, I do believe "respect" was mentioned quite frequently at that conference on Traditional Knowledge I went to. Funny how things like this move around in a circle.

A NATIVE PLAY BY ANY OTHER NAME

I remember seeing the New Zealand film *Once Were Warriors*, and noticing it stirred an odd, uncomfortable resonance within my First Nations soul, even though it was a Maori story. Same thing happened with *Rabbit-Proof Fence*, a movie about Australian Aboriginal children, and to a much more pleasant degree, *My Big Fat Greek Wedding*. All were films about different cultures that had an impact on me, and on a surprisingly Ojibway level. Little did I realize I was trying to achieve much the same resonance with a piece of my own writing.

Near the middle of this particular story, a car (a Saab, I believe) skids off the icy road and into a deep Canadian snowdrift. From the vehicle emerges a striking Native woman in her thirties. Her name is Janice and she is a successful entertainment lawyer from the city, dealing with returning to her rural Reserve community. She has come to meet her family. Her birth family. This is her first time there.

This character is the product of a tragic segment of Canadian history called the "scoop-up," where tens of thousands of Native children were cruelly taken away from their birth families by government and social service agencies, often for the flimsiest of reasons, and farmed out for adoption to the four corners of Canada. Seen by many as a project to assimilate Native people into the dominant non-Native culture, often these displaced children would find themselves forcibly settled in America, and occasionally in Europe and other far-off foreign countries they had probably never heard of before arriving there. Unfortunately, the results of these adoptions were often quite tragic, creating entire generations of people feeling at home in neither their original communities, nor in the communities where they were put. Their journeys home to that sense of belonging so necessary for one's self-esteem were frequently fraught with social obstacles and cultural difficulties, the most common of these being a simple ignorance to the existence of the subject.

In 1990 I wrote a short story, and later a play, about these events. Both were called *Someday* and told the story of this unfortunate Canadian historical practice, yet another of the many questionable by-products of colonization. The scoop-up is high on the "paved with good intentions" shelf, somewhere after residential schools and Reserves in the library of obscene Native programs. Since that time, there have been about a dozen theatre productions of *Someday*. I was always surprised by the success of this particular play, because I thought, foolishly, "How could other people relate to such an experience?" It had been, I concluded, a uniquely Native experience. Silly me.

Fifteen years and two sequels later, I have found out how wrong I was. It turns out that this same sort of domestic diaspora was a feeling felt not just in my own Canada, but in many diverse and far-flung places where knowledge of First Nations experiences was sketchy at best. *Someday*, a story of a single oppressed family dealing with blind government policies and entrenched racism that nearly destroyed them, was surprisingly accessible. More importantly, it was also tellable. People in other cultures didn't scratch their heads when they read my play, they nodded their heads in understanding instead.

In 2004, I had the unique experience of visiting one of the oldest universities in India, the University of Madras in Chennai. I was in the country on a lecture tour with my girlfriend and some other friends, and, as luck would have it, I got to see a production of selected scenes from *Someday* that was being put on by the university's English Department. Evidently, the play was on the theatre class's reading list.

Aside from seeing my play produced with an entirely Indian (South Asian Indian, that is) cast, speaking my Ojibway-tainted lines with noticeably inaccurate accents, I was eager to see their interpretation of its story. It was especially bizarre watching the scene where two Ojibways are discussing getting the car out of the snowdrift. It was easily forty sweltering degrees in Chennai, and highly unlikely anybody in the room had ever thrown a snowball, let alone had to deal with the greater Canadian experience of getting a car out of a snowbank. Regardless, I was flattered and delighted. More importantly, I was impressed.

While at that university, I was told the play was specifically studied there because, in its own way, it reflected a similar situation among India's Dalit community. Once referred to as the "untouchables," the Dalits have long been the disenfranchised, oppressed segment of the population, and existed deep below in the bedrock of polite Indian society until fairly recently. Most, if not all, of the students in that class were Dalit, as were the professors, and they found many parallels with the Native experience in Canada. Thus their interest. As is the custom in both cultures, just as much tea as conversation was brewed discussing those similarities.

By the way, *vedho oru naal* means "someday" in Tamil.

More recently, I have been contacted by yet another professor in an equally far-off land, interested in translating my humble play for the benefit of his students. His name is Abder-Rahim Abu-Swailem, and he is a professor at Mu'tah University in Jordan. He writes, "For me, I think the play is very interesting on both artistic and thematic levels. I think there are many things in common between the aspirations and the agonies of the Natives and the aspirations and agonies of the people in the Arab countries, especially the way they are perceived by the 'White man,' in a different way."

Hmmm, the scoop-up of an Ojibway child and her disenfranchisement from her family can be interpreted as a re-statement of Palestinian oppression? That's one of the things I love about literature. Anything can mean anything.

He goes on to add: "The fifty-year struggle with the Israeli occupation of the Arab territories, in addition to the biased stand of the US and England with the Israelis, made the struggle and yearning for freedom and legal rights a must for the Arabs. They want to put their own rules rather than to be dictated by the Other. Two thirds of Palestinians live abroad in camps."

Professor Abu-Swailem concludes by stating, "I am not a politician but politics are imposed on us and became part of our lives." That sounded vaguely familiar to me until I remembered that I've often been quoted as saying being born Native in Canada is a political statement in itself. We're not political by nature. We're political by birth. The Status Card is just part of the paperwork. Surprisingly similar perceptions abound globally, it seems.

In Arabic, Fi Yawmin Ma is the title of my play, though I'm told its closer to "Once upon a time ..." than "someday."

Admittedly I know little about the Israeli/Arab conflicts in that part of the world, only what I see on the news. I knew even less about the fight for equality by India's Dalits until I went there. I'm aware a little learning can indeed be a dangerous thing, and I try and keep that in context. But I've seen plays by Indigenous people in New Zealand, Australia, and a host of other countries scattered across the world, dealing with similar issues. Most of these plays are stories of survival. Of overcoming the ineffectual hand dealt to them by fate, and frequently, by foreign powers. Broadly put, these are themes of regaining control. Or finding purpose and independence. Of regaining destiny. A somewhat universal struggle for most of the world's minorities.

I've also had plays translated into Italian and German, but not for quite the same reasons, I would hazard to guess. The power dynamics are quite different. As everyone knows, the yoke of oppression makes for much better, and much cooler theatre.

There's a saying in the Native community: "And a child shall lead the way." In Someday, this child's name is Grace, until the dominant society changed it to Janice as she was being processed through the system. She was Ojibway, but she could just as easily have been Dalit, Arab, Maori, Aboriginal, or any other people controlled by another. As sad as it may seem, it's nice to know we all have something in common.

WAS HE TALKING ABOUT THE DOT INDIANS OR THE FEATHER INDIANS?

It's been some time since Stephen Harper's famous letter to the Ontario Federation of Indian Friendship Centres wishing them a happy India Republic Day—geography and history evidently not being one of the Conservatives' stronger suits. Now with National Aboriginal Day only a few days away on the 21st, I can't help but wonder if Harper's office is going to remain true to form and send India's Ambassador to Canada a card congratulating him on having such a vibrant First Nations culture. I mean, after all, what's a pow wow without a few tabla drums?

Should Stephen Harper manage to astound his detractors and actually become the prime minister of Canada, I'm sure his knowledge and understanding of Indian culture will come in handy. When, as PM, he travels the country visiting Native communities, I hope he will know what to expect from all those Indians. As somebody who's been to over 120 Native communities across Canada and the United States, I would like to offer Harper some advice, if I may, cuisine-wise. Always remember, if you want good curry, visit an Oneida community. Iroquoian curries are to die for. But if you're more interested in kick-ass samosas, I heartily recommend the Micmac. They really know their samosas. And if you want dahl, talk to the Salish. Their dahl is dahling.

Maybe he can also expect some sage advice from his new senior advisor and the national campaign chair for the Conservative Party, Tom Flanagan, controversial author of the book *First Nations? Second Thoughts*. Any man who has been quoted calling the Métis an "economically marginal, incohesive assortment of heterogeneous groups" and saying, "Perhaps the damage to Canada would be tolerable if it meant that Aboriginal peoples would escape from the social pathologies in which they are mired to become prosperous self-supporting citizens," must surely have something worthwhile to say about National Aboriginal Day. I think maybe somebody should send him a traditional Inuit sari to lighten up his mood a bit.

When I was growing up, it was safe to say that most Native people I knew voted Progressive Conservative. I remember the lawns of my community being awash in PC signs. This was not because most First Nations were freewheeling capitalists who believed in cutting income taxes (we didn't have any to cut, but don't get the Conservatives started on that), but more an acknowledgement, even an homage to the fact it was John Diefenbaker's Conservatives that gave Native people back the vote in 1960. It sure wasn't the Liberals, and back then the New Democratic Party was just a glimmer in the Co-operative Commonwealth Federation's eye. Who knows what state the Marijuana Party was in. Probably still having their policy meetings in jazz clubs.

How ironic, though, that a population collectively known as Canada's First Nations, were the last to get the vote, and as a direct result, the last to become legal citizens of that same country. And people wonder why voter turnout in Native communities is low. Or it could be that I have cousins who just can't find the polling booths every time they make their election pilgrimage to Calcutta.

However, taking my own completely unofficial, non-scientific, totally subjective poll, it seems times have changed. Most Aboriginal communities and populations have taken a decidedly NDP bent these days. Aboriginally speaking, Jack Layton's beads seem shinier. I wonder if Harper has ever even been to a Reserve, or bathed in the Ganges? Somehow I doubt it.

With the election a scant few weeks away, should Mr. Harper be granted a mandate by the people of Canada to govern as prime minister, I hope Grand Chief Phil Fontaine of the Assembly of First Nations, who's headquarters are located in the Taj Mahal, remembers to send a letter of congratulations to the Liberal Party of Canada headquarters ... not that it matters. They all sound alike anyways.

OPENING A CAN OF WORMS

Lately, our beloved prime minister has been making a lot of interesting promises as he settles into office, like for instance making his own government more accountable to the people. I think we all need a bit more accountability in our lives. I know I do. I think it comes from being called a "no-account" too many times.

I just hope Harper isn't forgetting he's still on what could technically be called "the electoral honeymoon." And as we all know, promises tend to come a little more easily and freely during that warm and fuzzy period, and are a little harder to fulfill down the road. Ask anybody in their second or third year of marriage. Reality, unfortunately, tends to work that way. By then talk is cheap and the proof is in the pudding, as they say. Maybe this is why I'm not married or have never run for office. I hate pudding.

Also, the prime minister plans to look into redressing the whole Chinese head tax issue. From the mid-1880s to the 1920s, a hefty admission fee was legally but unfairly charged to incoming Chinese immigrants who set foot on Canadian soil—a matter that's still fomenting understandable discontent a hundred years later. Still, you've got to give the government of those bygone days a round of applause. I've heard many a Native person say that it's a pity we didn't think of that, 500 years ago, for everybody wanting to immigrate to Turtle Island. That sure would have brought down the poverty rates in many First Nations communities.

Still, the Government of Canada addressing both the issues of accountability and the Chinese Head Tax is wonderful, fabulous, exciting, and honourable—and long overdue. I think Harper deserves some extra snuggle time in the post-election marriage bed for just tackling those issues alone.

But these two topics have got me thinking about potential repercussions. There is a possibility that Stephen Harper may be opening the floodgates of cultural accountability. I say this because I'm a man of the world and I've seen a few things. I've travelled to many parts of this globe, frolicking and cavorting with many of its Indigenous peoples. Trust me, the Maori, Saami, and Fijians do cavort, and occasionally frolic. And as has always been the case, we trade—things, ideas, food, t-shirts, and more interestingly, strategies.

Recently, Australia seems to be the place where interesting and some would say radical ideas are being developed by its original inhabitants. In 1998, tribal Elders from several Aboriginal tribes filed a motion with the country's Supreme Court. They were asking that their prime minister, John Howard, along with several other government officials, be charged with crimes that include: an attempted act of genocide by imposing conditions of life intended to destroy many Aboriginal peoples; causing them serious physical and mental harm; and directly and publicly inciting genocide. All this sounded oddly familiar, from a Canadian Aboriginal perspective. Alas, the motion never went anywhere and was dropped by the court.

But only last month the next phase of the battle was launched. Once more, Aboriginal Elders in Australia filed charges of genocide, crimes against humanity, war crimes, and crimes against the administration of the justice with the International Criminal Court. Only this time, the charges were against the sovereign head of Australia, Queen Elizabeth II, herself.

"Successive Australian Colonial governments have been and are unwilling or unable to resolve these fundamental questions of law. Therefore, the Queen of Australia is personally responsible for the crimes perpetrated against our people," said one Aboriginal Elder in a press release. "Queen Elizabeth II has been the sovereign ruler of Australia for the entire time that these laws have been in place and she has done nothing to stop the continuing genocide of our peoples, which is going on in this country." Now that will be an interesting court case, should anything ever come of it.

Could that happen here in Canada with our own prime minister, who's so new to the position, the paint in his office is still wet? I doubt it. Things like this don't happen that much in Canada ... I've heard there are still ex-Nazis in Canadian retirement homes goose-stepping down the halls with their walkers. Still, charging the Canadian prime minister with genocide would be a cool idea to investigate, though I personally wouldn't want to do all the paperwork involved. Just imagine the forms ...

Just one final word of advice to Mr. Harper though. Many of our Aboriginal leaders have been calling on you to fulfill many of the promises made by the Liberals before they left office. Otherwise, I'm sure there are a couple of Native lawyers out there who wouldn't be afraid to tackle the paperwork.

There's accountability, and then there's accountability.

WHEN GOOD INTENTIONS CONFLICT WITH GOOD INTENTIONS

Ponder this—you write something that explores a unique aspect of a culture or society in an interesting, fun, and critical context; however, on the journey to bring that exploration to the masses, it first has to be filtered through a process that could potentially rob it of some of its originality and reality. It's called editing. You may have heard of it.

In my case, it's a new book I've spent the better part of the last two years writing and compiling. It includes essays from various people involved in some way with the Native community, and in particular with its funny bone. Humour is, by its very nature, usually at somebody's expense—especially Native humour, where no prisoners are taken, even at our own cost. Depending on the nature of the joke, our humour can be racist (but in a funny way), sexist (but in a funny way), nationalist (but in a funny way), and exceedingly self-deprecatory (in every way). It reflects both attitudes towards us from outside the community and, as a direct result, attitudes we have towards ourselves within the community. Part of the point of the book was to detail the nature, origins, and characteristics of Native humour for others to appreciate. Academics love stuff like that.

Within the covers of the product of this exercise, *Me Funny*, are compositions dealing with the intrinsic humour in traditional storytelling, teaching, the Cree Language, and a variety of other topics including my own contribution exploring how Native humour often comes into conflict with that multi-headed animal, political correctness. Little did I realize the topic of my own essay would later become a critical point in the editing of the book. My next one should be on irony.

As the book was in its final stages of publication, my editor (a talented and well respected woman in the publishing industry) informed me that she had issues with some of the material contained within its pages. Specifically, she felt some of the jokes I'd gathered and was using to illustrate Native humour and separate the book's various chapters were sexist. She urged me to remove them in favour of less offensive material. As an avowed feminist (not that there's anything wrong with that), it seemed she was viewing the text through the spectacles of her own particular political agenda, something we all do to some extent. In fact, in one particularly unique incident, she suggested I change the gender of the central character in a joke, from male to female, in order to create a better sense of sexual parity. Otherwise, she was concerned that parts of the book would offend many of her "sisters."

Being a member of one oppressed section of society in editorial dialogue with another, I was, of course, sympathetic. However, as a member of the Ojibway Nation interested in presenting an honest perspective on Native humour, I had problems with having the authenticity of that perspective filtered through the consciousness of an educated middle-class White woman. I was afraid my creation was being "white-washed" and was having certain distinctive Native idiosyncrasies "whited-out" so as not to offend a certain segment of the population. I blanched at the thought.

Now it's important that I mention that some of my best friends are White. In fact, I've even been known to date a few—an ancient Ojibway belief states that we all look alike in the dark. I've always believed White people are an imaginative lot with an interesting and wonderful culture, and I've always held them, their cuisine, and their literature in high esteem. I have always been proud to support them in whatever way I can. I own several Stephen King and Pierre Berton books, and have an air conditioner (White people can be quite innovative and clever when they want to be).

Concerned that maybe I was being anti-feminist by wanting to include these various examples of Native humour in the book, I decided to test that possibility. During a summer barbecue, I invited ten well-educated people over for some traditional Aboriginal burgers and tandoori chicken; seven of my guests were women, eight of them non-Caucasian (mostly Native and South Asian), all of them were either attending, graduates of, or professors at universities. I brought up the topic of culturally sensitive editing and read them some of the jokes. Nobody was offended. In fact, they all found them quite funny and urged me to fight for their inclusion. It was generally agreed among us that White people can be quite grumpy about some things. Even the minority White people at the barbecue agreed with this supposition.

Since context is critical—any first-year university student can tell you that—what's the point in studying something if it may have been editorially corrupted? During the early 1900s, a photographer named Edward Curtis took many detailed photographs of West Coast Native people and cultures, but often posed his subjects and told them how to act, thus undermining their authenticity. There's one famous photo of a Kwakwaka'wakw man holding up the arm of another man, who appears to be dead, and biting the skin. This created the rumour that the Kwakwaka'wakw were cannibals. But legend says it was staged. Luckily the outfit the gourmand in the photo was wearing is supposedly genuine. So that's something, I guess.

To me I wonder if reading ideologically edited books is not somewhat similar to drinking today's absinthe; it looks and tastes the same, but without the hallucinogenic properties, is it really the absinthe Van Gogh enjoyed? It's healthier but not quite the same. In the same politically correct mode, if you took out all the references to "nigger," would Mark Twain's The Adventures of Huckleberry Finn be the same book?

Janine Willie, an Aboriginal PhD student in Native literature agrees. She says, "If you think of Aboriginal humour as a residual impact seen as a scar from colonialism, it would seem ridiculous to prioritize removing the scar over healing the whole person. Making cosmetic changes to the humour is not useful in understanding underlying causes and oppressions. In fact, it actually blurs the cause of the humour (patriarchy, Christianity, colonization, heterosexism, etc.) and actively works against or prevents an engaging, critical, feminist understanding of the humour. I think ultimately it could be counterproductive to a vital feminist, anti-oppression analysis of the subject matter. Hopefully, the humour would spark critical issues and questions for the students and hopefully the teacher would be able to facilitate a good critical discussion on it." Sounds good to me.

Now I am aware that by the simple fact that I am male, writing about what could be considered a feminist issue, I am pow wow dancing through a minefield. However, I've seen many non-Natives write about Native issues, so I guess my most relevant question is: is it legitimate to have a non-Native woman telling a Native person putting together a book on Native humour what jokes he may or may not incorporate in the project to best illustrate the Aboriginal funny bone, especially since I feel my original idea has been manhandled (or is the proper term womanhandled) in the process?

What little I do know of political correctness is that in many ways, it's no different from Aboriginal identity politics—the concerns and definitions of feminists vary from population to population. As I had it described to me once, the top five priorities of a well-educated, middle-class White woman are substantially different from those of a Native woman living on the Reserve (and from those living in the inner city for that matter).

So on my last trip home to my Reserve, I brought up the subject with Alice Williams, an amazing quilter and politically active Native woman. She also could not believe my story. "This is Indian humour. If you change it to what is acceptable to her and her class, then you have taken away the Indian humour; what it has changed to is no longer Indian humour. The idea of this book is to talk and tell and share about Indian humour. It is NOT to talk about the values of well-schooled middle-class White women and what they want to get across—even if it is 'politically correct,' this is not the place for anyone else to expound and use their privilege, prestige, power, position, and advantage to push and promote their agenda. Let them do it in their own writings and speeches. Goodness knows there's many more doors open for them than us to share and talk about stuff."

Perhaps I've heard it expressed most clearly by Anosh Irani, noted South Asian author of *The Talisman and the Cripple*, who told me during lunch at an author's festival in British Columbia, "Sometimes you have to be politically incorrect to make your point."

In the end, after terrific phone battles and blood-soaked emails, I believe I managed to maintain the integrity of my humble little book. It is indeed a fair and accurate exploration of Native humour. I managed to keep in it most of the sexually explicit but authentic Indian jokes. However, due to my editor's perseverance (by the way, don't get me wrong, otherwise she's an excellent editor), Me Funny is now fit for educated middle-class White women—who, after all, according to her, are my major audience base.

AN ABORIGINAL CANUCK IN KING BUSH'S COURT

Ann Arbor is a lovely little town about an hour west of Detroit. It's a university town, so logically enough, it's full of students. While I am here not as a student, I am however here in an academic capacity. Playwright-in-residence for Residential College is my official title, and as the title would indicate, I'm here to write a play for the Theatre Department, and offer up my experiences as a fairly successful playwright to the silly students who have opted to explore the world of theatre. Surprisingly, the course I'm involved in teaching—Introduction to Canadian Native Theatre—has limited appeal here. (Actually, come to think of it, I suppose even in Canada the appeal of this course might be somewhat less than universal.) So far, we have three students—though I am assured it will triple by next week. Even a "Philosophy of *Star Trek*" course would probably have a dozen more interested students than I have.

This is the first time I have done anything like this. I have never been a university student, but I hear it can be fun. I've seen all the appropriate movies. As a result, I've been kind of self-conscious about coming here under false pretenses. In the past, when compelled to think of the state of Michigan, it had to do with how Toronto is being forced to reduce the amount of garbage it sends there ... I think it's still wrestling with that problem.

Still, I am incredibly delighted to have been invited here by the Theatre Department. It's produced an effect on me like I've seen on many Native actors who occasionally get cast in a Shakespeare play or other roles of a non-Native nature: it's a validation of them as artists, not just an accident of birth. Countless times I've heard a young Native actor excitedly tell me, "I've got this really great role in a play/movie/television show, and I'm not playing an Indian!" They're so happy. And now, suddenly, it's the same for my situation. Needless to say the Native American studies program seconded my appointment, but I believe my point is still valid.

There's also a great alumnae history here. The University of Michigan is where Arthur Miller, author of *Death of a Salesman*, came to learn his craft. I walk in the shadow of greatness. The very college I'm teaching in once saw Madonna stay for a semester, as did Ted Kaczynski, also known as the Unabomber. Okay, so that shadow is getting a bit thinner ...

I am here for only a semester and this will be the longest I have ever lived in the United States. But already I'm getting acclimatized. I've applied for my first gun licence—why, I don't know, but everybody's doing it. I'm learning to use the word "Indian" again. I'm now suspicious of Cuba (even though I spent two fabulous weeks there on a beach once), and when I get back to Canada, I think the Canadian Army should invade a small, Third-World country. Like Newfoundland.

Still, I must remain focused on my purpose. I am here to spread the Good News of Canadian Native Theatre. I will speak the Gospel of Tomson, and how in 1986, he brought "the Word" to a small Native community centre in downtown Toronto, and how that Word changed the Canadian theatre community (and also the game of bingo). I will preach how the prophet Daniel David Moses spread the mighty waters of the Grand River to deliver the stories of his people into the promised land of freedom. I will talk about how Native Earth, De-Ba-Jeh-Mu-Jig, Centre for Indigenous Theatre, and other vessels of understanding delivered their message unto the population.

In the beginning, we were all dark.

And then God said educate the Whites and we did.

And it was good.

I am here to give them something to believe in.

The first thing I have told them is, "Be ready for rejection," whether you are a writer or a performer. I have been turned down by so many theatre companies, I feel like a Jehovah's Witness.

The second thing of importance in the study of Native Canadian theatre is a working knowledge of what I call B-cubed and R-cubed: bingo, beer, and bannock; rape, residential schools, and reserves. Most Native plays will have some variation on these themes scattered throughout the text. Sexual abuse, substance abuse, and in many cases, a sense of rebirth through the discovery of one's cultural roots pretty much make up what can be referred to as the Native theatre trifecta.

And thirdly, if you want to really understand the true essence of Canadian Aboriginal theatre … good luck. We have comedies, dramas, tragedies, musicals, one-person shows, even puppet shows. So essentially, Native theatre is as varied as its people and cannot be summed up in one or two sentences or experiences. Some of us who have worked in the field for a decade or two are still trying to figure things out. Hell, I should be taking my own course.

Regardless, Ann Arbor seems like a lovely little town and I am delighted to be here. I do believe, however, that it was preordained. It's been proven to me time and again that God/the Creator/whatever term you want to use, has a sense of humour. And I'm usually part of the joke. First: three days before I moved here, a Hollywood movie company came to Peterborough, a town about half an hour from my Reserve, to shoot part of a movie. It stars Samuel L. Jackson and Hayden Christensen. It's called *Jumpers* and is some sort of science fiction story. The film company dressed up the downtown core to resemble a small American town, and as I walked through it going for a coffee, I noticed there were a lot of Michigan references on the taxis and the window dressing, including numerous references to the

Wolverines, the U of M football team. Then I saw the water tower they had repainted for the movie. It said "Ann Arbor." The movie being shot a short drive from my home was to take place in the town where I was moving, and one of the stars was named Hayden.

And second: since I've been here, I've had quite a bit of trouble getting my university ID card. Today I found out why. There's already somebody here with my full name: Drew Hayden Taylor. Maybe I will be taking my own course.

If there's one thing I've learned over the years, you don't mess with karma.

APOCA-WHAT?

The shot in the film is of a Native man being chased by a bunch of other Native people. The movie is Mel Gibson's *Apocalypto*. Or it could be me admitting I've gone to see it and the resulting reaction from a bunch of annoyed First Nations people urging a boycott of the film. The release of this movie, which supposedly details the downfall of the Mayan Empire, has generated perhaps the greatest buzz in Indian country since the cancellation of the Kelowna Accord. And the odd thing is, all this fuss is over just an okay movie.

Granted the photography and camera work are truly amazing. The sets, costumes, and production values phenomenal. Other than that, it's basically an old-fashioned chase film with a remarkably simple narrative. A conventional car chase with no cars. And that's exactly how Mel has described it, "I've never done a chase movie before" he's reportedly commented. He just decided to set start the chase 500 years ago ...

Understandably, many Native people are upset over the portrayal of the Mayans. In the film, the Mayans are amazingly brutal; picture Nazis with big brown noses. They are so busy ripping the hearts out of sacrificial victims and tossing their headless corpses down the steps of a pyramid, it's hard to believe they found the time to discover "zero" centuries before Europeans.

As a result of that and numerous other visceral images, many Native people feel the movie is an insult to Indigenous people across the Americas and have urged a boycott. In fact, via the Internet, Rhiana Yazzie, a Navajo playwright currently living in Minneapolis, Minnesota, is urging people, Native and non-Native, not to see the film. "Its appalling representation of Indigenous people presents a chance to think about just how deeply ingrained the hegemony of colonial thought is among the mainstream and even in us as Native people." That last part of her statement dealt with the choice of the Chickasaw Nation Riverwind Casino in Okalahoma to have an official opening of the movie on their Reservation.

Yazzie goes on to say, "It's no longer acceptable to usurp voices from Native people and reinforce the image that Indigenous people are not human. This film is an assault not only on my culture but also on my life as an Indigenous writer." It's the newest battle in the Cultural Appropriation Wars.

I understand her indignation, and as an Indigenous writer, I sympathize and empathize. It doesn't exactly make the Mayans cute and cuddly. I don't think there's going to be any lovable stuffed Mayan dolls being sold for the Christmas rush this year. However, I felt it necessary to see the film. I was interested and intrigued by how Gibson would tackle a potentially politically volatile subject matter like this. And seriously, how can you be confident in criticizing something without ever having seen it? I remember the controversy back in the 1980s when the movie *The Last Temptation of Christ* was released, and many fundamentalist Christians urged a public boycott of the film, having never watched it.

With that being said, I saw the movie on the night it opened in Banff. I was there working on a project with Santee Smith, artistic director of Kaha:wi Dance Theatre, located in Six Nations Reserve in Ontario. She's putting together a dance/theatre interpretation of the Iroquois creation story with yours truly writing the narration. So, we (she, the dancers, a designer, and me) were in the mood to see something Indigenous-themed that night. So seven of us, six Native, one non-Native, trudged down the hill from the Banff Centre for the Arts, to the movie theatre.

After much soft drinks and popcorn was consumed, the common consensus was that we knew about four of the actors in the film (standard post-film discussion for most Native people who work in the arts). And that, overall it was pretty bloody and gory—the chief colour scheme being turquoise blue and blood red. Kinda fun too in its own way. And quite silly—one skinny Indian with an arrow wound running completely through his body out-running, out-fighting, and out-smarting eight burly, muscular well-armed Mayan warriors, and the final image of Spanish Conquistadors landing on the beach during the height of the Mayan civilization. Historically it's a bit wonky (wonky being an ancient Mayan word meaning wrong); there are about 500 years between the two events. And don't get me started on the little seven-year-old girl, who is dying of what appears to be small pox (before it was ever carried to this continent), suddenly becoming incredibly well-spoken, intelligent, and clairvoyant (evidently a little-known side effect of the disease) predicting everybody's death.

Still in the end, I found it very telling that amongst us it was the lone Caucasian woman with us who uttered the phrase, "If I were Mayan, I'd be very upset." The rest of us were laughing too much.

"Mel depicted the Mayans as psychos. He's trying to make a comment about contemporary society but I think the movie was more a reflection of him than of any Indigenous people or nation I know," observed Santee Smith. Gibson's views on cultures and beliefs other than his have publicly come under criticism in recent months.

Just last week I returned from a writer-in-residency at the University of Michigan in Ann Arbor where I co-taught an introduction to Canadian Native theatre. One of the things we had discussed was the possibility of arranging a class trip to see the movie, but one young woman, a very politically active individual, expressed some reluctance. "It would be like going to see *The Tempest*," she said.

I should point out that at that time, England's Royal Shakespeare Company (with Patrick Stewart) had just ended a two-month residency at the University. One of the three plays they were performing was The Tempest. This young lady, given the opportunity to see the production with Captain Picard as Prospero, wasn't interested. She believed the play was a prime example of colonialism, Eurocentrism, and several other "isms" thrown in for good measure. Specifically, Prospero's control over the island's original inhabitants (though they were spirits and monsters) made her uncomfortable as a Native person.

I would have loved to have seen the production for two reasons: Captain Picard (I am currently in treatment for Trekism); and the fact that this particular production was set in Siberia, with towering spires of ice and snow. Ariel and Caliban are representations from the Yupik Nation, an Indigenous tribe that inhabits the far north of Siberia. A unique interpretation, if nothing else. Alas, I never got to see it. Tickets were sold out months before I got to Ann Arbor.

But one of the best productions of The Tempest that I ever saw took place in Toronto years ago, where it was set on the Haida Gwaii islands along Canada's West Coast, with huge rotting totem poles scattered on the set, and Caliban running around with a tattered cape covered in West Coast designs. The political correctness of these two productions ... hard to say. Tomson Highway believes art is colourless. The beauty of the writing (Shakespeare, not Gibson), inarguable. Still, there is the uncomfortability factor. Most Native people who have studied anything about the media's portrayal of them know what I'm talking about.

As a writer I hate being told or being in a position to tell people what they should write, or see. As a Native person, I would prefer to ensure that non-Native people get a fairly accurate representation of who we are; past, present, and future. Over the years, the dominant society has viewed us with too many misconceived and misconstrued ideas, making us eager to make sure inaccurate or unflattering portrayals in the media are policed. The proverbial two masters to serve: artistic freedom versus political correctness. To some it's cut and dry. To others like myself, the edges are a little blurry.

Do I feel oppressed when watching The Tempest ... not really. Do I feel oppressed when I watched Apocalypto ... it was so over the top and inaccurate that I relegated it to the same category as Animal House being an accurate representation of my time at the University of Michigan. Most experts don't argue the fact that there was some bloodletting and beheading in the Mayan Empire, but the image in the movie is one of it being pervasive and an integral part of a typical Indigenous day. Thursday, 10:00—take kids to medicine man. 11:00 A.M—cut the beating hearts out of thirty captives and barbecue them. 12:00—lunch. 1:00 P.M.—turquoise arts and crafts. 2:00 P.M.—ritual beheadings. 3:00 P.M.—drop off feathered headdress at the dry cleaners.

And if truth be told, someday given the chance, I would personally love the chance to adapt The Tempest from an Aboriginal perspective. Picture Ariel as a vegetarian woman's bookstore owner and Caliban as a disgraced Bay Street stock broker. Would you feel threatened?

I also take great comfort in the irony that Pocahontas, when she was Lady Rebecca living in England, saw the original production of The Tempest in the early 1600s. Of all the plays for her to see ... "Oh brave new world that has such people in't." Unfortunately, I couldn't find any records of her reaction to the play. I doubt if she found it offensive though.

As for Apocalypto, I don't think it really matters. In six years it will all be a moot point; according to the Mayan calendar, the world is supposed to end in 2012.

THE NATIVES ARE RESTLESS

I'm sure that if the Fathers of Confederation were around today, and putting together this newfangled piece of legislation called the Indian Act, there would be a new provision in it—something akin to, "Under no circumstances will governments, corporations (Crown or private), or any other similar organization build a road, bridge, railway, or any other structure subject to potential blockade across Native land."

Once more the First Nations voice is being heard in Canada because of stalled traffic and irate commuters. The Mohawks of the Tyendinaga community near Belleville are using the ancient Aboriginal negotiating tactic of parking a school bus across a VIA Rail line to protest a related ancient Aboriginal tradition, growing frustration with Native-government negotiations. It's yet another tent on the growing campground of unfortunate yet forced Aboriginal reaction to stalled negotiations. There was Oka, or more correctly, Kanesatake, then other similar standoffs like Gustafsen Lake, Ipperwash, Caledonia, the list does go on. And on.

This time the issue seems to concern the disputed future of a gravel pit located in the community. Not exactly one of the pressing issues in First Nations governance that comes to mind, but as the saying goes, the Creator is in the details. The management of resources located on Reserve land is at the basis of this particular disagreement. In fact, the management of land is at the basis of most contemporary Native uprisings.

Traditionally, blockades were not part of our culture. Canada has too many wide open spaces for Natives to successfully blockade everything. But we are an adaptable people. After a while, we learned to hunt with guns. To cook with flour and lard. To ride in cars. To be abused in schools. To blockade roads and railways. It seems like a natural evolution.

Unfortunately this cultural development has serious drawbacks, other than the obvious. It's becoming far too familiar an image. It's the new stereotype. Canada's former favourite image of the drunken Indian is being replaced with the image of the camouflaged Indian. Children in today's schools are in danger of becoming more familiar with an Indian wearing a bandana to hide his face than with a mighty Indian warrior on a horse hunting buffalo. Not that long ago, I went to Los Angeles to see a play of mine. It was produced at a theatre owned by a large museum (the irony was immediately recognizable). As part of their outreach program, the museum handed out questionnaires to their patrons, interested in finding out why they had come to see the play/museum, and what they were most impressed by.

By and large, many of the audience members' comments centred around the fact that they didn't know there were any Native people still living in

California. A disturbing percentage thought they had all been killed off. Until all the Indian-owned casinos started popping up all over the state. That is the dominant image that most Californians have today of Native people—the Casino Indian.

Here in Canada, I have known many people who have been involved with blockades and other acts of civil disobedience. They do not make these choices lightly. Most of them know that if they get involved, things will get worse before they get better. Everybody remembers the tragic images illustrated in Alanis Obomsawin's brilliant documentary, Incident at Whiskey Trench, where Mohawks being evacuated from Kahnawake during the Oka Crisis were attacked and stoned by local White people, resulting in one local man dying of a heart attack.

It's also very easy to blame the government. But that's why they are elected. To take responsibility. When's the last time you heard anybody praise a politician? And the best way to avoid blame is to actually do something. In retrospect, most people have come to believe the incidents leading up to Oka (planning a golf course on disputed land, which also happened to be a traditional Mohawk burial ground) and Ipperwash (an entire community relocated and their land taken away during World War II for a military training site, and a failure to return it as promised) were understandable. All of these events involved many prior years of trying to settle things, but with little or no response from the federal government, the ante needed to be raised.

Today on the news I heard an annoyed VIA Rail passenger bitterly comment, "I didn't think they were allowed to do that, but I guess they can do whatever they want." Ironically, our Elders used to say the same thing about what White people did. Granted, if I were on that train—and three weeks ago I was—I would have been a little annoyed too. What these passengers need to know is that First Nations people don't enjoy doing this. It's not a field trip. They don't get paid for it. Oka was not a First Nations Woodstock. Ipperwash wasn't an Outward Bound for Political Aboriginals. Most of these people would rather have been home with their families, or making corn soup, or watching the playoffs (sound familiar, Canada?) Reality, however, frequently has a habit of forcing us to change our plans.

And of course there's always a threat that the police will come in with guns drawn, like in Oka, or Ipperwash, or Caledonia. That's always a huge inducement to participation in blockades at our "what will we do this weekend" meetings. Luckily (or unluckily, depending on how you see it) the police have never been very successful with that approach. Just ask Dudley George.

Remember when that ferry went down in British Columbia last year? Keep in mind it was mostly fishing boats from a nearby Native community that picked everyone out of the water and took them to safety. And contrary to popular paranoia, Aboriginal blockades are not going to spread across the country like wildfire. Take my community for example. It's on a peninsula with one road in and one road out. Putting up a blockade there would be kind of self-defeating.

I'm reminded of a lecture I did once at the University of British Columbia, after which, as I walked to my cab, I was approached by a gentleman with a perplexed and serious look on his face. He asked me why, in my opinion, the great uprising at Gustafsen Lake, which occurred in the mid-1990s, has been practically forgotten, when all the other Manifestations of Aboriginal Discontent (known as MAD) have entered Canadian folklore. Hell, they've even made movies about Oka and Ipperwash, he said.

It was difficult to answer, but I tried. Perhaps, I ventured, because the whole thing seemed ... tainted. A bunch of protesters wanting to practise the sundance "forcibly" took over some land belonging to White people who had originally allowed them to perform the ceremony on it. There was a bunch of gun-waving and shouting, but in the end it fizzled out when the protesters received little support. There were no bad White people or governments involved. It was a hiccup in the annals of Aboriginal protest. I told him not to expect a movie about the incident any time soon.

So simply put, blockading routes of mass transit is not a traditional Aboriginal activity. All those images you remember from the movies of your childhood, of multitudes of feathered and screaming Indians attacking wagon trains in the American West, are just a bunch of made-up Hollywood stories. So at the very least, the irate VIA passengers will have an amusing tale to tell their grandkids: "I was part of the great Tyendinaga Railway Blockade of 2007." And for those companies or individuals who may have lost money on this inconvenience, I'm sure their insurance will cover it. After all, I've never seen any sort of "Act of Indian" exemption clause anywhere in those policies.

I wonder if that's what the Fathers of Confederation would have called it.

WHY DID THE INDIAN BLOCK THE ROAD ...?

By now the whole country is aware that what's old is new again. In southern Ontario, First Nations people are blockading roads, bridges, and train tracks once again. That's when you know summer is almost here. In case you weren't aware, all great Aboriginal uprisings happen during the spring and summer ... Why? Because Native people are not stupid. That's when all the new camouflage outfits come out. And of course, most of these confrontations usually have to do with non-Natives wanting to build or develop something on Native land, because, as the old adage goes, in Canada there are two seasons; winter and construction.

This time around, all the confusion took place in two places.

In the first, Caledonia, just a few miles southeast of Hamilton, members of the Six Nations Iroquois community had a, what shall we call it, a "disagreement" with a company that intended to build a new subdivision on disputed land. Acting on orders from the courts, the Ontario Provincial Police went in to remove protesters from the premises with less than spectacular results. In protest against the OPP attack, Native people set fire to an abandoned minivan, which, to tell you the truth, I can't blame them for—on the highway, those things are impossible to see around.

The police, hoping to avoid another Ipperwash-like fatality, rushed the Iroquois encampment early one morning armed primarily with Tasers, tear gas, and pepper spray. Luckily, nobody was hurt—that is except for three police officers, one requiring stitches I believe, because he had been hit in the head with a bag of rocks.

Yes indeed. A bag full of rocks—the traditional weapon of the Iroquois Confederacy of which the Six Nations Reserve is a proud member. With all the current controversy about the effectiveness of Tasers, maybe the Province of Ontario should consider arming our police officers with bags of rocks. They seem to be a more effective non-lethal weapon.

One interesting footnote to this incident is that you can usually tell which of the Six Nations a specific combatant comes from by the particular rock he chooses to stuff in his bag. The Mohawks, known as "people of the flint," are obviously predisposed to flint. The Seneca have an unusual predilection for feldspar. The Oneida have a hankering for a bag chock full of pumice, and of course, the Cayuga like anything shiny, so they'll pick any rock with a vein of mica running through it.

Simply put, the OPP should have known better than to rush a peaceful encampment of Native people. It didn't work in Oka. It didn't work at Ipperwash. Maybe they were thinking, "Three's the charm." But in this particular case, it most certainly would not have worked if they'd done their research. In the area immediately surrounding the barricades, everything had been closed down by the conflict, including the supermarket and all other local stores. That is, except for the ubiquitous Tim Hortons. Like cockroaches after a nuclear holocaust, Tim Hortons will continue to flourish and prosper where everything else doesn't. After all, a warrior is simply not a warrior without his maple-glazed cruller.

This was a camp of First Nations people, armed with a righteous cause, and hopped up on sugar and double doubles. I'm sorry, but that's a hard army to beat—always remember there's even a Tim Hortons in Kandahar, Afghanistan.

The second tumultuous southern Ontario town this year is Tyendinaga. For Ontario Police Commissioner Julian Fantino, that small Native community may well still become his own personal Waterloo. Or maybe Little Big Horn would be a more appropriate metaphor. That little Mohawk hamlet, situated innocently near Belleville, had seemed for a while to be the centre of his professional displeasure, and now it's coming back to haunt him. With a passion. Mr. Fantino probably wishes he'd never heard of the place by now.

One man from that particular First Nation became a substantial thorn in Fantino's side, though one could say a self-inflicted thorn that he subsequently scrambled to self-medicate. Shawn Brant is a Mohawk protester who, with his pals, was largely responsible for blockading the 401 and the VIA Rail lines on Tyendinaga territory a few years ago last June. He says he did it to protest a local quarry, substandard conditions on First Nations Reserves across Canada, and as a response to Canada's sluggishness in resolving outstanding land claims. You have to admit it was an interesting battle technique, waging war on sluggishness with sluggishness. The 401 became more barren than Maple Leaf Gardens during the Stanley Cup finals. And VIA, for once, had a legitimate reason for running late.

Now, Fantino's response has come back to haunt the head of the province's police, both legally and professionally. Secret wiretaps, orchestrated by the OPP itself during the civil unrest, recorded the commissioner negotiating with Brant directly. Legally questionable, the wiretaps illustrated Fantino's highly unusual methods of "negotiation."

Fantino's mediation techniques included threats like: "I'm now telling you, pull the plug or you will suffer grave consequences." Picture your therapist saying that. Fantino also told Brant, "Your whole world's gonna come crashing down," and, "You're gonna force me to do everything I can within your community and everywhere to destroy your reputation." Anybody willing to drive, let alone blockade the 401, probably doesn't scare easy. And it seems to be Fantino's own reputation that's taking a beating here.

All in all, those are some pretty substantial threats coming from somebody allegedly trying to defuse a tense situation. And it begs the question: what exactly would Fantino have done to execute those threats and bring everything crashing down upon Brant; send the Mohawk man to a residential school? Retaliation like that has been tried in the past with Native Canadians in general, and that's probably one of the reasons Brant did what he did—he was just sticking to what he considered to be the tried and true methods of dealing with Native "unrest."

There are rumours afoot indicating Fantino's harsh language was all part of a plan the OPP had hatched to provoke Brant into saying something that would, essentially, hang himself, allowing Fantino and the rest of the OPP to move in and end the blockade. Presumably, the OPP was looking for just cause and had planned to use evidence from their wiretap selectively for that purpose.

Oka, anyone? I couldn't help remembering that television movie made about Ipperwash a few years ago. This could so easily have been *Ipperwash II—The OPP is back, and this time, it's personal!*

Brant, no hero to some Indigenous people who see him as merely a provocateur, was too smart to fall for it, and made no overt or actionable threats. Others who have read the actual tape transcripts find Fantino's approach not as antagonistic as reported—alleging that he was merely informing Brant of the potential consequences of the blockade. There are two sides to every story. So now we have the tapes, the publicity, and Fantino trying to deal with a year-old mess.

If that wasn't enough for the head man in blue to deal with, he and the rest of Ontairo learned about another disgruntled Indian in Fantino's cupboard. A certain chief of police from that same Tyendinaga community is rocking the canoe and plans on taking the OPP to court.

The year before, in an interview with a Native reporter from Loyalist College, Police Chief Larry Hay, himself a twenty-year RCMP veteran, called the RCMP "a racist organization," and went on to claim that "he came here to learn that the OPP and the SQ [Sûreté du Québec] are no different. It's deep-seated racism and they will do all kinds of things to show that it isn't so, but we know better." A few days later he was suspended with pay and the OPP's professional standards branch launched an internal investigation. Eight months later, Hay was officially fired. By letter.

Not much later, a report from a retired civil servant called into question the legality of that firing. It seems the Band Council of Tyendinaga was not consulted. Stan Jolly, a former senior policy and programs advisor on Aboriginal justice issues for the Ministry of the Attorney General called Hay's dismissal "clearly illegal" and a contravention of specific criteria under the Police Services Act that governs First Nations police officers. It seems Fantino's once again been the naughty boy, not Hay.

Bluntly put, that wasn't a good couple of weeks for Fantino. It was his summer of discontent. The Indians might be restless, but it seems he's the one who's losing sleep.

Does Fantino harbour malicious thoughts towards Canada's Native people, and specifically Tyendinaga? Hard to say. I wasn't there. As Will Rogers, the American humorist (and part Native) says, "All I know is what I read in the papers." And so far what I've read hasn't been very good.

Would I want the head of the OPP threatening me and my existence? Not if I could avoid it. It would upset my mother. Granted I, so far, have not blockaded any 400-series highways or any other paved roads, nor any train tracks. I do not have Shawn's ambitions.

It's been said you don't judge a man by his friends, but by his enemies. So Larry Hay and Shawn Brant must be pretty important people to have the head of the OPP harangue them. I just have Bell Canada. And Julian Fantino ... he just has an unemployed Native cop and Shawn Brant. God knows what he does when not blockading to curse him so.

So what's next? This is Canada and if there's one thing Oka and Ipperwash taught Natives is that Canada is a country of Inquiries. I think we all know where this is going. Today, there are now enough trained and eager Native lawyers to ferret out any and all inequalities imposed upon Canada's first inhabitants. There's a secret Reserve out west that breeds nothing but lawyers. This has become a double whammy for a White guy in power, meaning the lawyers and politicians, not to mention the media, on both sides of the blockade are already buying their bread to butter.

The ironic thing is, most Native people are used to getting grief from Italians in power. Remember Columbus's dealings with the first Americans? And then there was John Cabot (born Giovanni Caboto in Venice) and the Beothuks. But luckily for them, we don't have anything of theirs on tape.

NO MORE TEST PATTERNS

Remember the days that whenever you saw a Native person on television or in the movies, there was a good chance they were not actually Native? At least not to this country. More than likely, he was some dark-skinned European guy who had just learned to ride a horse the week before, and the only Indian things familiar to him were turbans and butter chicken. In today's politically correct world, it's inconceivable that any decent producer would risk a sizable public outcry by casting a non-Native as a Native character. We've come a long way.

In the early 1990s the Asian acting community was very vocal when English actor Jonathan Pryce (*Brazil, Glengarry Glen Ross*) was cast as the Vietnamese pimp in a production of the stage musical *Miss Saigon*. It was one of the few important stage roles available to Asian actors and they felt understandably insulted when a White guy landed the role. I'm sure the same would happen here in Canada's Native community. I mean, can you picture a movie featuring Christopher Walken as Tonto? Or if they ever remounted *North of 60*, and Pamela Anderson was cast in Tina Keeper's role, or Kelsey Grammer in Tom Jackson's? Actually, that would be kind of cool. I'd watch that.

Anyway, few outside the business know how much the Native sub-culture permeates the performing arts world already. There are First Nations people and all sorts of Aboriginal terms used in the industry all the time— sometimes where you least expect them. You just have to know where and how to find them.

For instance, how many times have you heard somebody at a rock concert say, when they are trying to get past security, "But I'm with the band." If they're Native, they probably are. I'm with the Curve Lake Band myself. I have a card that proves it. They could be with the Peguis Band, the Okanagan Band, or the Wapole Band. The point is, they are indeed with the band. So all security guards, take note. But do ask to see their band card. Too many people claim they have one, but can't back it up.

And if you really want to impress the groupies, tell them you know the guy who manages the band—the band manager. Girls will throw themselves at you. Well, at least in theory.

Another famous Indigenous saying, this time uttered by the stars and performers themselves, is, "If anybody wants me, I'll be in my Winnebago." It's no secret that many motor vehicles have been named after Native Nations or people, such as Pontiac, Cherokee, and I guess the Aztek. A Winnebago, for those who don't know, is more than a large mobile trailer. It's a tribe from the Great Lakes region of the northern US. So when these people say, "I'll be in my Winnebago," the phrase is not necessarily to be understood as a rather odd sexual reference. One hopes they are speaking metaphorically.

But my personal favourite moniker refers to this one particular Native person who must be the hardest working Indian in the business. This one guy has worked on practically every film and television show I have ever seen. And for as long as I can remember. The man is everywhere, and is an unstoppable machine. Years ago, I remember watching a film that had Native people in the cast and I idly wondered aloud to my friend if, perhaps, there were any Native people working behind the scenes. In today's day and age, there are Native directors, grips, caterers, camera people, flunkies, scriptwriters, yes-men (and let's be fair, yes-women), etc. all over the place. But back then, I didn't think so. They were more rare than a Stephen Harper appearance at a pow wow.

So there we sat, watching the credits roll on the screen, and I saw his name for the first time. I felt a rush of warmth, knowing he was there making sure all these people looked good, but still managing to hold on to his traditional name. And once I knew his name, I kept seeing him all over the place. His name was Chief Lighting Technician. A bit of an odd last name, and I don't know if he was an elected chief or a hereditary one, but still, clearly a proud Native person worthy of mention. Or credit. Or something. I think he should finally be up for an Aboriginal Achievement Award.

The next time you hear some White person call us lazy or on welfare or unproductive, just tell them to go look up Chief Lighting Technician's resume.

SHELVING THE IDEA

Several years ago, the Catholic District School Board in Halton Region pulled the book *The Golden Compass*, a children's novel written by Philip Pullman, from its library shelves for being too controversial—supposedly not because of anything in the book, but because the man who wrote it is an avowed and proud atheist. The man just does not believe in God. I heard that's legal in some countries.

Now, I am of two minds on the subject. First of all, I can, in theory, understand the school board's perspective. They are fundamentally set up to be fundamentalists. The idea of somebody not believing in God is akin to being a theological anarchist in God's government, and being paid with God's money for that can get under the skin of those in power. As a Native person, would I want somebody working at Indian Affairs who didn't believe in Ojibways? It's a difficult position.

On the other hand, as a reader and a writer, I have rather serious concerns about the concept of pulling books from public shelves. Simply put, it's not a good thing, especially when it has nothing to do with the content. If I remember correctly, Lewis Carroll liked to take photographs of prepubescent children. But *Alice in Wonderland* is a fabulous book and still pretty much available. I wonder where the Catholic School Board stands on him. And he was a reverend too. As for the possibility of banning *The Golden Compass*, it has more of an ideological precedent. The obvious analogy of Nazi bonfires of books by politically incorrect authors (mostly Jews, homosexuals, and members of the intellectual left) could be used here. Or perhaps more aptly, the burning of all Mayan books in Central America in the seventeenth century by Catholic missionaries, because they thought Mayan was the language of the devil. As a result, there are only five books in the Mayan language that have survived from that once-great civilization.

However, in the Halton Region's defence, I don't think any public school board was involved in that incident.

This whole issue makes me wonder if there's a double standard being practised here. Should the Bible be pulled or banned from schools with no religious connections because Matthew, Mark, Luke, John, and other contributors didn't believe in the theory of evolution? You see my point?

Currently, a review committee will be assessing *The Golden Compass* to see if it should remain on the shelves or be banished to the wilderness. Until then, the book will be removed from public display and be placed behind the counter—the librarians' equivalent of barbed wire or the Index—and made available for selective viewing only. So, using that same criterion, maybe the Bible should also be put behind the counter with *The Golden Compass* in more mainstream schools. At least it would have some company.

Trust me, banning or restricting any book makes it even more desirable. I know. It was in the mid-1970s when I went behind the counter and obtained secret peeks at Marion Engel's *Bear* and Herbert T. Schwartz's *Tales from the Longhouse*. That was one of the main reasons I spent so much time in the library. All the good books were back there. "Behind the counter" is like the VIP room for great books. It reflects society. Chicks always dig the bad boys. Readers have always desired the bad books, going all the way back to the variously banned *Huckleberry Finn* and *The Catcher in the Rye*. Think of "behind the desk" as your parents' liquor cabinet. Maybe this is one of those reverse psychology situations applied by the school board to get more students to join the Library Club. It worked for me.

The logic of these subjective literary exclusions always puzzles me. Philip Pullman's book was pulled because he was an atheist. What if he were merely an agnostic? Would the Catholic School Board in Halton Region then just wonder about pulling *The Golden Compass*? What if he were an orthodox Jew? Or a Muslim? Or is it simply a case of "it's not what you believe, it's just a matter that you believe something"?

I remember years ago, in my own county of Peterborough, there was a big stink over banning Margaret Laurence's *The Diviners*. I was kind of young at the time and the particular details escaped my attention. I was too busy reading *Dracula* and *Frankenstein*, the original novels. But somewhere in my adolescent mind, I do seem to recall thinking, "Wow, if they allow little kids like me to read about all this repressed Victorian sexuality and vivisection, about the power of evil and man's striving to do better than God, I can't imagine what goodies await me in that book." Needless to say, I was a little disappointed. I could not find a single decapitation.

As I said, I am of two minds on this whole thing. In a peculiar way, I'm for it. I think more books should be pulled and banned. A lot more. Back in the 1990s when a fatwa was declared on Salman Rushdie for his book *The Satanic Verses*, I saw many of my artist friends go out and buy his book on principle, never really intending to read it. That book now sits on so many shelves, unopened, and Rushdie, though forced into hiding for several years, became substantially richer for it.

I sure wish somebody would pull or ban one of my books. I recently had my first novel, aimed at teens, published. It's about an Ojibway vampire called *The Night Wanderer*. And he's an atheist vampire at that! If some school board out there would like to consider it, I'd be very interested in talking about a possible banning. Seriously. I could use the money.

So if any school board trustee is reading this and is interested in pulling my YA novel from the shelves, there's a twenty in it for you. Until then, you might as well go home and, for old times' sake, destroy some old Beatles CDs you might have sitting around the house.

And for those who don't understand that last reference, ask your parents.

IPPERWASH

What a Christmas present for the people of Kettle and Stony Points—their own provincial park. I bet you Santa just about had a coronary when he saw that on his list. But, as the yuletide story goes, he knew who had been naughty, and who had been nice. He, like Justice Sidney Linden, commissioner of the inquiry into the 1995 death of Native protester Dudley George, knew that the government of former Ontario Premier Mike Harris, and the federal government, had been on the naughty side. So, after sixty-five years, a week before Christmas, the status quo had been reinstated. The Stony Point people have a home again.

Sixty-five years. That's a long time, even by government standards. It was in 1942 when the federal government expropriated the land belonging to the Stony Point Band, which contained a burial ground, to build a military camp. White people wanted Native land to train White people to fight other White people on faraway White people's land. Somewhere, I'm sure, that makes sense. At one point, the Department of National Defence did say it was willing to return most of the land someday, but like many other promises to Native people, something was lost in translation.

We remember those good old days when things were promised for as long as the sun shines, the grass grows, and the rivers flow. But now with a diminishing ozone layer, the sun's become a dangerous thing, which is scorching and killing the grass. And the rivers and Great Lakes of this fair land are shrinking. So you go figure out what those words mean.

Sixty-five years. You know, if our governments were smart, they would take a page from the book of how Native people operate to explain the delay. It's worked before. They should just pay attention to the Iroquois people, who have proudly claimed for 200 years that the American Constitution was based on their Great Law, the basis of their government and spiritual beliefs. Well, the Stony Point people don't have a Great Law *per se* that the Canadian and Ontario governments can appropriate, but to me it seems they have appropriated something else particular to Canada's Native people: the concept of Indian Time.

It's an enigmatic and philosophical idea based around a unique cultural relationship with time. Simply put, things happen when they happen. There are not twenty-four hours in a day. Time is unlimited and impossible to cut up into chunks. If something is to happen at 11:00, it might happen at 11:01 or 12:26 or 1:11, A.M. or P.M. The universe has its own heartbeat, and who are we to speed it up or slow it down? To some, it's an excuse to be late. To others, it's a way to avoid ulcers.

Sixty-five years. Or on a different scale, thirty-five years since the minister of Indian affairs at the time, Jean Chrétien, noted that the Stony

Point Band was beginning to get annoyed at yet another broken promise, and perhaps the minister of defence should return the land or offer up another piece of land as compensation.

It's been seventeen years since Oka—more accurately Kanesatake—happened, proving once and for all that dangerous things can happen when Native people, burial grounds, provincial police, and indifferent levels of government are all poured into the same mixing bowl.

It's been fourteen years (1993) since the pissed-off (even for people who practise Indian Time) Stony Point Band members began moving back onto their land. In 1995, the military thought, "The hell with this," and withdrew. Evidently after fifty-three years, World War II was finally over and the need for the land had ended. That was twelve years ago. That was also just about the time an unknown Stony Point dude named Dudley George clumsily got in the way of a speeding OPP bullet and time ended for him.

It brings to mind the old adage: If you bury a bunch of Native people in the woods, and no White people are there to see it, are there in fact Native people buried there? What is it with White people wanting Native burial grounds? Have they never seen a horror film? Nothing good has ever come from wanting to develop any burial ground.

Part of the art of mastering Indian Time is also knowing how to manipulate the concept to your advantage. Just let another two to three hundred years pass, then point some unsuspecting archaeologists at the spot, and it immediately becomes a protected site. Ancient Indian burial ground, part of Canada's heritage. Up north of Peterborough, my community, Curve Lake, has a hand in the running of the Petroglyphs Provincial Park.

Unfortunately though, the Ipperwash land is soaked in blood and death. First of all, it was a burial ground. Secondly, people were trained there to kill other people. I'm sure that left some sort of psychic imprint. And thirdly, Dudley George, an unarmed man just trying to return home with his family, was shot there. Borrowing from an ancient Indian philosophy (the dot Indian, not the feather kind), it doesn't exactly make for good karma. It is believed by Native people that the land remembers what has happened on it.

Still, all is not calm in this province about Dalton McGuinty's decision. A casual glance at CTV's website showed a bewildering amount of disagreement over the return of the 109 acres. "We are all going to pay for this lack of thought on the government's behalf. I know, let's just hand over the whole province. Welcome to the Province of Ontario Indian Reserve." "They lost the land ... that's too bad ... I say that the Reserves should be removed completely ... and that they should become normal Canadians like the rest of us, and pay taxes! This is simply ridiculous." "Natives already

get far more than they deserve from hard-working taxpayers in this country."
You get the picture.

The ironic thing is, I've never met a "normal Canadian." And I am trying
to figure out what exactly I get from hard-working taxpayers in this
country, especially considering I pay taxes too. And trust me, we don't want
the whole province. You can keep all the clear-cut, strip-mined, toxic-filled
places that you've put so much effort into creating.

Sixty-five years. That's a long time. Even for Indian Time. But still, look
at the positive side. Income tax was introduced during World War I as an
emergency measure to help fund the war. It's been ninety years since. I
wonder when the federal government will get around to repealing that. I
think that war ended too.

LAST OF THE REDSKINNED LOVERS

Another Valentine's Day has come and gone, and many of us are no doubt happier with affirmations of love, and probably fatter from all the chocolate. Quite recently my mind has been preoccupied with the topic of love and sexuality, especially among Canada's Native people: the sexy Salish, the amourous Algonquins, the steamy Saulteaux, the delectable Delaware, and so on. That is because a book I edited and compiled, detailing the "ins" and "outs" of Aboriginal sex and sexuality, was recently published by Douglas & McIntyre. It's called *Me Sexy*. So as a result, I've got Indigenous sex on the brain. And it's all tax deductible.

Several years ago *Me Funny* was published, which explored and deconstructed the world of Native humour. I wrote it because I had always been concerned about the dominant culture's frequent misunderstandings of Canada's Indigenous people. One common stereotypical image of us is that we are all a tragic, oppressed, stoic, and generally unfunny bunch of people. Thus the need for a book like *Me Funny*. The other topic that had always intrigued me was the fact that in the dominant media, there is very little mention of, or discussion about, Aboriginal romance. Yet the latest census indicates we have the fastest-growing population in Canada, and now number over one million people of First Nations descent. So we must be doing something right.

Thus, in this post-Valentine season, I find myself continuously scanning the media for anything interesting regarding the passionate practices of this country's First Nations. Where I find a noticeable lack of representation is in the movies, both feature films and made-for-TV. To date, nobody has yet produced the classic Native love story. There is no Indigenous *Casablanca*, no Aboriginal *Ghost*, no Native *Titanic* (though some would say it's a movie about a giant sinking ship, rather than a love story. Regardless, the First Nations film community has not produced a movie about either topic).

There have been many notable movies made about this continent's original inhabitants, especially in the last thirty years. Yet very few of them, if any, delve very deeply into the topic of love, or specifically, the love between two Aboriginal people. And I can't help but wonder why.

If you look at the theatrical releases in recent memory, with Native themes at the forefront, it seems like more passion would be displayed at an Amish orgy. Take *Dances with Wolves* for example. Ninety percent of the cast is Native, and yet it focuses on the developing love between the only two White people for hundreds of miles around. I guess if you can find your life partner when surrounded by a bunch of Indians, it's a sign that it's meant to be. Of course there is that lovely sequence when Kevin Costner wakes up and sees Tantoo Cardinal and Graham Greene going at it in the teepee. Maybe four seconds. I act that way too when White people watch me.

Apocalypto is a movie by Mel Gibson purportedly about the Maya. There is a loving relationship already present at the beginning of the story, and the lead character struggles through adversity (and the movie) to get back home to his pregnant wife and child. However, I don't think anybody would refer to this film as a love story.

Shadow of the Wolf was a movie about the Inuit, made in the mid-1990s. It starred Lou Diamond Phillips and Jennifer Tilly, and they were so Inuk you could smell the muktuk coming off them. Well, you could smell something. They portrayed a married couple, but my desire stems from the need to make a "classic" love story, and *Shadow of the Wolf* is many things, but not a classic. *Atanajuat / The Fast Runner* is a much superior film with a married man and a couple in love (in fact I think he had two wives at one point), but again, not a love story *per se*.

There are many Native films that celebrate love of a more brotherly nature. In the early 1990s, *Powwow Highway* came out. It was about two Cheyenne men travelling together to bail a sister out of jail. It's a buddy film, and their relationship grows as they overcome many obstacles. Same with *Smoke Signals*, except this time the sister has been exchanged for the ashes of a dead father. Still, many hardships are faced and the buddies become better people and better friends.

Dance Me Outside has a similar feel to it. A couple of Rez boys getting into mischief, but there is dating in this film, and even the impregnation of a married woman by a past lover, but again, it cannot exactly be classified as a love story *per se*.

Many historical movies feature Native characters predominantly, though of a non-romantic nature. *Geronimo* didn't have one single kiss. *Last of the Mohicans* featured a love story of sorts, but once again between two White people surrounded by Natives. I guess it's easier for them to spot each other in the dark.

It should be pointed out though, that in both *Last of the Mohicans* and *Powwow Highway*, there was a Native person involved peripherally in a love story. But as is usually the case, it's with a White person. Eric Schweig's character bats his eyes at the younger White sister, but ends up being killed. I understand that happened a lot back then when Indian men batted their eyes at White women. A Martinez manages to survive in *Powwow Highway* when he develops a friendship with his sister's best friend, a noticeable blonde beauty.

And while on this topic, need I go into *Pocahontas*? One White man spurns her and the other indirectly gives her small pox. What's a thirteen-year-old girl to do?

On a similar but different note, Sherman Alexie's movie *The Business of Fancy Dancing* deals with a gay man returning home for a visit, leaving his

White boyfriend in the city. And if memory serves me correctly, Princess Tiger Lily had a crush on Peter Pan before that nasty White chick, Wendy, stole him away. The road of love has many potholes—an ancient Aboriginal saying.

Made-for-TV movies are no different. If you compare most of the crop from the last few years—*Cowboys and Indians, Big Bear, One Dead Indian, Dreamkeepers, Indian: The Oka Crisis,* and any of the Tony Hillerman adaptations—again, non-existent, established, or tentative advances towards romance, but no real love story.

Taking a slight digression, the popular music of today (and yesterday) does provide and explore the image of the romantic Indian, but of a more twisted and bizarre kind. *Kahliga* is a story about a wooden Indian falling in love with another wooden Indian, but like most men (deciduous or coniferous), he refuses to tell her. *Running Bear* tells the story of two Native youths, separated by war and a river, drowning together in each other's arms. Charming. *Indian Outlaw* is about a man who's "half Cherokee, Chocktaw, my baby she's a Chippawa," and proudly talks about prancing around in his underwear while beating on his tom tom. I think that could be described as a different kind of love.

Son, Don't Go Near the Indians tells of a man falling in love with a young Indian girl and wanting to marry her, until his White father (who kidnapped him at birth) tells him the girl he loves is his sister. Again, a completely different kind of love. And of course there is the classic *Halfbreed,* not exactly a love song you want to sing outside the window of your sweetheart.

It's a conundrum. My grandparents were married for over fifty-five years, and I'm fairly certain you cannot spend that many years together, raising fourteen kids, without having at least a passing knowledge of love. So I know that such passion does exist in the Native community. Add to that the fact I know we have Native filmmakers capable of making such a film. Somehow we just have to put the two together.

Some years ago, I remember appearing in a half-hour drama, produced by the Aboriginal film company Big Soul, where I was a "John" stabbed to death in a car by a Native hooker. But once more, that kind of love is a different story.

THE TRUTH ABOUT THE ARTISTIC LIFESTYLE

When I heard Stephen Harper's comments about the elitist lifestyle we artists lead, and how little we have in common with regular Canadians, I just about choked on my Kraft Dinner. I had been completely unaware that I should be eating sushi and drinking champagne all these years. I blame this on my agent. I may have to apply for a grant for that ... wait a minute, I can't. Harper also cut approximately $40 million from the arts budget.

I am an artist, more specifically a writer. I can proudly say that I have been shovelling coal in the behemoth known as Canada's artistic community for over twenty years now, and to the best of my knowledge—and I would remember these things—I have never been to the opera, worn a tux, or eaten caviar out of a duchess's bellybutton (though hope springs eternal). And I don't think it's just me. All those singers and actors who bring me my breakfasts, masquerading as waiters and such, seem to be equally misinformed. Stephen Harper's been watching *Entertainment Tonight Canada* far too much.

Granted I have been working in the extremely lucrative world of Native theatre, but contrary to what you've heard, the birch-bark stage is not paved with gold. Our sushi, if we're lucky, is raw pickerel rolled in wild rice—the very proletarian Uncle Ben's converted wild rice. The only champagne we see is the paint job on the 1988 Chrysler K-Car the rich one of us drives.

Maybe it's an attitude problem we artists have, because most of us, in whatever discipline, definitely did not get into the arts for the money. Most of our parents were right with respect to the prospects for financial security in the arts—they are about as likely and reliable as those of Canada's national lottery. Going into the arts for money is like going into politics to find true love. Its possible, but unlikely. That's why most actors can say, "Would you like fries with that?" in seven different accents and can recite the wine list in iambic pentameter.

And it's silly to think artists don't have anything in common with the "average Canadian," whoever and whatever that is. Most artists come from "average Canadian" backgrounds. Just like most "average Canadians" enjoy the arts ... whether it's television, magazines, novels, music, clothing styles, or poutine.

There is a severe sense of irony working here on several different levels. As a working artist, I do not live on grants. Other than the occasional writer-in-residency or travel grant to attend elitist soirées in hot spots like Thunder Bay and Saskatoon, I tend to live off my own earnings.

But I know I protest too much, and my hyperbole is making you rather sceptical, so perhaps I should come clean—I actually have hoisted many glasses of champagne over the years, and mingled with the well-dressed intelligentsia in various cities and countries, discussing elitist topics with considerable erudition. Some of the wine and food I've been treated to at these functions over the years has been quite magnificent. These galas have been mostly at embassy or political venues, when I have been trotted out as the token artist to spread the Gospel of Native theatre for the greater benefit of the tourist trade in my country. And at these places of excellent wine and the best salmon BC could fly overseas, I have usually been surrounded by ... politicians. In fact, almost every time I have been someplace where the food is great and wine is bubbling, it's usually been provided by, and for, politicians. Not "average" Canadians. How strange.

Here's the kicker. The few such black-tie affairs I have attended that were actually arts related in this country were usually sponsored by large corporations! Everything in the arts is always for sale. Do you really think actors, stage managers, costume people, and other related artists could afford an evening of cheeses from around the world? That's so unlikely it has even been mocked in the first season of that excellent (but probably snobby) show *Slings and Arrows*. The artistic director of a large theatre festival has died, and the funeral is sponsored by a company that makes cooked ham! I didn't realize Stephen Harper disagreed so violently with private companies sponsoring and supporting the arts. The Conservative Party might want to have a word with him about that.

Ninety-nine point nine percent of Canadian artists don't get free flights, have in-house maids (other than their moms), personal chefs (mom), drivers (mom), wardrobe consultants (mom), or a free place to live in Ottawa (mom's). I don't think it's the artists who are out of touch with the "average Canadian." I think the question is, does the "average Canadian" care about politicians?

THE ROCKY ROAD OF BEING A WRITER

In Three Parts

Let me share with you, if I may, some of the more problematic insights I have had over the years about the profession I have embraced. One of these involves trying to avoid other people's attention, the other involves trying to get other people's attention, and yet another deals with facing the limits of one's own talent. Nobody said the writing industry was easy.

Part One

There are many drawbacks to being a professional writer, some worse than others. For one thing, although I do a lot of writing, I don't particularly enjoy it. Sitting in front of a computer hoping what you create will be of interest to somebody you probably haven't met (and never will) isn't exactly what you'd call a pleasant social activity. Add to that the annoying knowledge that the Creator created spell-checkers to rub your nose in your orthographic challenges, and a lateral move to carpentry begins to seem like an attractive option.

But perhaps the most uncomfortable aspect of my career choice is the untold numbers of people out there who want to be writers—good for them!—and for one reason or another think that you (meaning me) can help them get their big break. I have been from one end of this country to the other many times, doing readings, lectures, and festivals, and on practically every trip, somebody has something they wrote that they want me to read.

I don't want to sound mean or rude, but there have been countless people giving me their poems, short stories, snippets of novels, screenplays, plays, etc., for reasons I don't quite understand. I don't know what to do with them. Seriously. One time when I was in Ottawa appearing at a conference, this older man followed me around both before and after the class, with what appeared to be a screenplay held tightly in his hand, and several times (I could tell by the way he kept hesitantly putting it on the table in front of me) he tried to get up the nerve to slip it to me. A few months later, in northern BC, I lectured at a high school about being a Native writer. That afternoon, a teacher came up to me and said her son had been in the class I had just spoken to and that I was "okay," evidently high praise from a teenager. She then casually mentioned that her son was working on a fantasy novel. Suddenly, there was a brown manila envelope in her hand containing the first forty pages of it. She asked me to read it. I get emails all the time from friends and strangers wanting me to read over their work. And universally, my question is ... why?

I would understand if I were a publisher, but I'm not. I would understand if I were an editor of some sort and could provide constructive criticism, but I'm not. I barely know how I write. Often, when pressed into a corner, I do read the material and send back a simple, "Yeah, it's good. Congratulations. Love the font." Other than that, I do not know what to say. And it's become quite embarrassing. Both my agent and my friend, the author Tom King, has strongly advised me not to read anything given or sent me, because down the road I could be accused of and sued for stealing an idea. And coincidences do happen—there have been cases of individual authors coming up with roughly the same storyline as someone else.

Now here's the irony ... I have a friend who knew, quite well, Margaret Laurence, the famous author who lived just twenty minutes away from my Reserve. At one point, early in my career, I had just started working on some short stories and was desperate to ask my friend to introduce me to the fabled Ms. Laurence. I was dying for her to read my work ... you get my point. But I don't know why—validation as an artist!? Was I looking for a mentor? To tell you the truth, I still don't know. But alas, she passed away before she got the chance, and personally I feel relieved that I didn't put her in that awkward position.

But every once in a while, there's a story that is an exception to the rule. I am referring to Dr. Vincent Lam and his book *Bloodletting and Miraculous Cures*. According to publishing mythology, he was a doctor on a cruise ship, and Margaret Atwood was one of the passengers. They started a conversation and he confessed he was working on some short stories about his profession, and asked if she would read them. She did. He was published. He won the Giller Prize a few years ago. There are two things of note about that apocrypha—I'm not sure, but I think Margaret Atwood has a bit more pull in the publishing industry than I do, and Dr. Lam, now a little more knowledgeable about the publishing world, has come to realize just how brazen and forward his approach was.

There is one positive thing I've learned about this issue—it has made me conscious of the professions of my friends. I have a cousin who's a plumber, and I am very careful not to ask him to check out my gurgling toilet when he comes over for a beer.

Part Two

When I lecture to young and impressionable playwriting students eager to hear the war stories of a battle-scarred playwright ... one who still has all his teeth and most of his faculties ... I often draw an analogy between playwriting and dating. The two are remarkably similar. Both can be heart-breaking, rewarding, life-altering, and involve way too much make-up. For instance, you spend hours, days, weeks, months, even years trying to work up the nerve to ask a certain artistic director out on a date. One that involves a two-act structure, five actors, and a plot twist that only you can come up with. You make your story as pretty and irresistible as possible. But more times than not, you end up spending that artistic director's prom/opening night at home, waiting by the phone, thinking, "They don't know what they're missing." But very occasionally, when all the elements fall into place, and you've managed to grab the attention of just that right AD—the one with the dazzling smile and the best set of performance spaces in the city—the rest, as they say, is history.

I remember my first date/production. It came after being stood up numerous times, and frequent calls that went unanswered. ADs can be so cruel and heartless. (That's why I'm a member of ADA—Artistic Directors Anonymous.) Yet even now, fifteen years and several heavy dates later, I still sit by the phone, hoping to be invited to Saskatoon or Vancouver for dinner and a show. And I tell these poor students, unless you have the raw animal magnetism or the irresistible sexual aura of Jason Sherman, Morris Panych, or Judith Thompson, get a good cable package 'cause it's going to be a long, lonely night. I personally recommend the Law & Order trilogy to ease the pain.

One of the other things I tell these naive future writers is that if, by some act of God, they actually get that fabled phone call from some interested AD, and lo and behold that first date goes swimmingly, resulting in a healthy and happy first production, don't get too cocky; the Canadian theatre highway is littered with the corpses of plays that got a single production, but no remounts. Take it from a man with just scar tissue where his heart once was—try not to get your heart broken after that first breath-taking date.

Sure, you've finally got that exciting and hard-to-get first date under your belt; you've got reviews and posters; and the hangover from some bland Canadian wine; but as all serial daters know, there's only one thing harder than getting a first date—it's getting a second one. Sure, everybody loves a Canadian or even a world premiere. But are you interesting enough to be worth a second look? Having been on the other end of the telephone, way back when I used to be the artistic chief of Native Earth Performing Arts, I was the one doing the phoning and dating. I also got the chance to watch other ADs in action with their playwright groupies.

And I was surprised at how many playwrights took their first productions for granted. There was a belief that "once you're in, you're in." They would strut and fret their hour upon the stage, and in the end, it would signify nothing. They would go home, believing they had made their mark on the world, and expect the world to start calling them, begging for the opportunity to produce their plays. But again, how often have you gone out on a date and the next day had the entire population of the opposite sex (or the same sex) phone you up screaming for your time? Alas it does not work that way. At least not at my house. That's why even I have a great cable package.

I tell these kids not to sit on their laurels. Everybody on this planet has a story to tell. Many have more than one. But there are only a few limited opportunities to tell them on a stage. And contrary to popular belief, opportunity doesn't often phone up saying it has a couple of dozen thousand dollars and nothing to spend them on. The squeaky wheel does indeed get the grease. God does help those who help themselves. Fortune does favour the bold. All those things aren't called clichés for nothing. I tell those students, "You have to want that second production as much as you wanted the first. And the third and the fourth."

Theatre and playwriting are lifelong affairs. You have to put as much time into your dates as you expect them to put into you. Like marriage, it doesn't stop with the rings and the honeymoon. That's where it starts. It takes effort. One-night stands are fine, but it's nicer if they remember your name a few years later.

Or so I've heard.

Part Three
One of the things that makes me nervous, as a writer, is constantly being asked to deliver or hold writing workshops. I did one in Yellowknife once, called "Wrestling with, and surviving in, the world of professional writing: scriptwriting, playwrighting, and prose writing." What gets me is that for some reason, these people seem to think I might actually know something about what I'm talking about. I always maintain that I am never interested in doing workshops because I've just managed to fake being a professional writer fairly well over the years. They, on the other hand, seem to think that because I am moderately successful at what I do, I might know how and why that is. I don't.

Success is subjective. Some are happy just to be published, or to publish their work themselves. Others need a large amount of public approval. I find it amazing that I have been able to survive as a freelance writer for twenty years, with no identifiable day job, though I think my mother still finds that embarrassing. A few years back, she suggested I, at the age of forty-five, take a few classes at night school and learn to be a teacher. This, after eighteen books, seventy productions of my plays, trips to sixteen countries around the world, and personally shaking hands with celebrities like John Raulston Saul and Jennifer Tilly.

My difficulty with teaching workshops is that I don't know what the hell I do as a writer. Honest. As the running shoe company Nike says, I just do it. I've never been to university, though I hear it's a blast; keggers and panty raids and all sorts of fun stuff like that. So I learned to write on the streets, so to speak. I learned by reading and listening. I also learned by doing. One of the benefits of a university education is that by being taught, you learn how to teach. But over the years I have learned to write just by sitting down and writing. What works, works; what doesn't, doesn't. It's hard to teach that to people who want you to help them be the next J.K. Rowling. For me, it's like telling people how to walk. When you think about, it's kind of hard to put into words.

There are two things I tell up-and-coming writers, though, that I am sure will work for them because it worked for me: First of all, read. Read. Read anything and everything. Read trash. Read literature. Read cereal boxes. Read erotica. Read the Bible. Read t-shirts. It's a process of osmosis. The more you read, subconsciously you soak in how a story is told, how characters are created, how dialogue works or doesn't work, often without even being conscious of it. All great writers are great readers. This is commonly known but its implications are rarely understood.

The second thing I tell aspiring writers is to have an interesting life. Most great writers have had great lives. Not always, but often. I don't think J.K. Rowling actually dabbles in magic, but I do know that Jack London and Herman Melville did live lives that contributed to their writing. If you are only interested in sitting around in your basement playing video games, chances are you probably won't have much to say or write about. That's why I urge young people who want to become writers to have exciting and passionate lives. Writing is based on experiences. So travel. Eat excellent food. Then fast. Get drunk and throw up in your parents' car. Sail across the ocean in a dinghy. Then swim back. Get arrested. Have your heart broken. Volunteer in the emergency ward of a hospital. Go to an authors festival in Yellowknife. When you least expect it, you will be setting the groundwork for your next piece of writing.

Though if you quote me or hold me responsible for any of these suggestions, especially the getting drunk or getting arrested part, I will deny it. The one thing most writers try to avoid is lawsuits.

CRY ME A RIVER, WHITE BOY

Aabwehyehnmigziwin—that's the Anishnaabe word for apology. That's what Prime Minister Stephen Harper delivered in the House of Commons on June 11, 2008 to survivors of this country's residential school system. Paraphrasing the immortal words of singer Connie Francis, he said essentially, "I'm sorry, dear. So sorry."

And the First Nations people of Canada listened. There were thousands of Native people on the front lawn of the Parliament Buildings alone, eager to hear this historic admission of responsibility. Televisions were set up in community centres in Native communities all across the country. And the people cried. They cried at the memory of what had been done, and at what was being said at last. Harper made a lot of people cry, but it was a good cry. A cathartic one. Psychiatrists and Elders will tell you that.

Since the late 1800s, over 150,000 Native children were forcibly taken away from their families, and shipped off to more than 130 schools scattered across seven provinces and two territories. There they were then robbed of their language, their beliefs, their self-respect, their culture, and in some cases, their very existence in the vain attempt to make them "more Canadian." The official apology alluded to how it was once, misguidedly, believed that "in order to save the child, we must destroy the Indian." Few knew how entwined those two could be. The thought processes of politicians can truly be baffling.

The official *aabwehyehnmigziwin* was a long time in coming, and hopefully it closes the book on this sad chapter of First Nations histories, and a new book can begin, this time hopefully with Aboriginal people as co-authors. All of the churches who ran residential schools have issued their own version of *aabwehyehnmigziwin* over the years. In 1998, then-Minister of Indian Affairs Jane Stewart offered kind of an early, wimpy version, something about having "sincere regrets." I have a lot of sincere regrets too. Most people do. For instance, I have had sincere regrets about some of my past relationships, but that doesn't mean I apologize for them. Big difference.

Perhaps it's my working-class origins and artsy nature, but I do find it odd that it was a Conservative government who found the balls to issue the *aabwehyehnmigziwin*. You would think the residential school system would be something the Conservatives would admire. On the surface, it would seem to fit with their political and economic agendas. In the days of the residential schools, the governments of the day managed to download much of the cost of educating the youth from over 600 Reserves that are spread across the world's second biggest country, as was promised in a number of treaties, to four churches. Sounds like a sound economic decision, doesn't it?

How could they know it would later be classified as—and I love this governmental term—a boondoggle. It has literally come back to bite them in their fish-belly-white behinds. Over one and a quarter billion has already been paid out to many of the 80,000 survivors and graduates of Manifest Destiny High. That's one hell of an expensive education. And the price tag is still rising. Canadian taxpayers will be buying bandages for the physical and psychological wounds their ancestors inflicted for generations.

I guess apologizing wasn't high on the to-do list of the Liberal Party of Canada. Pierre Trudeau didn't want to bother with an *aabwehyehnmigziwin*. He felt it would just open the floodgates to more apologies which would quickly become unfortunate speed bumps on the proud highway of Canadian history. And Jean Chrétien didn't believe current social beliefs should be applied to past issues. Yet it was Brian Mulroney's Conservatives who issued an apology to Japanese Canadians for some of the country's worst misdeeds during World War II. And now Harper's Conservatives issue an apology regarding Canada's historical treatment of its Aboriginal peoples. Who'da thunk it? It should also be mentioned that it was the Conservatives that gave Native people the right to vote in 1960. Way to go, Conservatives ... now there's a phrase I thought I'd never say. I guess that's why the Ojibways call Stephen Harper the *Kichi Toodooshaabowimiijim*, which literally translates as "the Big Cheese." Some things do translate.

And of course there's one spoilsport at every party: the one-man Conservative brain trust known as Pierre Poilievre and his amazingly insensitive comments about survivors just needing a stronger work ethic, and his opinion that giving "these people" reparation money was a waste of time. Otherwise, things might have been just fine and dandy. Evidently Harper took the boy out to the proverbial woodshed, and a new and additional apology by a contrite Poilievre soon followed.

I am very fortunate. Neither I nor any of my immediate relatives attended a residential school. Instead we were schooled at the Mud Lake Indian Day School, located directly on the Curve Lake Reserve in eastern Ontario. Still, many of the residential school policies extended to our communities. My mother tells of not being allowed to speak Anishnaabe on school grounds, which were located just a few hundred metres from where she lived. Just the other night I heard her reminiscing with one of her sisters about how they made sure they never played under the windows of the school, so the teacher wouldn't hear them talking in Anishnaabe. One usually doesn't think of one's shy, seventy-seven-year-old mother as a rebel. Maybe that's why it's still her first language, and English a distant second. And that certainly didn't make her any less Canadian.

Many of the Native people watching that historic *aabwehyehnmigziwin* were not actual survivors of residential schools. But I think it's safe to say they were all affected by the practice in some way. We all know somebody, often several somebodies, who went to one, or were descended from a survivor, or related to one, and as a result has been forced to deal with the repercussions of that experience. The experience now permeates our culture. Harper and Canada's apology was to all of us. Just as all Jews were affected by the Holocaust in some way (if I may be allowed to say that), all Native people were victims of what happened in those institutions. I think it's called collateral damage.

Was the *aabwehyehnmigziwin* sincere and do I buy it? Yes I suppose I do, naive as that may sound. But I also know that by very definition politicians shouldn't be trusted or believed any more than a *Jerry Springer* guest should. Especially when it comes to their commitments to Native people. But Harper looked sincere. So did Dion, Duceppe, and Layton—all privileged White men eager to curry First Nation favour. It's amazing how a good education can make you the empathetic leader of a federal party, and a bad education can get you an *aabwehyehnmigziwin*. To warm up, they all probably listened to Connie Francis and her songs. Nobody could apologize like her.

I know a lot of people were a little cynical about the sincerity. That's their right. If an abusive husband apologizes to his abused wife and kids, however sincere it might sound, some might doubt the authenticity of that apology. Same in this situation. But the healing must start somewhere. And an admission of responsibility is as good a place as any to start. Ask any lawyer.

What happens now? I don't know. Maybe Phil Fontaine and the gang should contact Maher Arar. He might have some suggestions. If memory serves me correctly, Mr. Arar was kidnapped for no logical reason, taken far away from his family for a long period of time, beaten, starved, and terrified for the greater good. He finally returned to his family a changed man, who is now seeking justice. Geez, you'd think he was a Native kid or something.

As the sympathetic Connie Francis—who by the way was neither Native nor a residential school survivor—sang those many years ago: "I'm sorry I made you cry. Won't you forget, won't you forgive. Don't let us say goodbye."

Harper couldn't have put it better, though I am glad he didn't sing the *aabwehyehnmigziwin*.

THE REZ SISTERS

Is everybody ready for Introduction to Native Theatre 101?

First things first: most of us in the Aboriginal arts world believe the contemporary Native theatrical renaissance began in 1986. November 22, I believe it was. Eight P.M. The wind was out of the east and as usual, the Maple Leafs were doing badly. That's when a little play called The Rez Sisters premiered at the Friendship Centre in Toronto. Even back then, people knew the play was something special. The Bible of Native Theatre, when written, will read: "In the beginning there was The Rez Sisters, and it was good."

Today, The Rez Sisters, written by Tomson Highway, could arguably (if you're the arguing type) be called a classic, if not the only classic, of Native theatre. Of course that's keeping in mind this is a genre that's less than twenty-five years old, and there's still much more to be written and reviewed. It also asks the question if anything that is only twenty-five years old can be called a classic. I'm not even sure if cars or books can become classics in less than forty years. Still, when one thinks of the most influential and famous of the dozens of Native plays produced since the mid-1980s, The Rez Sisters pretty much stands alone. As well it should. It may not have been the first play written by a Native playwright, but it certainly was the first to shake things up in the larger Canadian theatrical community and gain international notice. And it is undoubtedly the most successful. There's a production of it somewhere in this country every two or three years, along with regular productions as far away as Japan and Scotland.

Think of the play as being on par with Anton Chekhov's The Three Sisters, a known inspiration for Tomson's play. I guess if you combined both Chekhov and Highway, you'd come away with The Three Rez Sisters ... but I digress. One of the latest productions of The Rez Sisters opened at the Market Square in Peterborough, Ontario. This production will tell you more about bingo, fundraising, and life in a typical (if such a thing exists) Reserve than you would ever have expected. One woman with a toilet fixation, one semi-divine bingo caller, a broken down van, and a lesbian biker chick ... think of it as just another weekend in Curve Lake.

When it was first produced over twenty pounds ago (by my own measurement), half the cast was Native, and the other half ... well let's just say, they tended to burn in the summer and didn't know what a residential school was. Back then, trained and experienced Native actors were few and far between, primarily because in order to be trained and experienced, there had to be an industry to train and experience them. It's hard to be a successful sculptor if you don't have a chisel or a rock. Today, such a multicultural production would be highly unlikely and unnecessary. The cast of the current production is all Native, with several local performers wielding their own bingo dabbers quite effectively. As is the case with classics, many of the performers have appeared in various productions of the play before, in different parts of the country. They are as seasoned as an Indian taco.

If I sound like an unabashed fan of the play ... well I guess I am. This play swung the doors open for an entire generation of Native playwrights. While twenty-five years might not make a classic, I do believe it constitutes a generation. It was one of the first works of literature to prove Native people had interesting things to say in interesting ways that people of all nations could appreciate and enjoy. I am looking forward to this production ... hopefully it's good. I have my dreamcatchers crossed. If it weren't for this play, I'd probably be working at the Curve Lake Band Office, embezzling money from the Department of Indian Affairs.

One of the ironies of this play is that it helped to change and correct many of the stereotypes people in the dominant culture had developed over the centuries about Native people. It did this by replacing them with others. I'm referring to bingo. The story is essentially about seven women wanting to go to the largest bingo game in the world, located in Toronto. Bingo has now become a cliché in Native theatre. I know very few Native women who, as suggested in the play, embrace the world of bingo like a Weight Watcher let loose in McDonald's.

Back to the actual production. Unfortunately, I was deep in the Prairies spreading the Gospel of Native literature to the populace when it opened and therefore unable to attend. But from everything I've heard, it was an excellent production—even the local reviewer had a few positive things to say about it. However, there was a comment buried deep in her review that caused me to pause and ponder about her interpretation of the play. In her review she says, in part: "Eurocentric theatre is not a medium that is natural to Native cultures. Theirs is a storytelling culture ..."

I found that phrase oddly disquieting. It bugged me. Porcelain toilets were not a medium that was natural to Native cultures either, but we seem to have mastered their usage quite well. And believe it or not, I have it on good authority that theatre, in its many forms, is dramatic storytelling. To me, this is more of a case of Eurocentric theatre-reviewing. I know. I asked a White person, and they know everything.

As somebody who has been writing plays for twenty years, won a few awards for it, and had over seventy productions of my work in four countries, I find I must object to her rather bold statement. I believe it implies we are at a disadvantage in this particular field of the arts because of our heritage. I know of no such disadvantage. Yes, we never had the proscenium stage or iambic pentameter, but most theatre throughout history never did. Just ask the Greeks.

With the explosion of Native theatre since *The Rez Sisters* premiered all those years ago, so called "Eurocentric theatre" seems to have come pretty naturally to us. In fact, it quickly became the medium of choice for a lot of Native writers. Since ours was an oral culture, and theatre is an oral genre, and stories are told via the voice, not through written prose, the transition from storyteller to playwright came fairly easy to us. We knew how people talked. Therefore, Native people took to the possibilities of theatre far more quickly than say ... a culture versed in the written word.

As a result of that first huge popular success of The Rez Sisters, spread across Canada are almost a dozen Native theatre companies, most of them classed as professional companies. We have many trained, experienced, and talented actors, directors, and playwrights, many of whom were involved in this very production in Peterborough. Not bad for people doing something culturally unnatural. As an Ojibway playwright, I know all the proper Eurocentric theatre terms: dramatuge, thrust stage, box office, workshop, and plagiarism.

I must also point out that Tomson Highway is a classically trained pianist who, for a period of time, struggled with whether to devote his life to becoming a concert pianist or a playwright. Classical piano is also not something that is natural to Native cultures. Evidently, I suppose, ours is a drum culture. Yet Tomson is exceedingly good at tickling the ivories, though I have no knowledge of his drumming capabilities.

Let's expand the discussion here, sort of. Theatre is not a medium that is natural to many African-Canadians or African-Americans either, probably due to that slavery thing. Yet they too are no strangers to mastering the art of the theatre. Just ask playwright August Wilson or Canada's own Andrew Moodie. I wonder if a reviewer could or would dare say that "Eurocentric theatre is not a medium that is natural to African-Canadians." Jade is not a medium natural to Canadian Native cultures, but visit the Vancouver airport and witness the work of Haida artist Bill Reid, sitting there proudly, and then ask me if that observation is at all relevant to anything.

Paddling canoes is not something that is natural to Caucasian cultures, but rumour has it there are quite a few good ones out there. In fact, during the summer Olympics, I believe there is a kayak event and I severely doubt if an Inuit has ever won a gold, silver, or even a bronze medal. Yet ironically, there is an extremely talented Inuit hockey player named Jordan Tootoo. Again, while perhaps hockey is culturally "natural" to Canadians in theory, one might say it is not so to the Inuit. But perhaps I'm rambling a bit.

Since writing columns for newspapers is not a medium natural to Native cultures, maybe I shouldn't be writing this at all. Of course, I could always blame it on my White side. Or maybe I could argue my case in pictographs or petroglyphs. But to be culturally correct, I suppose I should be presenting my case via storytelling ...

Okay, there were these three little Native playwrights ...

DANCES WITH WORDS

An Aboriginal Writer's Search for Words

I think it was James Joyce who once said, "I am forced to write in a stranger's tongue." Geez, he could have been Native. It definitely seems both the Irish and the First Nations of Canada have similar concerns. Most First Nations authors write almost exclusively in English and, to a lesser extent, French. Unfortunately very few of our writers are able to, or have the opportunity to, write in their own Indigenous languages. Most of these dialects and languages are dying of neglect, or are being elbowed aside by this arrogant new language called English.

Our original (ab-original?!) tongues are thousands of years old. English, on the other hand, is perhaps a thousand years old at best—a loose cobbling together of German, French, and various local dialects spoken in those islands to the east of us and to the west of Europe. English is the new kid on the block and a very popular one at that. It's tough, aggressive, and definitely ego-centric. It's also practically viral. Plus, if you wanted to add insult to injury, most of us now write down what we have to say—in fact what you are reading and holding in your hands right now is not only written in English, but is also printed on this thing called paper, using their/your alphabet. It seems our primary methods of telling stories have gone from voice to print. What did Gutenberg have against oral storytelling anyway? Now stories have even gone electronic. Ironically, audio books are becoming increasingly popular. Could we be reverting back to an oral/aural culture? Our teachings say that life is indeed a circle, but I just wish those White guys would make up their minds.

Back when I got started marking my path on this literary trail, I was but a young buck, unversed in the ways of the literary publishing industry. But I was lucky because I was fortunate to have appeared on the scene during what I refer to as the contemporary Native theatre renaissance. That's when an unknown play by Tomson Highway premiered at, of all places, the Native Canadian Centre in Toronto. Called *The Rez Sisters*, it blew the doors off the large Canadian theatrical community and made the drama pundits sit up and wonder what the western wind had blown on stage from the local Reserve.

A lot has been written about that play and its ushering-in of Native storytelling for the stage. Suffice it to say, for the next six to ten years, Canadian theatres were burning with Native stories by Native playwrights. Theatre, for a period, became the premier method of expression for many Native artists. Of course almost all of it was in English. With the occasional dabbling of Indigenous linguistic flavouring scattered through the text, these plays heralded in a new movement, one of telling our stories our way. The Indians had found their voice in a "stranger's tongue."

It wasn't an accident that this suddenly popular preoccupation with Native literary expression was through theatre. It was logical. Theatre is essentially oral storytelling, with some blocking and costumes thrown in. Most of us First Nations writers were born into what could be called an oral culture. And as your high-school English teacher may occasionally have pointed out, theatre was and is primarily dialogue. It is telling a story through the human voice. And most of us back home on the Rez had lots of experience with that method of communication. For example, the number-one problem I find with many first-time dramatists is their inability to clearly delineate characters through dialogue. Many of their characters sound alike, if not identical. Were it not for their names at the top of each dialogue passage, most of them would be indistinguishable. No two people say things the same way. Native people know this, whether it is in Ojibway, Haida, English, or Esperanto.

So, that's when I came along and added my stories to the canon of Native theatre, having had no specific training in theatre, other than one semester in the first year of college—a very broad overall introduction to the world of Canadian theatre, including text analysis, acting, directing, and set-building. It was also the one and only time I ever appeared on stage. I was Dingle, a Christmas elf in *The Year Santa Didn't Come*. It was embarrassing, uncomfortable, and I didn't understand much of what the fuss was about. So I temporarily lost interest in all things theatre. I don't even remember what my final mark was that semester. I think I passed though. What my actual future, my income-earning future was meant to be, I didn't know or care back then. I was young, off the Reserve, and thin.

So, as you may have surmised, my education did not destine me to be a playwright. The drama I had studied in school while growing up on the Reserve had taught me that theatre was essentially about dead White people. And I didn't know any. I didn't speak iambic pentameter, or know what a proscenium arch or a thrust stage were. A potential career in such a discipline seemed beyond the pale. Oh well, I'm sure I'm not the only one who has ever said, "Things were not supposed to have turned out like this."

My search for suitable words was doubly difficult. To put it bluntly, I woke up one morning and discovered I was a playwright. It was a rather rude awakening. Thus, I had to embark on a rather steep learning curve in order to do something with my newfound career. Also, most of the theatre artists I have known nurture a burning need to change the world, perhaps to illustrate some horrible social or political injustice in the world, or merely seek to engage the imagination of an audience by taking them places they have never been or seen before. Unfortunately, I lacked most if not all of those motivations. I got into theatre for the money.

It's a long story, but essentially Tomson Highway, then-artistic director of Canada's premiere Native theatre company, Native Earth Performing Arts, phoned, offering me the job of playwright-in-residence for the company. It was twenty weeks' work, offering a nice honorarium, and a godsend, for I had a very hungry landlord and few options for other career opportunities. So I quickly re-evaluated my sense of theatre and found its merits had risen substantially during the length of that phone call. I was now a potential playwright—but that was like saying I was a pilot who'd never flown. A swimmer who'd never swam. A drunk who'd never drunk. The proof, as they say, is in the pudding. And I had never made pudding before ...

Theatre is a truly strange mistress. She doesn't pay well. In fact, she often costs more than she gives. I think in the world of literature, only poetry has less financial potential. Yet she can be infectious, and not necessarily in a bad way. There is a unique feel about the process. It can begin with sitting in your room, huddled over a computer trying to be funny or dramatic, saying lines of dialogue aloud to yourself, or to some poor fool who happens to be in the vicinity: "Hey, does this sound funny?" or "If somebody said this to you, would you believe it?" Theatre is a world unto its own. Movie and television stars, who make more money in a day of shooting than they would in a week of acting in the theatre, will nevertheless eagerly tread the boards in search of a pure theatrical experience. Also, there's slightly more caché in saying you're a playwright than saying, "I write episodes of *The Young and the Restless*."

Since Tomson's phone call so long ago, I have worked in almost every conceivable field of writing known to man. I have laboured over television shows, documentaries, short stories, creative non-fiction, plays, essays, articles, novels, awards shows, and even a musical. But I've always come back to theatre and a certain romance particular to that medium. The money and the food are definitely better in film. There is the potential for more fame and fortune in novels. But theatre has remained my seductive mistress for over twenty long, hard years.

And remember I mentioned that sense of devotion and dedication most theatre artists have to their discipline? While I have tried to embrace that heartily, I've obtained only limited results. You don't spend twenty years working in an area you don't love and respect, I know that for sure. However, I never quite managed to grasp the sense of ... I guess you could call it a sense of fundamentalism that a lot of people in the industry seem to embrace. I guess you could say pragmatism has darkened my soul. I remember this one time we were workshopping a play of mine and the dramaturge, currently a well-known artistic director working in Toronto, was having difficulty with a section I had just handed her.

Seeking answers, she gazed intently into my eyes and asked me, "Drew, why did you write this play?" I responded as truthfully as I could, searching for those right words to convey my motivation precisely. "To get paid," I said. She didn't like that answer, at all. In fact, she got visibly angry.

Yet, in so many ways, it was an accurate answer. We were getting paid for the workshop. I had signed a contract indicating how much money I would receive for how many days the workshop was to last. Keep in mind though, I'm not quite as money-focused as this may sound. As anybody in the industry will tell you, if I wanted to get rich, theatre would not have been my path. And Native theatre didn't even warrant a path. In fact, keeping with the metaphor, that path has become an overgrown weed bed.

Please understand. I enjoy theatre. You can see, hear, and feel the audience's response to the work instantly. It made me who I am. And as the saying goes, it sure beats digging ditches and working in a cubicle. But I think, in this woman's eyes, I had dared to sully her pure and untainted world of theatre by introducing to it the stain of monetary avarice.

That had not been my intention. I merely answered her question truthfully. Perhaps I should have said that I don't know why I write what I write. The story comes to me. I see it somewhere. It says, "Write me," and I do. Why did I write *The Baby Blues* or *alterNATIVES*? Because I wanted to. Why did I want to? I thought it might be fun and I'd make a few bucks. That's about as introspective as I can get. I am not trying to change the world or make the world a better or more understandable place. I am merely a storyteller. A contemporary storyteller, that is. Where the stories come from, and what they mean, and why I write them, other than the obvious, is beyond me. What was it Michelangelo once said, when asked about how he was planning to carve a horse from a big block of marble? "I will just chip away everything that doesn't look like a horse." See! No big deal.

As the years creep by and I find myself becoming a grand old man of the Canadian Native theatre scene, I'm beginning to think maybe I should have put more thought into why I write, because people keep asking me that question. More recently, about fifteen years after that first encounter with the fundamentalist artistic director, I was once again engaged in a workshop at a well-known and well-respected theatre in Toronto. As I was wrestling with a new draft of my play *Dead White Writer on the Floor*, the literary manager of the company, clearly wanting to help, asked: "Maybe if I knew specifically what themes you wanted to express, I could give you some direction."

Appreciating her offer of help, I sat there for a moment, pondering her question. The only problem was, I didn't know what themes I was wrestling with. Didn't have the foggiest clue. Themes ... it had been a long time since my high-school English class. You see, I don't work that way. I've always believed that what I may want to say as a writer is completely irrelevant to the story. It's what my characters do or say that's important. You want to know their themes, ask them.

Years ago when I wrote *Someday* and *Only Drunks and Children Tell the Truth*, both of which explored the world of Native adoption, I wasn't interested in standing on my soap box and telling the audience what they should or should not feel and think about the topic. That was just the environment of my characters—and if the audience wanted to come along for the ride and thought there were larger themes involved, bonus. I also find my characters are usually a lot smarter and well-read than I am. So when it comes to writing, over twenty years of experience has boiled it down for me, and you can quote me on this. Basically, when I write, I just want to create interesting people, who have interesting stories to tell, who take the audience on an interesting journey. That's about it.

Upon reflection, evidently my approach to writing has not been too advantageous. The theatre company that I had been working with soon lost interest in my play after my admission of the woefully non-academic approach I take to my craft. I should have searched for better words to explain my process to them. I could have said what I usually do when presented with a problem like this: "It's this language of yours. English. I am not comfortable with this tongue. It ... it ... confuses me." Sometimes they buy it, sometimes they don't.

It has now gotten to the point that when I do publicity for plays or books, I always start interviews by telling the journalist that there is one question (actually two, but they are variations of the same question) I refuse to answer: "What are you trying to say with this play/book?/Why did you write this play/book?" I will leave that question-of-the-ages to all the students writing their master's theses to ponder.

But life ... and theatre go on. In my search for words and how to express them, I have moved on to other genres. Novels, most recently, seem to have captivated my eye. I've written two in the past four years and so far, I have never been asked about themes, or what I am trying to say. That is a good sign.

And as I get older, the hunt for words continues. And I think that's a good thing. In fact, I know it's a good thing. As a writer, I live in fear of two challenges: not finding the words I am searching for, or thinking I already have them all. Writers are hunter/gatherers. We cannot be complacent with what may already be there—pretty soon we'll exhaust the local terrain. We have to search for our sustenance. And if we can't find it, then maybe it's time to learn to say: "Would you like fries with that?"

I do know that I am getting more and more selective about what I want to say and where I will say it. My younger days of "will do a reading/lecture for food" are rapidly receding. Instead, I want quality, not quantity. And there are times when words do fail me. Most poignantly and recently, at my mother's funeral. I was asked if I wanted to do the eulogy ... and I could not. Instead, my cousin Shelley delivered it, with a few paragraphs contributed by me. I travel the country and the world lecturing and talking. I am no stranger to people looking at me, waiting for me to talk. And I have written probably millions of words by now. But that's my professional life, not my private life. I was there to mourn, not to talk.

Strange, huh?

After all those hundreds of writing projects, and millions of words, my most difficult hunt for words was for what to put on my mother's tombstone. I am an only child of a single parent. While not being much of a reader and definitely not a writer, my mother had somehow managed to encourage that curiosity about language in me. I had to come up with something that would address that. So I thought about it for quite a while and consulted a few people. Now, standing in a graveyard in Central Ontario, on a small Reserve in the Kawartha region, is a tombstone that says at the top, "N'dodom." It means, simply, "mother," in Anishnaabe, the language of my mother and our community. But it also says so much more …

Oddly enough, it is a word that is not in the language of our conquerors. So maybe James Joyce wasn't so right after all.

FADE TO RED

Everybody knows that movies are cyclical. No industry feeds on itself more voraciously than the film industry. Every couple of years, romantic comedies are popular for a while, then science fiction movies are in vogue. Next to catch the audience's eyes are teenage comedies, or horror flicks. Remember the year of *Armageddon* and *Deep Impact*, when earth-destroying asteroids were box office boffo? And when *Dante's Peak* and *Volcano* gave geological pimples a certain caché in Hollywood within months of each other? And don't get me started on the two movies about Christopher Columbus that came out in the early nineties. Not surprisingly, it's the same with movies celebrating or featuring Native people. Every once in a while, unexpectedly, a string of movies dealing with Aboriginal issues or characteristics wash over the local Cineplex.

A few years back, two major Native-themed movies were set for release within a few months. Terrence Malick's *The New World* and Mel Gibson's *Apocalypto*. You can't get much more popular than that. I saw *The New World*, staring Colin Farrell, and it sort of reminded me of some dates I've had: overly long, dull, and occasionally pretty. There's no love story quite like a thirty-something sailor sweeping a thirteen-year-old girl off her feet. I think there's a word for that kind of love.

White guys were bad; Native people good. Five hundred years of colonization, and that's the best they can come up with?

Now Gibson's latest great epic, *Apocalypto*, or, as I like to call it, *The Passion of the Maya*, proved interesting. It's a period movie that takes place in Central America during the height of its civilization, and to tell you the truth, the production values were awesome. However, I can't help but wonder if Mel Gibson is the right person to tell this story. I mean, he was born in America where approximately 500 Aboriginal nations were oppressed; raised in Australia where around 600 Indigenous nations once thrived; owns an island in Fiji whose people were successively colonized by both Europeans and South Asians; and his father purportedly had Nazi sympathies. With a heritage like that, he needs neither a bullwhip nor a cotton plantation to get in touch with his heritage.

And now, it seems we've hit a new cycle of fad movies.

Everybody in the world has seen *New Moon*, the second installment of the *Twilight* teenage vampire romance series (three different genres right there, in one movie!) The plot is awesome! Basically, some of the local Native teenagers are werewolves, and they have an ongoing disagreement with the non-Native teenage vampires, which as you know, can make dating a bitch. Taylor Lautner, who plays Jacob, sports thirty extra pounds of muscle for the role, as do several other fine examples of Native beefcake (or would that be moosecake?) Recently, I got back from a lecture tour of Germany, where unfortunately I had to tell the German audience that contrary to what they may have seen in the movie, alas, those young men are not typical examples of Native youth in First Nations communities. Where once we actually did put the ab in Aboriginal, baloney only has so much protein. And baloney can't be brain food, since the characters spend most of their time running around the Pacific Northwest, in winter time, dressed only in shorts. So while I ventured to guess that transmogrifying might at least be good cardio, there was a groan of disappointment from the German girls regardless.

Several other movies that are out right now have hints of Native content, though obviously not as much as New Moon. Quentin Tarantino's Inglorious Basterds, for example, features Brad Pitt as an American from Tennessee, who runs around World War II Germany with his men, literally and graphically scalping Nazis, the reason being Pitt's character claims to have diluted Native blood, somehow giving his actions inspiration and legitimacy. Remind me never to attend a pow wow in Tennessee.

Then there's 2012, a story of global destruction which also claims to have an Aboriginal origin. Supposedly, according to the Mayan calendar, the world is supposed to end in December of that year. The problem is, most contemporary Mayans have publicly stated that is news to them. Not only that, they consider it a highly unlikely event as most of them have car and house payments extending well beyond 2012. As the old joke goes, "I can't die now. I owe too much money." Mortgage and credit companies now have more of a say in our destinies than the gods do. Welcome to the New World.

Most interestingly, the science fiction epic Avatar introduces some novel twists on a lot of familiar ideas, especially about "noble savages." This movie, in its own way, is more Native than most dreamcatchers. It is an unabashed futuristic version of Dances with Wolves. I am not joking. An obviously American company of marines (or cavalry) on a distant planet is planning to forcibly remove or relocate (or exterminate, if all else fails) the Indigenous population in order to gain access to mineral wealth that exists underneath their village. At one point, the colonizers had even built schools in an attempt to educate and civilize the savages, but with limited success. They just won't budge. One soldier, sent to infiltrate the local population, slowly begins to develop a better understanding of the people and himself. He even falls in love, and chooses to betray his own people to help the Natives in an epic battle. Is any of this sounding familiar? Add to this, Wes Studi, the famous Cherokee actor, is the unmistakable voice of the wise tribal chief. You can practically smell the corn soup.

In particular, one of the lines of dialogue in the movie grabbed my attention. It's spoken by one of the corporate leaders, hungry for the mineral unimaginatively called "unobtanium." In discussing strategic options, he says ironically—"Killing the Indigenous doesn't look good." Wiser words were never spoken. Just ask the OPP near Ipperwash or the Saskatoon police department. We kind of find it annoying ourselves.

But perhaps the most subversive movie of the past six months is *District 9*, a fascinating and well-made film. Since it took place in South Africa, many would argue that it was more of a commentary on the now-dissolved apartheid regime that once flourished there. But several of the key influential filmmakers in the project were from Canada, and I like to think about it as an Aboriginal "what if ...?" There are "strangers" in your country and instead of taking over the entire land and imposing such bizarre concepts as a harmonized sales tax and *Canadian Idol*, you put them on plots of land that they are forbidden to leave. You also control every aspect of their poverty-stricken life.

Hey, there's something oddly familiar about this storyline ...

DOES NATIVE THEATRE HAVE THE SAME BITE IT USED TO?

It was a little over twenty years ago today that Tomson Highway taught the band to play. And it does seem that since then Native theatre has been going in and out of style. In those scant two decades, a lot has changed. It all began with a spectacular play way back in 1986. Oh, there had been other plays by Native authors prior to that, *Jessica* by Maria Campbell and Linda Griffiths being the most notable, but for one reason or another, they had not tapped into the larger Canadian theatrical consciousness. Plays by Manitoulin Island's De-ba-jeh-mu-jig Theatre Group had been entertaining summer audiences since the early 1980s, and Native Earth Performing Arts, Canada's premiere Native theatre company, located in Toronto, had been producing urban-based collective plays for years, again, with little fanfare, but none kidnapped and captivated the public's attention the way Tomson's masterful play did.

But most theatre historians will say the contemporary Native theatrical renaissance began on a cold November evening. That's when an impoverished theatre company named Native Earth produced a play by an unknown playwright, Tomson Highway, about seven Native women's preoccupation with bingo, at a Native community centre in Toronto. The play was called *The Rez Sisters*.

From those humble beginnings the world for Native theatre artists changed. Like the Big Bang, Native theatre rapidly expanded exponentially. The following year, the same company that had struggled to produce that play by an unknown Cree playwright found the interest and financing to take that same play on a cross-country tour. Then in 1988, *The Rez Sisters* was invited to the Edinburgh Fringe Festival, one of only two Canadian plays featured that summer. It should also be mentioned that *The Rez Sisters* won the Dora Mavor Moore Award for outstanding new play in 1986 and received a Governor General's Award nomination. Not bad for a play about bingo by an unknown Cree playwright. And that in 1989, its sequel, *Dry Lips Oughta Move to Kapuskasing*, once more shook up the Canadian theatrical community.

Many tales are told in the Aboriginal theatre community of how, during the early weeks of the original production of *The Rez Sisters*, staff and cast had to give tickets away on the street in front of the Native Friendship Centre to guarantee an audience. Since then, Canadian (and many foreign) stages have been set ablaze with performances by and about Native people. Now, in any given year, half a dozen or more productions by Native writers can be seen on stages across the country—stages not necessarily operated by Native people, but main-stage companies that have embraced the Aboriginal way of theatrical storytelling.

Montreal's Centaur Theatre, Saskatoon's Persephone Theatre, Vancouver's Firehall Arts Centre, Magnus Theatre in Thunder Bay, and Factory Theatre in Toronto are just a few among many that have taken a bite out of the Native theatre apple. Perhaps the apotheosis of this interest came in 1991, when three of Canada's biggest theatre companies joined forces and co-produced a remount of *Dry Lips Oughta Move to Kapuskasing*: the Manitoba Theatre Centre, the National Arts Centre, and the Royal Alexandra Theatre Company are rumoured to have spent over a million dollars on the production.

But, some ask, do those plays still have the same bite as when we in the Native theatre industry were young and full of bravado so many years ago? Have we all since got old and tired? It's hard to say. Our stories told of the results of 500 years of colonization, of residential schools, of being put on Reserves or thrust into the city without a community, of a sort of internal diaspora. Native theatre became a sort of cathartic release after so many years of our voices being silenced. It was a way to bitch, artistically. Back during those formative years, it was Tomson Highway, Daniel David Moses, and I who garnered most of the attention. Tomson kicked the door open and in doing so broke the lock and hinges in the process. *The Rez Sisters* and *Dry Lips Oughta Move to Kapuskasing* are still the standards by which the rest of our plays are judged.

Using a presumptuous Beatles allusion, Tomson was the John Lennon of the group.

Daniel David Moses, on the other hand, was George Harrison. Quiet, introspective, his work was very different. There was a definite poetic flair to his plays, probably due to the fact he was a poet by nature and profession. *Coyote City* and *Almighty Voice and His Wife* have an almost serene, ethereal quality to the writing.

And then there was me, somewhere between Ringo and Paul. I was more prolific, but my material was more kitchen-sink drama, lacking the esoteric nature or vision of the work of my two pioneering colleagues. They were and are true artists in every sense of the word, whereas I remain perfectly content to be a competent storyteller. I was also the only one not to have gone to university. And not to be gay. Talk about feeling left out ...

There were of course many other writers who contributed to Native theatre's success during those early years: Ben Cardinal, Shirley Cheechoo, Joyce B. Joyce, Tina Mason, and John McLeod to name just a few, who had exhibited early promise but never proceeded much beyond their first play or production for a variety of reasons—possibly because most were never published or aggressively promoted. One of the ironic twists about being a Native playwright involves the challenge of self-marketing. In the Native community, it's considered impolite and un-Native to promote oneself over anybody else. The community is more important than the individual. As a result, many new First Nations playwrights would get the attention of a Native theatre company for their first play, but lack the self-confidence or the know-how to proceed much beyond that. In the world of playwriting, it is literally the case that the squeaky Indian gets the grease.

It wasn't that long ago, maybe eight years or so into the Aboriginal theatrical renaissance, when a former artistic director of a theatre for young audiences who had just returned from an extended trip to Europe confessed something to me at a barbecue: her view of the then-current mainstream Toronto theatre scene was less than enthusiastic. She said, "The only interesting theatre these days is coming out of the Native community." Those were indeed exciting times.

Awards were being won. Every new production garnered much publicity. Books about Native plays were being published. Ours was a theatre that asked some tough questions about Canada and its original inhabitants. And more and more new writers were coming forth with stories and tales to be told. Frontiers were being crossed. And Canada was listening to us. And paying us for the right to listen (though that's a relative term in the non-lucrative world of theatre). We all shared in each other's success. It was like being on the Left Bank of Paris in the 1920s.

Many things have changed in the intervening years. Native theatre is no longer the exception to the rule; it's now part of the established Canadian theatrical community. But the irony is that whereas there are now a lot more professional Native theatre companies spread across Canada, there are growing concerns that the quality of theatre isn't as earth-shattering as it once was.

Tomson Highway's third venture into what was anticipated to be a seven-play cycle was the mega-musical Rose. Many have described it as the most famous play that wasn't. Grand in scope with over twenty characters and live musical accompaniment, it brought together many of the characters from the preceding two plays in an orgy of music, violence, and humour. But it was vast in imagination, bold, and therefore very expensive to produce. There were also the controversial issues of several rapes, and the crucifixion and castration of a main character on stage. Many thought it was unproducable, even though the music was sublime and the action truly amazing. As a result, other than a student production at the University of Toronto, it has yet to be fully realized on a professional stage.

Almost a decade later, Tomson's first main-stage show in a dozen years, Ernestine Shuswap Gets Her Trout met with limited response, though many agreed it was still vintage Highway. He now spends half the year in the south of France, eating cheese I assume, and writing mostly novels and children's stories. Rumour has it he's now working on several cabaret pieces.

Daniel David Moses has been living the life of quiet academia at Queen's University, with little of his unique theatre making it to the masses. Primarily still a poet, Dan tells me he still does tiptoe through the pond of Native theatre occasionally, when inspired. Recently, a remount of his play Almighty Voice and His Wife was toured by Native Earth in England.

Perhaps the last few great hurrahs by Native playwrights occurred when Ian Ross burst on to the scene, winning the Governor General's Award for his play FareWel in 1997. Since then, he too has been keeping a low profile, producing little other than writing some Winnipeg-based radio and print commentaries. Like many playwrights, Native or non-Native, occasionally they have one story to tell or one play to write, and then they retire. Witness Margaret Mitchell and that little story she wrote ... I think it was called Gone with theWind. Same with Harper Lee and To Kill a Mockingbird.

Native theatres themselves are feeling the bite of leaner economic times. It was reported in a study tabled at a conference on Native arts in Banff a few summers back that one of Canada's most influential Native theatre companies, Les Ondinook Theatre, run by Yves Sioui Durand, existed for over twenty years and had become a fixture on the Montreal and national theatre scene until it shut its doors that year. Funding difficulties were rumoured to be the primary reason. Two other companies, located in Western Canada, are at a crossroads as to how to proceed further, also due to funding issues.

To be fair, the waters of First Nations theatre are not completely still. The Turtle Gals, with their amazing Native Earth show The Scrubbing Project, made us all gasp at the possibilities of what could be done. It was a unique blend of song, theatre, and political commentary, produced with a sense of the sheer enjoyment of performing that made it extremely infectious and satisfying.

And for its 2006–07 season in Ottawa, Métis writer Marie Clements premiered her new show Copper Thunderbird at the National Arts Centre, the first Native-authored play ever to premiere there, thanks to its new artistic director, Peter Hinton. The bonfire, while no longer burning as brightly as it once did, does seem to flare up occasionally.

Case in point: in 2010, history repeated itself when another Native playwright won a Governor General's Award for his first play. Keven Loring snagged the prestigious prize for his play Where the Blood Mixes. An actor/playwright, hopefully we'll see more of Kevin's work in the future.

This sense of plateauing in the Native theatre arts could merely be a sign of acceptance. We are no longer the new kids on the block, the colour of the month, the flavour of the week, as it were. The rebels may have joined the establishment. It has been two decades, and the initial shock and wave of interest in what Canada's First Nations had to say and how we said it may no longer be as fresh or as interesting to mainstream theatre audiences in Canada as it was in its youth. It seems the honeymoon is over. Is this the metaphorical seven-year itch? If it is, we must be right in the middle of the fourth time around—1986 was, after all, twenty-four years ago.

However, it now seems the real Indigenous theatrical excitement is coming from below the border. Since the birth of The Rez Sisters, Canadian Native artists have been conscious of how much more fully developed the industry is up here than in the USA. Astonishingly, most Native theatre performed in America had been imported from Canadian sources. At almost every Native theatre festival held down south (the few that have occurred), two-thirds to three-quarters of talent (playwrights and occasionally actors and directors) have been of Canadian Aboriginal ancestry. In fact, one company's board of directors complained to its artistic director about the constant importing of Canadian First Nations talent.

This is primarily because we have those twenty years of Aboriginal theatrical history in Canada to call upon. We now do know what we're doing. Often in America when there is a call for scripts to be developed, it's the Canadian Native playwrights who submit completed first drafts. According to a Native artistic director, many Native American writers (admittedly not all) usually submit one or two scenes. Or just an outline. Or a paragraph. Theatre is not new to us. We know the game.

In America, they are just waking up to the possibility of what theatre holds for its Native population. And we have that training, and the talent.

That's why it seems Americans have lately begun taking the forefront in pushing the Native theatre envelope. Last year, Trinity Repertory Theater in Providence, Rhode Island, produced a comedy of mine. It is one of the five largest repertory theatre companies in America, and that production was rumoured to have had the largest budget of any Native play ever done in North America. Native Voices, the predominant producer of Native theatre in California, regularly develops half a dozen plays a year at their Los Angeles festival, and produces, on average, two a year. They are developing an excellent reputation for the work they do and the support they provide to the Native theatre community.

In Minneapolis, Minnesota, a well-respected theatre company ironically called Mixed Blood Theatre recently embarked on an ambitious endeavour. They contacted fifteen Native playwrights from across Canada and the States, contracting them to write four- to eight-minute short original plays dealing with a social or political point of view. It was their attempt to "produce an opinionated snapshot of Native America in 2007." They high-lighted them later in their season during an evening featuring all the short pieces. One of their guidelines suggests: "Write as if your whole audience is Indian."

Perhaps the future of Native theatre lies further abroad, across the eastern and western oceans. In the last six months, I've had one of my plays, *Someday*, translated into Arabic at a University in Jordan, and also into Czech. The same play is part of the course of study at the University of Madras in India. There have been productions of various Native plays in countries as diverse as Germany, Italy, and Japan. I wonder how the word bingo translates into Japanese.

Western theatre has been driving people to exotic places for over 2,500 years, and we've been riding in that car for only two decades. It's hard to say what the future of Native theatre will bring. There are still so many more stories out there to tell, and so many more storytellers waiting for their chance. Theatre has always been an essential part of traditional storytelling. It's the ability to take the audience on a journey using your imagination, your body, and your voice. It can be timeless. Like skinny ties, I'm sure Native theatre will go in and out of style in mainstream Western theatre. I say this because everything from Christianity to jazz goes in and out of style. And Native theatre is as versatile, as exciting, and as creative as anything else out there.

It will be interesting to revisit this article in twenty years' time to see if it needs revising.

South

South is typically represented by the colour yellow, for that is where the sun travels across the sky in the northern hemisphere. Because it also represents the wind, of the four elements, south represents the air. It is the direction of exploration and discovery—both inwards and outwards. Summer, light, and preparing for the future come from the south. It represents maturing life, like the lives of young men and women. It is a direction of full understanding, generosity, relationships, sensitivity towards others, and emotions. It is sometimes referred to as the place of heart knowledge.

STARLIGHT TOURS

Its not often I have brainstorms about topics outside my usual realm of expertise (in this case, tourism), but if anybody is interested, I do believe I have a wining idea for the city of Saskatoon. It's a unique way to get some free publicity for a service that already exists there!

I got the idea in Ottawa, of all places, attending an Aboriginal policy conference on, ironically, many things Aboriginal. More Native people milling about there, drinking their coffee, than you could shake a talking stick at. Later that evening, as everybody was decompressing and decomposing in a local establishment, a gentleman from the Prairies leaned over to me and for some reason saw fit to mention he was from Saskatoon. I've always thought of that place as a fine town with a fine Native theatre company.

During the rest of the conversation, he confided in me that he had been on one of those famous Saskatoon Starlight Tours, so thoughtfully provided by the local constabulary. I, like many Native people, had heard about these tours, but to me they were like the stories about sasquatches—you hear about them, but they seem kind of rare, and you are very unlikely to run into one, let alone in an Ottawa bar. But I was wrong.

For those not quite up to date on their Aboriginal civil rights violations, Starlight Tours are routine events where Native people are picked up by the local authorities and deposited some distance out of town, to fend for themselves in an often hostile environment. Evidently this is usually done for the mere amusement of those same authorities. To further increase the humour quotient, the Native people's coats and shoes generally remain in the police car as trophies, while their lucky owners trudge off in search of justice, often through the snow in the middle of winter, getting back in touch with the land.

The most famous recipient of such a unique tourist opportunity was Neil Stonechild, who was found frozen to death in a field outside the lovely city of Saskatoon some years back. However, it seemed to me, living all the way out in Ontario, that these so-called "tours" were few and far between—hardly an epidemic. But my Ottawa friend told me these Starlight Tours are far more common than most of us Canadians are aware. In fact, my decompressing friend's nonchalance about the topic and his own adventure startled me. "I figured it was just my turn," he said casually. Evidently that is an attitude shared by many. It's just what the police do out there, it seems.

I figured the Saskatoon cops must have really gotten enthusiastic about my buddy and dumped him just outside of Ottawa instead of Saskatoon this time. That's probably what they call their National Tour. But luckily, the man still had his coat and shoes on. And a story to tell.

So, I started talking with this Prairie dude and we got to thinking about how we should pitch something to the Saskatoon Chamber of Commerce about this unique and untapped resource. Starlight Tours—how to experience the Aboriginal lifestyle without being Aboriginal! I mean, there's only so much wheat around to keep Saskatoon in the money. Think about it— the police pick you up right from the airport and let you off somewhere well outside of town. Aerobically it's great, with all that walking and occasional running. Lots of fresh, brisk air. You will need a decent health plan though. And just like a visit to the plastic surgeon, it's all kept really confidential. Nobody will ever know you're there.

In tourism terms, it won't be much different from going to the Niagara region of Canada on a wine-tasting tour. The fee: a donation of your jacket and shoes to the Goodwill.

I don't know if the Saskatoon Chamber of Commerce or the Police Board would go for it. God knows the Starlight Tours are providing enough publicity for the city already, but they're not really making any money on them yet. Maybe it's just a matter of perception. Maybe they should think of this revenue-generating opportunity just like Alberta thinks of its oil— it's already out there, just waiting to be tapped. But unlike Alberta oil, eco-tourism is a highly renewable resource. Lots of Indians and lots of cops. A symbiotic relationship.

Christmas will be here in nine months—think of a Starlight Tour as something to give somebody who has ... nothing.

GETTING FOXY

Ah, to be forty-one and single. Like most men of a certain age, the hunt/dance/chase is requiring a little more effort these days. It's only been recently that you've learned of the term "cougar," which you're told refers to women in their thirties and forties who, shall we say, go on the prowl for men. You wonder if there's a male equivalent. "Tomcat" would be the closest parallel, you suppose. At least it's in keeping with the feline metaphor.

You realize that you've been dating in one form or another for almost twenty-five years now, with varying degrees of success. Paraphrasing a once-popular country song, you could say you've been "looking for love in all the wrong Nations. Looking for love with too many Caucasians." And in the end, what has it got you: three moderately healthy plants and the ability to understand both kinds of music—country and western. Maybe it's time for a change.

When your last girlfriend told you she no longer required your services, (one of the reasons being that evidently you didn't dress well enough to impress her—you still maintain velour is a much-underappreciated fabric), you toyed with the idea of swearing off love. Permanently. You figured there's no point in falling in love anymore—you should just order in from now on. It would probably be cheaper in the end.

Even so, with all the young bucks out there, you still find yourself tempted to try anything to catch the eye of all the pretty young things out there. You have visions of being hip, with it, cool, you want to get down and dirty with the homeys. Thongs are in, you hear. You decide to get one. A cool, Indigenous one. One that's beaded. For grip. You find out later that this may have been a big mistake. You can still wear it as a headband though.

You end up wondering if other people are beginning to smell your desperation, because over a one-week period, at least three people you know have forwarded you a link to www.rezfox.com, the first online dating service for Natives by Natives. This is where you go if you're a lonely Nish with a wish to fry some fish with a beautiful dish. And the scary thing is, you decide to investigate. You don't end up joining, but you are intrigued. Overall, you find it quite progressive, Aboriginally speaking ... From the '49er to the Internet. From the social to the website. Who says Native people are stuck in the past? Either way, you can still get a nasty virus.

"Whether you are looking for a life partner, or just someone to hang out with, here you'll be able to find exactly who you are looking for, locally or around the world. Rezfox was created to assist Native people of Turtle Island [North America] to find other Natives with similar interests and dreams and to help create lasting relationships or maybe even love." That's a tall order.

They ask you for a profile: gender, age, city, religion, whether you drink or smoke, education, languages, interests, whether you call it frybread, scon, bannock, or Indian bread—you know, all the usual stuff. And of course, a photograph of some sort. You are pleasantly surprised to discover the vast majority of people listed, at least 75 percent, are Canadian. If you wish, you can give your real name, or a cyber *nom de plume*. Some of the more curious names you find in the female catalogue, which you strenuously maintain you perused strictly for research purposes, included such creative monikers as Anishnababe, Nishdish, Naughty Cree, and your personal favourite, Life'stooshortto49withuglymen. You acknowledge that she's brutal but honest.

Amongst the men, the same sense of fun prevails—after all, what's dating without a little fun? Some of the men online who are looking for someplace hot to bake their bannock include such creative Natives as Buck Naked (who obviously watches too much *Seinfeld*), Nationwide Threat, Does My Inner Child Need a Spanking, Tongue Kung Fu Master, and Nish4U. Oddly, nobody has yet made the obvious joke: I'm looking for either a bush Cree or a Cree bush. You admire their restraint, but not your own. Participants from places farther afield than Turtle Island are trolling the Cyber Sea off the island. There is one from Turkey, not apparently named after the American bird. And of course, a handful of ubiquitous Germans, eager to hit the Aboriginal motherlode.

But at the end of the day, when all's said and done, and all the dishes are put away, you are still sitting at home, alone, playing with your hard drive, and you begin to understand the appeal of bingo.

ENWEYING—THE WAY WE SPEAK TOGETHER

The Way We Speak Together ... a noble and fitting title for this conference. The Way We Speak Together ... or for the academics in the audience ... The manner in which we communicate as a group of individuals.

Many, if not most, of us come from some sort of an oral culture, and speaking together harks back to those days of our ancestors when the history and teachings of a people could be told over a campfire. I remember one Elder telling me, "Writing something down is asking permission to forget it." I didn't have the heart to tell him I was a writer. I guess that means I forget for a living. But to me it only seems fitting to be holding the conference here at this university, because it's one of the leading institutions for Native studies in Canada (I believe there's some sort of PhD program here), and it's also a little-known fact that the word "Trent" is an ancient Ojibway word that loosely translates as "101 things you can build using cement." In case you hadn't noticed.

First of all, I want to thank the people who invited me to be a part of this evening. It's always good to come home and be amongst friends. For those who don't know, I grew up about twenty-five minutes north of here, in a little hamlet called Curve Lake. I think I was five when this place was built, on an ancient immigrant burial ground.

I love conferences like this, but I don't know if I'm the right person to be up here, for as a writer I lead a very solitary life. Solitude is part of being a writer. It's often just me, my room, and my dreams. When I speak, more often than not it's alone in a room. Yet ironically, the type of writing I produce quite frequently, theatre, is collaborative by nature—actors and directors almost always have a great deal of input into the final production. Even the audience can make every performance something new. So in a manner of speaking, I guess maybe in the end we all do speak together. Some processes just take longer than others or take different forms.

That is what I do for a living. A teller of literary tales to earn my bread, I guess it could be said. I "speak" through my art. I educate, I reason, I explore, I teach, all through my writing. And I will be honest with you ... I educate, reason, explore, and teach myself just as much as other people in that process. Because if you do it properly, you can't help but learn, as you teach or write. That is the beauty of art. It gives and receives. I've heard it said (where, I'm not sure) that there is no word in most First Nations' languages for "art." I disagree. Sure there is. It's called B'modsawin—or for those not fortunate enough to understand Ojibway—my life. For me, the two are the same. Life is the novel you write or the canvas you paint. Without life, there can be no art. Without art there could be no life ... at least not one worth living.

The way we speak together; speech ... communication ... language ... there are many ways of addressing this theme. Or exploring it. And the basic human need to speak among ourselves can be found in all places. Last August I was fortunate enough to visit India. In that fascinating country, they speak approximately 600 languages, I'm told ... I lost count after about seven. They say in India that the only great thing, besides gin, the British brought with them was the English language. It allowed them all to communicate. It united them. So now there are 601 languages. In India they tell real Indian jokes, and all the road signs are in English.

In Australia, oddly enough, about the same number of languages are spoken by its Indigenous peoples. And if you take into account the 500 First Nations in the United States and add what we have up here, it comes out to roughly the same. Six hundred seems to be the magic number in the world of languages. That's a lot of Indigenous people talking, with or without the ubiquitous kitchen table.

When I was in Mexico the previous year, I was asked to speak at a PEN International conference on Indigenous languages. I spoke specifically on being a First Nations writer, but one who did not speak or write in his Indigenous tongue. Unfortunately that's me. So, amongst all those educated scholars, somebody saw fit to put me on a panel with four PhD'd professors ... and I can barely spell PhD in any language. The situation reminded me of that *Sesame Street* song "One of These Things Is Not Like the Other."

Anyway, as a person in my predicament, I talked about how I suffer from a linguistic syndrome. Picture this if you can ... you have a dog. You tell the dog to sit. The dog hears you. It sits. It does what you say. But the dog cannot respond in the same language that it heard the original command. Now, my mother tells me in Ojibway to put the kettle on. I hear her, I understand her, and I put the kettle on. But I cannot respond in the language in which I heard the original command. That's what we call the Dog Syndrome. This is how many of our Indigenous tongues are being neutered.

In many other ways, we do not always speak together.

These are changing times among our people. Things are happening faster and faster. Things inside our communities are developing at incredible rates. At one time, formal education was thought a frivolity, something not actually needed or wanted by the average Native person. It was not really necessary to lead a full and meaningful life. My mother, the oldest of fourteen, had to quit school at an early age to help raise her younger siblings. When I got to the age where I was contemplating what to do after high school, I brought up the topic of coming here to Trent to take Native studies. Let's just say she wasn't exactly amenable to the idea. Her response was: "You want to study Indians ... Just take a look at me. And that won't take you four years." My mother can be very subtle. Thus ended my brief flirtation with the idea of getting a university education.

But to be fair to my mother, I'm guilty myself of that kind of narrow rationality sometimes. You are guilty of that too. We all are. Sometimes we need to step back and see what others have to say. Step outside the box, as they say. Or outside the teepee in our case. If life is a test, then sometimes you have to deviate from the standard course curriculum to find the right answers. Several weeks ago, when I was last visiting my mother, we were driving into Peterborough, and there was a commercial on the radio about taking French classes. And my beloved mother said rather wistfully, "I wish I was bilingual." I looked at her and said, "Mom, you are bilingual." She looked puzzled until she realized I meant Ojibway and English. She had never considered herself as bilingual. In Canada today, it's almost always associated with English and French or either of these "official" languages with another foreign language. That day, I taught her something new.

It's been said that the best way to learn a new language is across the pillows in bed. I disagree, 'cause if you're talking, it ain't working. Or maybe that's just an Ojibway thing. The only non-Ojibway or English word I ever learned across a pillow was, of all things, a Cree word. And I think it was … Awuss—it means "go away." I tried not to take it personally.

But if there is one thing I have discovered in my travels across this earth, it's this: humour is the greatest communicator. It builds bridges and forges alliances. You want to make friends, make them laugh. You want to teach something to somebody, wrap it in a joke and serve it covered with smiles. Few things bond like a good laugh. People will share jokes, giggle together, huddle together over the warmth of a good belly laugh. And no one does that better than Native people. That is one of the reasons I love to do what I do. Humour connects. It heals. It unites. Simply, it feels good. And anything that feels good, people will quite probably want to do again. And again. They might even bring a few friends along. There may be 600 words from 600 languages on this continent for laughter, but the one single sound of a good laugh is universal. I find it to be one of the few sure signs of a Creator. Because while nature is beautiful and awesome, the ability to laugh is divine. Just study a child when he or she laughs.

We in First Nations communities talk a lot about Native humour, how unique it is. It can be empowering, it can be teasing, it can be self-depre-cating, and it sure can be politically incorrect. For example: "What did the Indian say when he walked into a bar? 'Ouch.'" Or, "Okay, these two Indians walk out of a bar … 'out of a bar'—Hey, it could happen."

So when we talk a lot about Native humour, we're presupposing that it is something specifically Native … Maybe, maybe not. True humour is universal. In the communities we come from, humour is everywhere. It may be tinged with ab-originality, but we all know the source of that river of humour. It's allowed us to survive 500 years of oppression and colonization. One of the projects I have coming out this winter is a book of essays exploring and deconstructing, if that's possible, the world of

Native humour. It's being published by Douglas & McIntyre and it's called ... and this is the whole title, Me Funny: A far-reaching exploration of the humour, wittiness and repartee dominant among the First Nations people of Canada, as witnessed, experienced and created directly by themselves, and with the inclusion of outside but reputable sources necessarily familiar with the Indigenous sense of humour as seen from an objective perspective. Everything you need to know about Native humour should be in that book. Though I'll be honest with you; I really don't think you can deconstruct Native humour. You have to be there, in the moment, and understand the situation. But what the hell, Douglas & McIntyre brought the idea to me and I had to make it work.

In doing my research—and I should clarify this point—much like calling life and art synonymous, I have to call life and research synonymous because for me, most of my research comes not from books but from living. I always tell first-time writers that if you want to become a writer or storyteller, you have to have a life. You have to do things, go places, succeed and fail. Sitting in the basement playing video games all day will not help you deal with the complexities of either life or writing. Being a writer requires experiences, and vice versa—experiences require a thoughtful, articulate life. And an interesting life is cheaper and often more fun than spending the afternoon in the library. And don't get me wrong—I love books. Books give you knowledge. But life gives you wisdom.

So, in doing my forty-two years of research for this book on Native humour, I can safely say I have been to over 120 Native communities across Canada and the US, and everywhere I've visited I've been greeted with a smile, a laugh, and usually a joke. And like t-shirts and spoons, I collect funny stories from the places I travel. Stories that show us how we speak and laugh together. And funny stories are sweeter than home movies.

Like ... I don't know if anybody here has ever heard of a far-off land called Wiky. It is a land of beautiful women and twenty-four-hour bingo. And more often than not, the two are indistinguishable from each other. I know a woman from that community. Her name is Audrey. And she has one of the thickest, most delightful Rez accents you will ever hear. A mutual friend of ours who has since passed away, his name was Larry, was trying to teach her better English diction. After all, she was getting involved in the world of theatre and someday she might be required to inhabit a role other than that of a Rez-sounding woman. Going, "Oooohhhhhooo" might not be required. So, for some reason, she just could not manage the "th" sound so common in the English language. It kept coming out as a "t" sound. Instead of thirty-three, she would say "tirty-tree." It was adorable and very Wiky. But for some reason Larry was determined to make her his own Eliza Doolittle. Every time he caught her saying the "t' instead of the "th" sound, he would correct her. Pretty soon she caught on.

Then she came to Toronto for a visit. I took her out to dinner with some friends and introduced her to some new ethnic cuisine. Soon, she went back to Wiky with some new big-city adventures to brag about. Larry asked her if I had taken her to dinner, and what she had had to eat. She stood erect, and said with as much pride as she could muster, "I had Thailand noodles!" Of course the correct diction does not use the "th" sound, as Audrey had. Larry just shook his head, laughed, and never attempted to correct her again. Heaven help her if she ever decides to do Shakespeare's "Otello" or "Macbet."

So based on this little bit of information, I one day decided to write a sketch about a similar situation for a Native comedy show I was putting together. It sort of illustrates the unique humour of our communities. If you have a moment, I'd like to share it with you. Picture this: a woman enters a small cubicle with a tape recorder. She puts a cassette tape in it. It's one of those speech therapy tapes, to help get rid of an accent. She puts it in, and out of the speaker comes a voice saying something like, "Today, we will focus on the 'th' sound that is unique to the English Language. What I will do is say a sentence three times. You will repeat the sentence immediately after I say it, paying particular attention to pronouncing the 'th' sound perfectly. Let's begin." There is a pause, followed by:

"I thought I heard the thunder."

"I taught I heard da tunder."

This is repeated several times until at the very end, the student manages to say it correctly: "I thought I heard the thunder."

After this, the tape says, "Very good," to which she responds … "T'ank you."

One time, I was working on a play in Wiky, and Floyd Favel-Starr was there co-directing. He's a well-known Cree theatre director from Saskatchewan. As we were working, he commented on how much he liked the shirt I was wearing that day. He really liked it, he said. I was flattered—I'm not exactly known for being a flashy dresser but I'll take any compliment I can get. So I thanked him. And then there was this awkward pause. Then he gave me what I like to call a lesson in Cree etiquette. He said: "Well you know, where I come from, when somebody says they really like something, you are obligated to give it to them. It's our tradition." He paused, then took another admiring glance at my shirt. "Yep, I really like that shirt." I began to catch on.

Now I have always tried to respect other nations and their customs, and who was I to deny an ancient Cree ritual? So, capitulating, I started to unbutton my shirt to give it to him. Then I casually said, "Floyd, I don't think I've ever mentioned this, but I really like your girlfriend." Now, much to my surprise he insisted I keep the shirt I was perfectly willing to give him. I guess maybe I was just a little more traditional than he was.

The way we speak together … I have been very fortunate that I have been given the opportunity to speak about my career so much, and to have so many places in which to speak about it. And I'm constantly astonished that there are so many people out there who want to listen. In the past two years alone, I have spoken about Native literature, humour, and identity in Mexico, Germany, Belgium, France, Italy, Australia, India ... and yes, I loved being an Indian in India, but oddly enough, they don't talk there like they do in Wiky. And this August, I will be making my way to Finland. It will be like a homecoming for me because I've always been told I look more Saami then Ojibway.

And in those travels I've seen or heard some pretty interesting things: asparagus-flavoured ice cream in Germany; roast beef-flavoured potato chips in England ... A play of mine, The Baby Blues, was produced in Venice, where a bunch of Italian actors were running all over the stage yelling, "Ille Pow wowa." In Germany I went to a West Coast art launch. In Australia I bought a dreamcatcher.

But there can be a danger when people think we do all speak together. I am referring to the constant threat of pan-Indianism—the romanticized idea of the "universal Aboriginal." How many times have we heard the question, "What do you people want?" Evidently, we are all one people. We're all salmon-fishing, sweetgrass-burning, birch-bark-biting, seal-hunting, bingo-playing, throat-singing, lard-frying, snow-snake-throwing, sun-dancing diabetics. And that's just in this room. But slowly the world is learning.

Not that long ago I was conducting a lot of research on the world of Native erotica for a documentary I wanted to do for the National Film Board of Canada. A few years earlier I had done one on Native humour called Redskins, Tricksters and Puppy Stew. My working title for this erotica project was The Night Was Dark and So Was She. Alas it never came to fruition but it did involve a lot of rather unusual research, shall we say. Luckily, because the producer was a government organization, I was reimbursed for a lot of the expenses ... and you should have seen some of the receipts I had to turn in. Even stranger, I had to occasionally ask, "Excuse me, could I have a receipt for that?" But in the end, a non-Native friend of mine asked what I had discovered about the difference between Native erotica and regular mainstream erotica, and all I could think of for a response was: "Our tan lines weren't as noticeable."

The reason I bring this up is that times are changing. Our subject for this conference, The Way We Speak Together, reflects the fact that while not that long ago we were prevented from even speaking our languages, now you can take courses in them. What was once forbidden is now embraced. The unpopular is now popular. There's a line in a play I wrote called The Buz'Gem Blues, where an Ojibway Elder at an Elders' conference ... (I don't know if anybody here is familiar with them), comments, "When I was young, the government tried beating the language out of us, now they're paying us to speak it. I just wish those White people would make up their minds."

All sorts of things we as a people knew and embraced are now being embraced by the dominant culture.

Today, contemporary Native people and our cultural baggage are hot! Thirty years ago, Indian wannabes were few and far between. Nowadays, they're helping to support a thriving beaded-earring industry all by themselves. As proof of this cultural transformation, ask yourself how many non-Native people go to pow wows, Elders' conferences, and things like this gathering here, with only a minuscule percentage of those non-Native attendees being anthropologically oriented by nature. How many non-Native people are taking Native studies courses at this university? It seems our secret is out. We're a fabulous and interesting people. Well, most of us.

But I'm sure you all know this already. None of this is really new. You are all smart people who no doubt follow the conference trail like the Plains Indians used to follow the buffalo. And as part of the tradition, I hope no part of this conference goes unused. Now, instead of the tools of the fur trade, we share our information technology. The leg-hold trap of today is the computer. And I hear there has been an increase in reported cases of people gnawing off their mouse arm to get away.

Far wiser things will be said this weekend, I'm sure. So thank you for inviting me here today and I hope the rest of the conference is far more interesting and important than my contribution this evening. I have been up here speaking alone, and now it's time for the speaking together part to start.

Meegwetch and co-obmen.

I'M CONFLICTED ABOUT THIS

Have you ever been in a situation where somebody of reputable standing and excellent credentials tells you something about your particular cultural group, and you go: "I didn't know that!" and it leaves you feeling like somebody back home forgot to mention it as you were leaving the Reserve? It can make you—or in this case, me—feel less Ojibway. As luck would have it, I have been Ojibway for about forty-two years now, starting pretty much at birth, and I'm still learning something new about my people. That can be both a good and a bad thing.

I have a friend who sees a psychiatrist on a regular basis. She is Native, but not Ojibway. While that's tragic, that alone is not worth seeing a psychiatrist about. The doctor in question is neither Ojibway nor Native (a double tragedy), but evidently he has spent a lot of time in Northern Ontario working with and in Ojibway communities. In fact, he is regarded somewhat as an expert in the field of Aboriginal mental health, and often has Native clients are referred specifically to him by others.

Somehow the topic of Ojibways came up in a session and this gentleman commented on what could be called his Oji-research and Oji-conclusions, concerning how we as a people deal with the concept of conflict. In small communities, conflict can often be blown way out of proportion—dumping your leaves on somebody else's lawn, dating and breaking up with somebody's cousin, gutting and cleaning your fish underneath somebody's window, the usual. Now granted, each culture has its own unique way of dealing with this type of conflict. We're no different.

It was this psychiatrist's belief that Ojibways deal with conflict through avoidance in three specific ways: the spreading of rumour and gossip; humour/joking; and bad witchcraft/medicine. Two of those three methods are pretty cross-cultural in the conflict-avoidance world.

In my opinion, the spreading of rumour and gossip is quite pan-cultural, and the very fact that I'm writing this article for publication might just fall under that category ... not that I'm spreading rumours about the doctor or anything. Perhaps I am simply asserting my Ojibwayness. So the more I gossip, the more I am merely an Ojibway avoiding conflict. So if I don't spread rumours and such, does that mean I am neither Ojibway, nor avoiding conflict? This is why I am not a psychiatrist ... these questions get way too complicated way too fast.

As for using joking and humour as a method of conflict avoidance ... this psychiatrist walks into a bar and buys a drink. It costs $9.50 and he gives the bartender a ten-dollar bill. The bartender asks, "Hey, buddy, do you want change?" To which the psychiatrist responds knowingly, "We all want change." I think I've made my point. I've been accused of using humour to avoid conflict on many previous occasions.

It's the third option for conflict avoidance that has grabbed my fascination—the use of bad medicine or witchcraft. That was a new one on me, so I asked my mother if she'd ever done anything like that, in between visits to church, and oddly enough her answer was a fairly firm no. But that wouldn't explain the bags of human hair and fingernail/toenail clippings under the kitchen sink.

However I'm not saying this particular practice doesn't exist out there in our communities. I've heard too many stories and travelled to too many places. But it's important to know that traditional beliefs and spirituality are rife with primarily good practitioners (and a few bad ones). Like in any culture, there are two sides of the moral coin, and accordingly, the Creator gives us the choice of using his gifts for good or bad.

But what has me so bemused is that the use of magic and witchcraft is evidently so popular and ubiquitous among the Ojibway, as I have been informed by this psychiatrist, that seemingly it is the number-three method to deal with conflict resolution through avoidance. That means it's more popular than calling the police, moving, shooting your opponent's dog—you know, all those tried and true practices common to most cultures. I didn't realize there were enough people practising this type of medicine to crack the "top ten" methods of conflict through avoidance in our communities. That's what's news to me. Unlike the other two, I can safely say I've never been accused of this one … so I decided I should go home and check this out.

I asked my aunt about the possibility of using magic and witchcraft in our community and her reply was a dignified and strong, "ick," pronounced with a strong Ojibway accent. (In the Native community this kind of thing is classified under the "ick" factor.) To her, and a lot of people like her, the idea of skulking around, trying to find your enemies' hair and nail clippings is pretty high on that factor. But then again, we are classified as a southern Ojibway community. Peterborough can hardly be called the Far North. So maybe we're exempt. Apparently there's no witchcraft south of Sudbury. I'll have to check with the Assembly of First Nations.

It also makes you wonder what the top three methods of conflict resolution through avoidance would be in other Native cultures. The Iroquois for example. Or the Cree, or the Salish. Most of the other people I know from those cultures have pretty much the same methods of dealing with life and its difficulties as the Ojibway. They tell jokes (though not as well as the Ojibway) and they gossip (far more than the Ojibway), but the whole witchcraft/bad medicine thing … it just doesn't come up in conversation that much. I'm sure with the Iroquois it probably has something to do with corn, and with salmon for the Salish. I wonder if other psychiatrists have made similar observations and studies of them, and if their conclusions concur.

I just might do a little research of my own and see what the Native people of this country think about cultural psychiatry. If I remember correctly, in some cultures playing with people's minds is considered witch-craft. Hmmm ...

BE CAREFUL WHAT YOU WRITE ...

Just the other day, I encountered a rather uncomfortable display of two different types of stupidity, demonstrated by two different types of men. Unfortunately I was one of them. The situation didn't happen recently. In fact it happened several years back, but it was only a few days ago I found out about it. And it's left me feeling ... I guess odd would be the best way of putting it.

I have an acquaintance—for the sake of argument, let's call her Mary. Both being members of the arts community, our paths would cross every couple of years or so. Evidently the last time I came into contact with her was during a book tour I was on some time ago, where she interviewed me and got me to sign her book. I'm not even sure what I wrote, but being genuinely fond of her in a platonic sense, in a playful and teasing mood, it ended up being something to the effect of: "Mary, you're fabulous. Let's run off together and get married. Drew." And then she disappeared for a few years.

I recently ran into this woman again at an arts function. After some brief salutations, Mary filled me in on the intervening years. After our last encounter, she told me, she took the book home and proudly showed it to her boyfriend. He read my inscription and, to use her words, proceeded to "beat the crap out of her." Because of my flippant dedication, he automatically assumed there was more to the joke than there was, and decided to register his disapproval in a brutally physical manner.

When she told me this, my jaw just dropped. Immediately, feelings of anger, guilt, surprise, and a host of other powerful emotions swelled up inside me. Basically, I was responsible for a woman being beaten by her spouse. Always a strong advocate against domestic abuse, this news struck me to the core. I was stunned. Unfortunately I've been in situations before where I say or do something in a joking fashion that is wildly inappropriate, only for it to have unfortunate and embarrassing repercussions. I think everybody's been in a position like that. But this, by far, took the proverbial cake for me.

Mary then told me that for the next year or so she was understandably furious and very angry with me, and looked forward to confronting me about the result of my clever and witty little comment. Had I known all this had happened, I would have gladly presented my neck for ritual decapitation.

Instead, to my surprise, she thanked me. Once more I was stunned. Because of this horrible, violent act, she said, I saved her life. I'm paraphrasing Mary but evidently it took her a while to properly assess the environment she had been in. She had placed herself, unconsciously, in a very controlling situation with a man who was both her fiancé and tutor for school. That assault precipitated her leaving the relationship. It wasn't until then that she had the time and the distance to better reflect on what had happened. Her friends who had always had concerns about the man supported her and told her she was lucky to get out of that relationship when she did.

As a result, she doesn't blame me anymore for what happened. All I did, Mary said, was to force the issue to the surface where she could see her fiancé for what he was. Basically, my attempt at humour had forced him out of the closet, so to speak. In fact, she hugged me after our talk. Now she's off on her own, having a wonderful and exciting career. So, I guess it was a good thing that it happened. I guess ...

Still, I feel weird, conflicted. Indirectly (or directly) I was responsible for the abuse of a woman as a result of a thoughtless gesture on my part. That turns my stomach. It never would have happened if I hadn't written that dedication, I said to her. She countered that, yes, it quite probably would have happened, eventually. There would have just been a different trigger, maybe when she wasn't in a position to leave so easily. To use a bad metaphor, it's something like having heart surgery. It's painful and scary, but in the long run, it's better than the alternative.

Ironically, I make my living as a humorist (though some might disagree). This whole episode reminds me of a comment made by Dick Gregory, one of the two leading and most influential African-American comics (with Richard Pryor) of the 1960s. When he decided to give up the stage, people asked him why.

"After a while, things stop being funny," he said.

So Mary's at peace with the world and has gotten on with her life. Now it's my turn to try and reason this all out. That, and why it is that some women never get the men they deserve. And vice versa.

And that book I signed all those years ago that started this all ... she says she still hasn't read it. I don't blame her.

WHERE THERE'S SMOKE, THERE'S FIRE

For years, philosophers, Elders, and people who work in the Membership Department at Band Offices across the country have been battling with the age-old question of what is Native and what is Caucasian. What separates the two, and where one belief system begins and the other ends—truly complicated questions worthy of serious pondering. Well, I believe I may have the answer. And it's quite obvious. I expect no praise or rewards for my discovery, merely the credit. And maybe some understanding.

The answer came to me while I was working with the Saskatchewan Native Theatre Company in Saskatoon. They're a fabulous company doing fabulous things, and I would urge anybody in the area to check them out. But it was the contract I signed with them that may shed some light on this puzzling question of the ages. I was there to work with a group of youth, eighteen and over. Buried deep within the contract was a small three-line stipulation. Specifically, in section two, paragraph A—right there between making all necessary payments to Revenue Canada (money going out), and the copyright and ownership clauses (money coming in)—it states: "that as a mentor and role model with the program, the playwright will respect the true intent and spirit of the healthy lifestyles work environment as a component of the Theatre's Healing Journeys Through the Arts Project."

Basically, as I was led to understand, this meant no drinking and drugs. Fine. No problem. I understand and fully support a healthy lifestyle. Besides, I have more interesting vices. But then I began to notice a slight contradiction between what was perceived as a healthy lifestyle and what people were actually doing. Throughout the week I was there, we kept taking small breaks during the day, at least twice in the morning and twice in the afternoon (not including lunch hours), for these vitamin-enriched, low-calorie, zero-transfat, low-impact things called cigarettes. Now, call me silly (and I have been), but I always believed that smoking was not part of a healthy lifestyle. Granted, tobacco definitely has Native origins, but I was always taught it was for spiritual and ceremonial purposes. I don't remember hearing about our great-grandfathers having a twenty-pipe-a-day habit. And I understand the tragic history we have with alcohol. Still, why is one equally damaging habit better than the other? Is it a matter of choosing the lesser of evils? If so, why?

My conundrum was put to the test later that week when I met up with an old friend I hadn't seen in a few months. Somehow we ended up in a bar and the waitress asked me what I wanted to drink. I was about to order a beer when I remembered the contract I had signed a few days earlier, but then I also remembered the image of all those students, and several of the staff, huddled outside the office door, smoking and shivering in the winter cold. Surely that couldn't have been all that healthy—smoking cigarettes outside in the Saskatchewan winter. I found myself hip-deep in a moral quandary. What to do? I decided to break even. "Have you got a light ... beer?" I asked her. I figured the lower alcohol content would limit my stay in purgatory. Evidently my word of honour was worth a Blue Light that night. Now that's sobering.

Smoking contradicts the concept of living a healthy lifestyle. Most doctors will agree, and in fact they'll tell you that one to two glasses of wine a day are actually good for you—for your heart and for your blood. I'm quite positive the same cannot be said of tobacco. Now do not misunderstand me, I'm not advocating anything here, just making a point. Other Native organizations have had similar stipulations. Until fairly recently, the Aboriginal Arts program at the Banff School of the Arts had a prohibitive drug and alcohol policy. In fact, their lounge was drug and alcohol free, and yet smoking was allowed. Evidently smoking isn't considered part of an unhealthy lifestyle in any of those contracts. That's probably because the people who drew up those contracts were smokers.

Yet, out there in the White world, it's practically the complete opposite. You'd have to be deaf, dumb, and blind not to notice the gradual tightening of the noose for those who smoke. It has become practically impossible to light up in restaurants, any form of public transportation, bars, anywhere in public. Tobacco advertising has been officially banned for most, if not all, sporting and entertainment events. I'm sure they would go nuts if they ever saw the air quality in a Native bingo hall—I've been to some where you'd need a NASA space suit just to cross the floor to get to the bathroom. But beer and alcohol companies can advertise to their hearts' content. I love all those "I AM CANADIAN" and Blue Light commercials. In the dominant culture's world, you are more of a social outcast if you smoke than if you drink. Notice the difference?

So basically, what the argument boils down to is: Native people ... smoking okay. Alcohol bad. White people ... alcohol okay, smoking bad. I guess if you're a mixed-blood or Métis, you have the option of picking the best—or worst—of both worlds.

SUFFER THE LITTLE WRITERS

I was flipping through the television channels the other day and came upon an interview with the award-winning author Joseph Boyden. His two novels, *Three Day Road* and *Through Black Spruce*, have had the success most of us writers can only imagine. Not bad for a self-described Métis boy now living in New Orleans. I'm a self-described Status Ojibway now living in the Curve Lake First Nations. I think I need a better agent.

Be that as it may, it was late in the interview when the host asked a particular question that caught my attention: "Do you think writers need to suffer in order to write?" he inquired. Admittedly, I don't remember Joseph's answer because I was stunned at what I considered the stupidity of the question. "Do writers need to suffer in order to write?" That question just floored me. I still grind my teeth at the thought of it.

Why? Because it's silly. Sure, we are all familiar with the romantic stereotype of artists suffering for their art—the image of the lonely artist slowly starving to death in a rundown Paris flophouse as he or she struggles to paint. Or the Charles Bukowski legend, living on skid row, drawing inspiration for his poetry from wallowing in alcohol and urban decay. I always found that route to creativity a little problematic. Call me a radical, but being well-showered and well-fed can be just as conducive to art as anything else. Maybe moreso. I think I would have trouble focusing if I were on death row.

I have always believed, and lectured, that if you want to be a good writer, one of the things you have to do is lead an interesting life. If not interesting *per se*, at least an event-filled life. Do things. Have a full life. Rack up some frequent flier or frequent events miles. Sometimes that definitely does include suffering. Yes, suffering provides loads of experience and a certain understanding necessary to certain kinds of writing. But so does surfing the other end of the spectrum. Travelling the world with your kids can produce just as many interesting books. Hemingway didn't exactly suffer like the romantic ideal of a writer. In fact, he probably thought that was for wimps. Instead, he led an interesting life. Stephen King or Kurt Vonnegut didn't exactly start out begging on street corners, or cutting off their ears either. They had family and kids to support.

It's like asking if all pilots need to crash in order to be good at flying. Hopefully not, but I'm sure the experience would provide a unique perspective. Again, there's that word "experience." But being an excellent pilot can also come from performing a perfect landing every time. Do accountants need to gamble in order to have a better understanding of the ebb and flow of finance and chance? Maybe, though not necessarily. But you get the point.

I know I've suffered in my own way. Granted I'm not dying of consumption or learning to walk after a tragic car accident, but last year I had to deal with the death of my mother—I'm the only child of a single parent; you do the math. In the larger context, I've had broken hearts, weathered unkind public criticisms, and more recently, I've marked the passing of the television show *Lost*. I have yet to find a country song that properly reflects that particular pain.

Basically, everybody suffers, or more precisely, to quote the band REM, "everybody hurts"—it's not a country song, but it will do for now. And to tell the truth, I don't think I've ever met anybody who has never suffered. Sure, some people may suffer more than others, whatever suffering may be—but then again, some people eat more than others, play tennis more than others, laugh more than others, cry more than others—it's all relative. And obviously, as Native people, we are no strangers to the art of suffering. Five hundred years of colonization tends to do that to a people. But hopefully you do not have to spend ten years in a residential school, or several months in a rehab centre, in order to be recognized as a decent author.

Writers don't have to suffer to write, any more than we have to sneeze to write. We do, same as convenience store clerks, waitresses, and people who sell discount cigarettes. For some reason, people just expect us to.

That being said, I don't think I could imagine a world without suffering or pain. Geez, think of all the unemployed country singers that would result in. Now that would be a tragedy.

GOING TO AA (ACADEMICS ANONYMOUS)

Not that long ago, I found myself walking the halls of one of Canada's newest (and its first Aboriginal) universities, logically enough named First Nations University, but affectionately known as FNU (as we say in the humour business, the jokes about the acronyms just write themselves). The gentleman who was giving me the tour bumped into some of the faculty and introduced me. One woman said she didn't need an introduction— she knew of me and my work: "In fact, I use him in my human sexuality class." My first thought was ..., "As well you should." But alas, she was referring to some articles I had written about my research into Native erotica for a proposed NFB documentary. To me, this encounter was yet another example of my tenuous and immaterial relationship with the world of higher education.

I have two years of community college under my belt. Some might argue that it's not as good as four years of university, but at least it's better than two years less a day of someplace else. Yet because of my profession as a writer, I find myself constantly mired in the world of academia, surrounded by the pursuit of knowledge and understanding in an increasingly complex world, in which my train of thought frequently gets derailed.

Once when I was up in Prince George, BC, lecturing at the University of Northern British Columbia, I casually mentioned to a sea of fresh-faced students that as a writer I had no idea what postcolonialism or postmodernism were, nor did I care. It wasn't important to me. When I'm writing stories about my childhood, my family, or my adventures, putting technical or academic name tags on them somehow makes them less interesting or less personal. With my writing, it's a straightforward case of "I don't know how I do what I do, I just do it." How many traditional storytellers can deconstruct their pre-contact oral narratives? Perhaps the better question is, how many would want to?

After telling the English/Canadian literature class this, I got a round of surprisingly rousing, enthusiastic applause, about forty seconds' worth, from the students. Evidently the kids loved my disregard for what the professors were trying to drill into their young, impressionable minds. Afterwards, like a bad boy, I was metaphorically called into the principal's office, where one professor chewed me out for so flippantly dismissing two important components of modern English study. Evidently I was being blasphemous. To the best of my recollection I had not urged them to hang William Shakespeare or Michael Ondaatje in effigy, but this man with letters behind his name did not like what I had said. In fact, he felt I was implying that all this stuff the teachers were attempting to teach these kids was irrelevant and unnecessary. There was a chance, I was told, that they might believe me. This situation reminded me of a man I once met who told me he never takes medicine when he's sick. He just doesn't believe in it. He trusts Aspirin less than he trusts a cold. I, on the other hand, who heard him say these things, still take an Aspirin when I get a headache and talk to academics who put way too much emphasis on what I say and/or how I say it. But what do I know? I've never been to university.

But this unpleasant little confrontation did remind me of the time I was at a birthday party for a professor at York University a few years back, when I'd only had a half-dozen books or so published. This individual, who was understandably well-lubricated at his own party, stopped me on my way to the potato chips to engage me in an interesting bit of conversation. Basically, he said: "How can you, as a leading Native playwright and writer, validate your literary existence without having any academic credentials to support you?"

My first reaction was that I wished I'd gone for the popcorn instead of the potato chips, because they were in a completely different room. My second reaction was to say, "Well, for one thing, I prefer to work for a living," but I figured that would sound too mean-spirited. God knows, I wouldn't have wanted to start an all-out academic brawl—there'd be dangling participles, deconstructed paradigms, and theoretical pedagogy splattered on the walls before you knew it. Instead I excused myself and went to the bathroom where I wrote a treatise (as opposed to a treaty) on the effects the introduction of alcohol has on social birthday discourse. I'm hoping to get an honorary degree for it.

The bizarre thing is, I support, encourage, and celebrate all forms of higher education. Learning and academic achievement should never be discouraged. But neither should somebody sit in judgment on the direction your career is going based solely on your academic credentials. Should the day come when I have children, damn right they're going to university. Then maybe they'll explain what postmodernism and postcolonialism are to me. It will give us something to talk about over the holidays. Until then, I can wait.

LET'S HOPE IT WAS WORTH IT

It's finally official—as official as it can get until the cheques actually clear. One point nine billion dollars to the tens of thousands of Native people who were physically, sexually, and emotionally abused at residential schools by those in the service of God—hopefully it will provide a little bit of karmic closure. Perhaps. The deal will give the survivors a lump sum of $10,000 each, plus $3,000 for each year spent in the schools. That will buy a lot of therapy and Band-Aids, I suppose. It's better than the decades of runarounds survivors have experienced. But is that what this is really all about? What has me puzzled is the federal government seems to be footing all these compensation bills, and while it is more than culpable, I don't see many of the churches cracking open their chequebooks to help make this regrettable part of history go away any time soon.

I do recall that there have been some apologies from various religious denominations, but I have it on good authority that doesn't add up to much in a court of law. Maybe I'm a little cynical. Maybe I'm a lot cynical. We destroyed your life … sorry—that's about it. Geez, if life were that easy, I'd be a much happier man. It's that absolution of sins thing that probably allows them to sleep nights. I don't know if it would work for me.

I guess what's upsetting is the apparent contradiction of doing God's work, which on the surface seems good, and abusing children, which on the surface (and for quite a few layers below), seems bad. Granted, I haven't read the Bible cover to cover, but I've seen most of the movies, and watched 7th Heaven on television. So I have a working knowledge. Yet I must have missed the part where Christian beliefs endorsed and condoned such highly questionable behaviour. I thought I'd found a reference in the Gospel of Mark, 10:14, where it said something about "suffer the little children." But seriously guys, I don't think God meant that to be taken so literally. However, I'm not a theologian and maybe it's there somewhere between the lines. I never went to Bible study. Such situations also make me wonder about that phrase Christian people are urged to consider when faced with moral decisions: "What would Jesus do?" I certainly hope nothing like that with children.

Just recently, I read that a priest who had been relocated to Mexico was found guilty of abusing a lot of kids several decades ago. He was called to the Vatican where his wrist was slapped when his behaviour became unavoidable public knowledge. Then he was placed on leave and told to pray and seek forgiveness. That's about it. No demerits on his driver's licence. No rescinding of his library card. No being told to jog around the Vatican fifty times. Because of his age (he's in his eighties) and his declining health, it was thought some quiet pennance would be more humane.

I'm sure it was. But still, you know the old adage: "Spare the rod, spoil the priest."

Remember the good old days when it was quite common for devout families to give 10 percent of their income to the Church as a sign of belief? I think it was called a tithe. Wouldn't it be wonderful if the tables were turned and the Church had to give 10 percent of everything it took in to everybody it hurt? But I guess that makes too much sense, and heaven knows we can't have that. Instead, the federal government pays a large chunk of money out of everybody's taxes. Maybe that is why the gas prices went up so suddenly last month. That money has got to come from somewhere.

In 1876 AD, the new Dominion of Canada devised an interesting little document called The Indian Act. In 1960 AD, Native people were given the right to vote in their own country. In 1986 AD, Bill C-31 was passed, giving thousands of Native people back their Status. I guess we can add 2006 AD to the list of pivotal periods in Native history that affected us intensely, but did not originate from us. An entire industry has been built around protecting us, empowering us, abusing us, and compensating us. Talk about a micro-environment.

Ironically, for most Native people, we always thought, rightly or wrongly, the term AD meant After Death, and BC was believed to have meant Before Christ. Now I suppose they will mean After Dispensation and Before Compensation. Native people must and will change with the times. We have little choice in the matter.

Oh well, maybe I'm a little paranoid about this whole Church and compensation thing. But it does make you wonder what Jesus would do in this situation. Maybe he wouldn't know about it. Maybe he'd be like the CEOs in those big Enron and federal-sponsorship scandals. After all, he's way at the top, removed from the doings of those toiling along way below him, and just doesn't know what the little people who work for him are up to. I've been told a lot of religious organizations are run like corporations.

Never mind. I think I should just keep my mouth shut and maybe curl up tonight with a good book to take my mind of things. I have it on good authority The Da Vinci Code is really interesting.

WHAT'S AN INDIAN WORTH THESE DAYS?

You may not have noticed it yet, it's so subtle, but trust me, it's happening. If you take the time to pick up on it, you'll notice there seems to be a shift in Canadian society's perception of Native people. Believe it or not, we seem to be a lot richer these days. In fact, a lot of mainstream Canadians are under the impression that many of us are substantially well off.

That's news to us. Even moreso, it's somewhat of a shocking surprise, considering only twenty or so years ago we were considered the tragic, poverty-stricken, forgotten, and victimized segment of this country's population. Practically the shame of Canada. A lot has changed in the last decade or so. The problem is, we didn't notice it had happened.

In the collective memory of most Canadians, our Reserves are little more than Aboriginal wastelands, dirt roads awash with abandoned cars and three-legged dogs. There were hundreds of our communities that existed far below the poverty line, and their residents, victims of a social system that doomed them to fail, at best, marginally existed. Substandard housing, poor diets, lacklustre health care, indifferent governmental bureaucracy, all were to blame for the dire economic straits our people were condemned to live in. We were the fourth world—an oppressed nation within a nation. We led bleak and pitiful lives.

But luckily, happy days are here again! According to word on the street, we all are dripping in money. What a difference a few years can make. I even heard one person ask a friend of mine, "So, what are you going to do with all the money you're getting?"

"Money from what?" my friend asked.

"Oh, you guys are getting money from everywhere. It's in all the papers."

Evidently, when I wasn't looking, our standard of living suddenly rose so high it went through the roof. I definitely must read those papers more often. I say this because on more than one occasion now, I too have talked with numerous people of non-Native ancestry who are of the strong belief that Native people are currently riding a wave of substantial financial success. They are convinced prosperity now smells of sweetgrass and buckskin. Alas, the papers notwithstanding, my accountant and I both know the sad truth.

Public perception says that because of such notable sources of finance as free post-secondary education; royalties from casino, oil, and mineral rights; and residential school payments, Native people are sitting pretty. We're pricing Tom Thomson paintings and drinking subtle, yet powerful chablis.

Due to a cap on post-secondary school education that was established back in 1989, Native people do not have a free ride in universities and colleges. Contrary to popular belief, Native youth do not have unlimited financial support (though it's a nice thought), and most have to claw and scratch their way through the pillars of higher education like other non-Native people. Each band sets its own education policy, so statistics can vary wildly from community to community. In some areas, only 25 percent of college students receive Band funding, and only 15 percent at the university level, though some Reserves do have a higher support rate. There is often a waiting list, and the living allowance for post-secondary students, $675 a month, hasn't changed in decades. Keep in mind the dropout rate in most First Nations high schools is double, and sometimes triple the national average. Also, for those who do qualify for Band assistance, Reserves sometimes give a limit of four years to achieve whatever degree or diploma they intend to pursue before their funding is cut. Additionally, Native students are expected to locate other sources of educational support, like most people from our colour-challenged society must do. The road to a bachelor's or master's degree is not paved with gold. Culturally, we never had roads, or gold.

Luxurious royalties pouring in from casinos are another collective public fantasy. In Ontario, the money coming from Casino Rama, for example, has more strings tied to it than a government arts grant (I speak as an artist). First of all, casino money is constantly in flux. Payments vary constantly, depending on how well people lose annually, so it's hard to budget for what each yearly cheque will bring in. Additionally, the payment can only be utilized by five branches of Reserve governments: education, economic development, infrastructure and capital, culture and language, and health. Distribution of casino royalties to individuals on a per-capita basis is illegal.

Also, the casino royalties distributed to each separate community varies anywhere from approximately $15,000 to over $50,000, depending on a simple formula: 50 percent of the estimated payment is allocated to the community; a further 40 percent is tied to the population of the band; and the other 10 percent depends on the community's remoteness. Again, Aboriginal pockets are not overflowing with those orange and green bills, never mind the brown ones.

As for oil and mineral rights, only a handful of Aboriginal communities across Canada have successfully managed to maintain ownership of those lucrative properties, mostly in Alberta. In the last few days, several people from the Ardach Algonquin First Nations were released from jail, after spending two months there for protesting against the exploration of minerals in their back yard, and their lack of legal standing in this rapidly growing issue.

Residential school payments would perhaps be the subject of the most laughable misunderstandings, if the situation weren't so tragic. About 78,000 former students across Canada are eligible for compensation, a substantial number of them passing away each year—this, while as many as 21,000 claims are still being processed. However, it's still not a cakewalk for survivors of those schools. The Federation of Saskatchewan Indian Nations reports that more than 2,300 people have been rejected in that province alone. Each survivor gets a flat $10,000 if they attended a school, with an additional three grand for every year they spent there. Also, there is extra money if you can prove you were physically abused there—each claimant must provide such proof, in whatever way they can. So when you take into consideration that, according to the 2001 census, there are over 1.3 million people who self-identify as Aboriginal in Canada, the numbers really don't justify the creation of an Aboriginal Billionaires' Club. Yet. Hope springs eternal though, especially in Native communities.

I wonder if the people of Kashechewan in Northern Ontario know how well off they are. They're not abandoning their homes every year because they are fleeing a flooding river, they're actually going to Turks and Caicos to work on their tans and look more Aboriginal. Every Native person who's anybody goes there—everyone knows that, don't they? Lubicon Lake has a five-star hotel, I hear, near the polo grounds. And that place in Saskatchewan where those two little girls froze to death, never mind what the papers said about them—they were downhill skiing at the Reserve Resort.

All this just goes to show the damage that misinformation about a people can cause. It reminds me of the time I was having a conversation with two people of the Jewish persuasion in Toronto one day. For some strange reason, we had been commenting on that tiresome rumour that Jews secretly (or not so secretly) run the world, especially its finances. One of my friends said to the other: "Oh, by the way, did you get your world-domination cheque this week?"

"Yes, but I had to turn most of it over to my ex-wife," said the other. "Forgot to put that in the pre-nup."

I mentioned this growing rumour/belief to several First Nations friends of mine. They burst out laughing, including the chief of my Reserve—that's perhaps the best response.

NOT-SO-SECRET SOCIETIES

The year 2000 doesn't seem all that long ago. We were all a little bit younger, waiting for the Y2K computer crash to end the world. We would have gone from using BlackBerries to communicate to eating them to live. Well, the world didn't end, but something really amazing occurred down here in Ann Arbor, Michigan. I wish I'd been here then. I'm here now, at the University of Michigan as the writer-in-residence for the semester. And I heard a story that involves one of those things you hear about all the time, but don't actually think exist, or have anything to do with you, directly or indirectly. It's about a "semi-secret and self-selecting honorary society" for university senior men. Rich White students who loved to dress up as Indians, but who wouldn't allow Indians to join them to dress up as Indians.

In 1902, a group of White men, twenty-five of the best "leaders" on campus, formed an organization based on service to and pride in the university. Their strong sense of institutional honour and prestige was enhanced through their creation of a savage warrior ideal, based on stereotypical and romantic images of American Indian men. The leadership dubbed itself the "tribe of Michiganua," and began a legacy of adopting images, rituals, and artifacts of Native American peoples into the identity of their organization. They hung out in a part of the university donated to them by a former alumnus (and there's a plaque on the wall honouring him), a guy known as the "Great Scalper," Fielding Yost. A letter from him dated 1933 states, "and now Michiganua plans its own home, a real wigwam." This was a large room located on the seventh floor of one of the university buildings—ground zero for one of the most bizarre organizations I have ever heard about.

Stories still abound about faculty and students walking down the street, hearing the most unsettling chanting and singing coming from the open windows of this "wigwam" as the adherents of the society conducted their initiations and meetings. Supposedly, though it's hard to confirm, these members would dress up in pseudo-Indian clothing, in a room wallpapered with birch bark, adorned with Aboriginal kitsch and some legitimate, though tragic, Native artifacts, and do whatever it is semi-secret societies do behind closed doors. According to a roster that's been found, each member had a unique Native nickname. They ranged from "Squaw Give 'um Itch Pantowach" to "Face in Fur Hennigar" to "Squaw Stalker Sharp." What is that old saying? "Boys will be boys?"

All this changed in 2000 when a group of concerned students "raided" and liberated the place. They were called the Students of Colour Coalition. The group was composed of students from various ethnic backgrounds— Native, Black, Asian, and Latino. They occupied the site for three weeks, took photographs, and began cataloguing objects found in the room, including what appeared to be an authentic ceremonial pipe and a photo showing a Michiganua member holding it in one hand and a beer in the other.

When I first came to Ann Arbor, I thought to myself, "What a cute little university town." But like Peyton Place, you never know what you'll find beneath the surface. Part of me, the part that likes to rubberneck on the highway as I pass a car accident, would love to have seen that room. Reportedly it was quite tacky. Another part of me, the politically correct part, is aghast that such an institution existed for almost a hundred years.

Now, I would like to point out here that while I'm highlighting one isolated organization's prostitution of Aboriginal culture in these august halls, other than that, my time here at the University of Michigan has been very well received and I've enjoyed my residency quite a lot. There is a vibrant Native students' organization on campus, and the curriculum includes classes in conversational Ojibway. Any university that offers conversational Ojibway can't be all bad. And the teacher is from my Reserve, proving this place is even more civilized. Given the chance, I would return here in a second.

But still, the thought of an organization such as the Michiganua persisting into our modern era is quite disconcerting. So, on pondering this issue, two possible avenues of response seemed obvious. The first, which is what the Students of Colour Coalition did: direct, decisive action at the crux of the situation—and it worked in this case. The second: copying the idea and just doing it better than them. I call this the "Asian car-making strategy."

I think all universities, whether in Canada or the United States, with a sizable Native student population, should set up their own version of the Michiganua. Picture it if you will—Chuganosh Clubs (CC for short), where Native people dress up in three-piece suits and they have evening gowns for the ladies. They stand around singing bad imitations of opera, reading the *Wall Street Journal*, giving each other standard Chuganosh (Caucasians in Ojibway) titles like "CEO Kakagamic," or "Chairman of the Board Cardinal," or "Guest Conductor Toulouse," or "Cheats on His Taxes Maracle."

It's so silly, it might actually be fun!

WHEN DID GETTING A GLASS OF WATER BECOME SO COMPLICATED?

India and Canada have many things in common. For instance, both are members of the British Commonwealth and both have prime ministers. Both are surrounded on three sides by water. Both have lots of "Indians." And unfortunately, in many places, both have a boil-water advisory in effect. For Indians.

Kashechewan is not located in India. In fact, it's the name of a Cree community located on the Ontario shore of Hudson Bay. It is a name that, I think I could safely say, was unknown to 99.9 percent of Canadians until a few years ago. That was when the country became aware that the quality of their water had made life unbearable and downright dangerous. That's when it also became a pawn in the battle between the Ontario and federal governments over jurisdiction, responsibility, and who could get the better public relations opportunity from this community's, shall we say, "unfortunate" circumstance.

Normally when you think of Native people and water, something to do with canoeing pops into your mind. Rivers and lakes were, after all, traditionally used by First Nations people to travel from place to place in canoes. Now, however, because of the bad water in Kashechewan, practically the entire population of that community has travelled, ironically this time by plane, to a half-dozen communities across the province for refuge. They have travelled many kilometres merely to gargle. Through no fault of their own, they have become a sort of Indigenous diaspora ... which may or may not be a contradiction in terms.

But what to do? Last month all the premiers met in Kelowna, British Columbia, at a first minister's conference, along with the leaders of the major Aboriginal organizations, to discuss this and other related issues. No doubt on all their tables were nicely filled bottles of chilled and distilled water. Many would argue that's all the Kashechewan people wanted. At least for a brief period, all of our political leaders had water on the brain. In Ontario alone, it was recently reported that thirty-four Native communities had posted some sort of water warning. So if these statistics are correct, somewhere, quite probably within driving distance of where you are reading this now, turning on the tap can possibly endanger your life. Taking a shower? Potentially suicidal. Brushing your teeth? Instead of Russian roulette, Canadian roulette. It is a truly scary thought. Death by water.

For a country with the largest fresh-water resources in the world, a conference like this could seem unnecessary, even indulgent. But times have changed. Remember that old treaty saying: "As long as the rivers flow and the grass grows?" Well the grass is now genetically modified, and the water is still flowing but you can't drink it. I guess it's an aesthetic thing. You know those government guidelines suggesting you drink eight glasses of water a day ... did you ever think you'd see the day when eight glasses of Coke might be considered safer?

The final result of the conference? The promise of millions of dollars of financial aid to Native communities across Canada. I wonder if it will be the same amount of money that was spent to plan, orchestrate, and hold the conference. One can't help think it would have probably been better just to not hold the conference, and hand over that money to the Native people. Eliminate the middle-man. But regardless, from what I understand, none of those financial promises is concrete. It's more of a conditional promise right now. Most of it is dependent on the Liberals getting back into power.

Let's hope at least the premiers managed to come through with those grandiose promises of money and other fabulous things to make our lives easier. After all, it's been several months—the people of Kashechewan are probably getting kind of thirsty. And let's face it, the governments' track records haven't exactly been the best. A lot of us Native people are still waiting for the full implementation of the Royal Commission on Aboriginal Affairs recommendations, which was released almost ten years ago.

Speaking as a Native Aboriginal First Nations Indigenous Person (NAFNIP, to my friends), let's say I'm hoping more than idle promises will come out of that conference. Just like the water in Kashechewan, those promises are getting kind of hard to swallow.

BLACK AND WHITE AND RED ALL OVER

I am sure everybody felt the same way I did when I first heard the news. Two children on the Yellow Quill First Nation in Saskatchewan froze to death, clad only in t-shirts and diapers. The reason? A drunken father, it would appear. A drunken Native father to be specific. Once the shock of the news wears off, another equally unappetizing thought occurs to me. Once more, the dominant culture's impression of Native people will be reinforced. Native people + alcohol = tragedy. Definitely an unhappy equation. Some would call it the algebra of marginalization.

Canadians (and quite probably Americans too) may not consciously think thoughts like that. Or maybe they do. But I know they are there, not far below the surface. Like a grave.

I really don't know enough of what happened in that faraway community to offer an opinion on the situation, other than the obvious. The facts are still coming out. Evidently the community had been struggling with substance abuse problems for a number of years and these two children were just the latest casualties. It has been said that children are too often the first victims in such situations. Some might call it a war between what was and what should be.

Astronomers often talk about still being able to see, using special telescopes, shock waves from the Big Bang, an event that created the universe fifteen billion years ago. Some might consider misfortunes like these shock waves from a different kind of Big Bang, 516 years ago.

Luckily these kinds of tragedies are few and far between. Granted, other Native people have frozen to death in the cold Prairie winter. Neil Stonechild comes to mind, a man who was taken to an abandoned field outside of Saskatoon, relieved of his coat and shoes, and told to walk back to the city by the police. He never made it. There were no drunken fathers involved in that situation, just non-Native cops. Many people, especially Native people, now think this is a regular occurrence—that there is a constabulary shuttle service of sorts between urban and rural areas existing in all major Canadian communities and Natives should beware. But unfortunately, many Canadians will think the Yellow Quill tragedy happens all the time in Native communities, because of this one incident.

It's the power of prejudice, of media reinforcement, of painting with broad brushes. This brush was populated with well over a million bristles, according to the last census.

It seems a thousand years ago that I left my Reserve to attend college in Toronto. I was young, unsophisticated, unknowing in the ways of the outside world. But I was armed with cowboy boots, a metro pass, and an eagerness to see what the country of Canada outside my sleepy little Reserve had to offer. (I must point out here that, incidentally, and to my knowledge, there is no case of anybody freezing to death in Curve Lake in recorded history, drunk, sober, or narcoleptic.)

So, during my first year, I found myself sharing a house with several people. One of my new roommates, who became my closest friend for many years, came from a town near Sudbury, an exotic place called Falconbridge. After I had moved in, he informed his family up north about me, and that I was Native. I still remember him telling me that his older sister, an average middle-class Caucasian like himself, had cautioned him about letting me move in, because, "you know how Indians like to drink!" If memory serves me correctly, he got drunk just as frequently as I did, if not more. But this being college, I'm sure our statistics were skewed.

At the time, I was puzzled by my friend's sister's immediate and controversial concerns about me and my presumed vices, but I just chalked it up to weird things White people say. I just put blind faith in the benevolence of a people who invented Tasers.

When, several months later, I was introduced to her, I casually brought up her sight-unseen assessment of me, looking for further clarification. Flustered, she immediately chewed her brother out for daring to tell me what she said, then tried to justify her original statement by adding, "Well, up where we are, Indians do tend to have a drinking problem." Since then, I've been up to Sudbury quite a few times, and have done some field research in a few bars, especially those patronized by local miners, and wouldn't you believe it, there were few dark-skinned faces to be seen in that hard-drinking crowd. So I can't help wonder who was doing all that hard drinking? I wonder what she would have to say about that.

Actually, I don't hold a grudge. If anything, I am somewhat grateful for what my roommate's sister said. Since that long-ago time, I have travelled to sixteen countries around the world, doing talks about Native culture, identity, humour, and literature. I frequently mention her and what I must assume is her amazing clairvoyant perception of me when I talk about the innate racism that sometimes exists under Canada's calm and cool exterior. It's generated much interesting discussion and I appreciate that. I must buy her a drink next time I see her.

True, that was way back in the early 1980s, and I'm sure a few naive optimists believe that things have changed since then. God bless them. It makes me want to ask them, "What colour is the sky in your world?" Or maybe, more accurately, "What colour is skin in your world?"

In geological times, a quarter of a century is a millisecond. Not even a blink of an eye. The same can be said about how long it takes for attitudes to change. In a nearby restaurant/tavern close to my community, my girlfriend overheard somebody discussing with a waitress the possibility of holding a wake in this working-class establishment. The waitress thought this was odd and jokingly asked, "Is the guy Irish?"

The man said, "Actually he was part Native." Almost immediately, most of the patrons in the restaurant/bar burst out laughing. And it wasn't a pleasant laugh. Once more, I don't have any recollection of any Native person ever having had a wake in a restaurant/tavern. It must have been his White side wanting that. Maybe his White side was Irish, after all. You know how they like to drink.

I don't think people are laughing in Yellow Quill. Once those poor girls are buried, the legacy of their passing will unfortunately live longer than they did. You have to wonder.

It's been a bad week for children overall. A young girl is abandoned in a Toronto parking facility—she looked to be of African-Canadian extraction. Two kids, left in a car in minus-twenty-seven-degree Calgary for over half an hour, while the mother ran "errands." No comment on their nationality. But I bet you, these two incidents will be forgotten way before what happened to the two girls in Yellow Quill.

THE NEW LEXICON

With the growing complexity of everyday life on the globe, the once solid and stationary world of the North American First Nations has had to adapt and evolve. Over the years, Aboriginal Nations have had to find ways of translating words like AIDS, the Internet, and satellite, just to name a few, into their own unique tongues. In order to preserve their language, the Inuit are particularly adamant about finding Inuit translations for modern terminology. For instance, a television satellite becomes *qangattaqtitausimajuq*, which literally translates as: "it has been made to fly," and the computer becomes *qarasaasiaq*, a "little artificial brain."

Part of that evolution has been additions and augmentations to this language that we have been forced to use—English. New phrases and concepts are constantly being created as a way of describing the changing face of being Native in the twenty-first century. Language, like everything else, evolves. Below are some of the newer First Nations-related terms currently being bandied about out there in our communities and cities.

The Identity Wars

I came across this one at Michigan State University. It is in reference to the situation facing two faculty/staff associations for people of Native ancestry on campus. One association had in its original founding documents a clause restricting membership to only those faculty or staff who were members of federally recognized tribes, or had the Bureau of Indian Affairs equivalent. After four years, some members wanted to add a clause that allowed those faculty/staff who could show "community recognition" to become members and hold office in the organization. The entrenched association members were reluctant, prompting some of the disaffected to start up another faculty/staff group with bylaw membership language that is more inclusive. As a result, there is much animosity between the two groups. One association is under investigation for "maintaining a persistent and pervasive campaign of ethnic intimidation which has created a hostile world environment." It should also be mentioned that two other phrases from this dispute can be added to the new Lexicon: "Melanin Police," which refers to those who are in a position to assess who looks Native and who doesn't; and "Ethnic Fraud"—somebody of mixed-blood ancestry who fundamentally embraces their Native heritage, but physically looks more European.

Indiginate/Indigenize

The practice of taking rituals or objects from another culture, usually the dominant one, and giving it an Aboriginal overhaul. A form of reverse cultural appropriation. For instance, making spaghetti with a moose bolognese sauce. More sadly, rumour has it that somewhere in the Western provinces, somebody is putting together an *Aboriginal Idol* contest.

More-nig

Again, I came across this term in America—along the eastern seaboard. On a visit to the area, I was inquiring about the local Native population, and its proximity to the city I was visiting—I always like to search out and visit nearby Native communities when I'm on the road. I was given some rough directions, but warned not to expect too much. "They're more-nigs." Not being familiar with the tribe, I mentioned that I had never heard the term before.

"It means they're more nigger than Indian. More-nigs."

Once I got over my shock, I understood the historical significance of the word, as offensive as it might be. For hundreds of years, many escaped slaves would seek asylum in Native communities where White men often feared to tread. In such circumstances, a little DNA transfer can be expected. It also seems natural that two of America's most marginalized populations should find comfort and understanding in each other's arms. It's often quite easy to see, more than in Canada, African-American features at many American pow wows.

Marry-ons

It is a dismissive and derogatory term. Marry-ons refers to, specifically, non-Native women who marry Native men. It has more of a Reserve application than an urban one. However, it has less of an impact in the post-Bill C-31 age when non-Native women no longer get Status upon marriage and the issue has become less volatile.

Oddly enough, I have never heard it used to refer to White men who marry Native women. Yet.

The New Buffalo

This term has sprung from the American Plains and the Canadian Prairies. And of all things, it refers to casinos. For untold millennia, Native people in these regions relied on the buffalo for their very existence. The buffalo was so integral to their way of life, virtually every part of the animal was utilized. Many believe it was the systematic destruction of the vast buffalo herds that allowed for the conquest of the Lakota, the Cree, the Métis, and many other tribes dependent on its bounty.

In today's society, casinos are now the cash cow—or better yet, the cash buffalo for many Native communities. For some, they have become the main source of survival and success in perilous economic times. "New Buffalos" has become such a catch-phrase that recently there was a conference in, of all places, Europe, on American Indian casinos called, simply, The New Buffalo.

Two Teepees of Separation

This is in obvious reference to the more popular variation of "six degrees of separation." The chance that two Native people, be they from different provinces or parts of the country, might know each other or somebody the other person knows, is astronomically more probable than in the general population. Normal greetings among Native people also make the chances of that discovery more likely. Indigenous introductions usually begin with any variation of, "Where are you from?" or "Who are your parents?" (or if off-Reserve) "Where do you work?" With those three items of information, a network of geographic, familial, and vocational contacts makes itself immediately obvious.

This belief even works on different continents with different Indigenous groups. Several months ago I was in Australia, sitting on a small island at a bar, having some lunch and drinks with some local Aboriginals. One commented that he spent a couple months living on the Six Nations Reserve in Ontario. I asked with whom and he told me. I knew the wife of the man he had been staying with. I hadn't talked to her in years, but in Australia I managed to catch up on her life.

MUSING ABOUT MUSEUMS

I admit it, I'm a big fan of museums, and have been fortunate enough to visit museums all over the world and see some amazing things within their walls. Twice I've been to one of the most amazing in the world—the British Museum in London. I've stood a scant few feet from the Rosetta Stone, the amazing chunk of rock discovered by Napoleon's troops that helped decipher the ancient Egyptian hieroglyphs. And just because I know all this doesn't necessarily make me a geek.

Interestingly enough, on that same floor was an exhibit featuring Canadian Kwakwaka'wakw canoes, clothing, and artifacts. The juxtaposition of those two diverse cultures was quite interesting. I guess that's one of the amazing things about having a worldwide empire, you can bring everything the world has to offer in both time and space into one humongous building. Of course the flipside of it is, a worldwide empire has the power to take anything it wants from you, remove it, and house it in a single building on the other side of the world. The Greek government is still trying to get the Elgin Marbles back, a series of marble sculptures taken from the Parthenon in Athens by a British guy named ... Elgin.

Native people are no strangers to depatriation. There are smatterings of totem poles, medicine bundles, canoes, and bones spread across most of Europe (and let's not forget some of the finer museums on this very continent) that are currently the focus of repatriation efforts. Many of these objects were taken from their owners in less-than-hospitable circumstances. While standing there in the British Museum, I couldn't help wondering if I could possibly stuff one of those war canoes in my luggage and take it back to Canada. It would have beaten the hell out of a duty-free chocolate bar.

More recently, I've been spending time in Washington, DC, at the Smithsonian National Museum of the American Indian. It's a whole building dedicated to celebrating America's Aboriginal history; past, present, and future. Whereas most museums have an unusual fondness for dead and departed things, the NMAI's mandate seems to lean more towards highlighting living cultures. It's quite cool. And as all people know, the measure of any institution, whether in Canada, the USA, or elsewhere in the world, is the cleanliness and hospitality of its bathrooms and cafeterias. People may forget an excellent and fascinating exhibit of creation stories from across Turtle Island, but you give them a messy toilet and crappy food, and that's all they will remember. Tourists, like me, can be so shallow.

However, quite intelligently, the cafeteria is part of this museum's cultural allure. It's like a food court, but with food from all over the Americas, broken down culturally. There's the Northwest Coast station, which offered cedar-planked fire-roasted juniper salmon with oyster stew, made with acorn squash and wild leeks, or a seaweed and wild mushroom salad. The Northern Woodlands station (my neck of the continental woods) offered roasted crab apple and pumpkin soup or free-range rabbit soup, the main course being either a maple-brine roasted turkey with cranberry relish, or a traditional mincemeat pie consisting of venison, black barley, dried fruits layered in flakey pastry shell, served with a port huckleberry sauce. Kind of puts that burger and fries I get up the street at home to shame.

Obviously most of the foods being served there are supposed to arouse Indigenous taste buds, but oddly, the little bottles of wine being offered were generic Californian. I asked if any Native communities in the States had ever had wineries, and received a bewildered look. Evidently not. That's where I did my little bit for Canadian Aboriginal cross-border selling and told them about the Okanagan Band that's been running a successful winery for years. Hopefully they'll get a few bottles in.

The weirdest aspect of my trip to Washington and its museum came the night before I left. After my reading, I went out for dinner with a couple that I'd met on previous trips there. He's Lakota and they both work for the government and attend all Native functions, even Canadian ones.

So there we are, having dinner at a Thai restaurant, and I should have figured something weird was afoot. The man brought his current wife, and his first wife. There were three of them. Man, ex-wife, and current wife, all sitting together having an amiable dinner with me. Very unusual. But here's the strange part—throughout the conversation, I asked the first wife what she did, and quite seriously (I'm not joking) she said she worked for the CIA. I looked at the man and he nodded. I figured, who else are you going to meet in Washington?

So I took a sip of my wine to ponder this unusual development and that's the last thing I remember. I woke up in a cab on the way to the airport, luggage all packed, trying to figure out what happened and that's when I remember, quite dimly though, answering questions, mostly about the Band Office on my Reserve. You see, my aunt is married to the chief, and I have an aunt and uncle on the council.

That's when I got that cold, sweaty feeling. The CIA now knows the deep, dark secrets of the Curve Lake Band, chief, and council. What have I done?

COMPENSATION FOR EVERYONE

As most Canadians are no doubt aware, many victims of Canada's residential school system are receiving financial compensation for years of physical, sexual, and cultural abuse from the government and God's representatives on earth. For most of the twentieth century, generations of Aboriginal kids were taken away by government agencies and farmed out to large authoritarian residential schools, run by a hodge-podge of religious denominations: usually Roman Catholic, Anglican, and United.

Most people—Native and non-Native—would agree this was a grievous and abominable practice. Or so I thought. A few years ago, I wrote a column about the June 29 First Nations Day of Protest where I said "WE DEMAND the federal government apologize to survivors for over half a century of abuse at the hands (and other body parts) of residential schools. There are just some things children should not learn in school." I and many Native writers believed this apology (and the compensation package) were long overdue. Finally it was delivered by Prime Minister Harper, and was accepted by Canada's First Nations. The healing was beginning.

One reader had a spectacularly different perspective on the issue. In a letter to the editor of the *Peterborough Examiner*, Zoltan Bank wrote, and I am paraphrasing: "Many residential school residents are now receiving cash settlements for being sexually victimized by a few bad apple priests/teachers. What is missing are some letters from Native Indians who praise the White man for his generosity financially and otherwise to educate them when they were children. Many of them have found good jobs over the years after being educated free by the White man. It is dishonest and not fair; all we hear from them are the few sexual cases being compensated but nobody thanks us for their free education. Our ancestors did not have to do it; it was due to their good religious hearts."

Could this man be right? Are we overlooking the obvious? Over all, are we, the Indigenous people of this country, better off? Does the cost of this attempt to save the child by destroying the savage within through cultural genocide and systematic pedophilia justify, years later, the additional cost of supersizing their former students' McDonald's Happy Meals? But before we can explore our own situation, let us look to the dominant ethnic cultures to see how they fared in our exploitation wars.

After all, this whole apology/compensation thing could backfire and bite us in the ass.

In 1876 when Custer and the 7th Cavalry were wiped out by a combination of Lakota, Cheyenne, and a variety of similarly disgruntled Natives, it could have potentially set the stage for its own compensation case. The descendents of those over 250 men could, today, potentially sue the Lakota

Nation, amongst others, for emotional distress, demanding financial compensation and apologies. Stranger things have happened.

Here in Canada, look at the legions of Jesuits who, in the sixteenth and seventeenth centuries, came to the New World determined to spread the Word of God, and as a result, got a little hot under the collar when they met with resistance and a bonfire. Maybe the Catholic Church, in a bit of "turnabout is fair play," could demand some compensation from the Iroquois and other Nations for the trauma suffered by that particular sect. It could be viewed simply as a case of "what's good for the goose is good for the gander." But of course, this case would be complicated enormously by the fact that none of those Jesuits had any descendants—at least none that they would know of or admit to. Evidently, Jesuits don't breed. Vows of abstinence have more than one drawback.

So who knows? Maybe Zoltan has a case. Don't get us wrong. We do praise the White man for the education he gave us. We praise him for educating Native lawyers who have allowed us to pursue and win this case; for educating our doctors and psychiatrists who are helping to deal with the recovery; and for educating us to write about what has happened, what is happening, and what should happen in a "just society."

Thanks, Zoltan.

ABORIGINAL HOT AND HEAVY

Years ago I had a female friend whose life ambition—well, one of them anyway—was to write a book detailing the hundred most beautiful places in the world to make love. Needless to say, I was very eager to co-write that book with her, but alas, both it and the woman disappeared into the mists of what might have happened. Still, I thought it was a very cool idea at the time, and, upon reflection, I still wonder if writing such a book might be possible.

For obvious reasons, I would attempt to approach the project from an Aboriginal perspective, and select a title like: *The 100 Most Beautiful First Nations in Which to Make Love*. I can't really say how popular it would be, but it would still be fun to put together: I could write about the austere beauty of Saskatchewan's Gordon's Reserve; I could wax poetic on the oolichan-scented breeze of Hartley Bay; or try my luck with a passionate moment bathed in the lights of Casino Rama. I could even write the whole thing off as a business expense. My accountant would like that.

We all know the topic of love is there waiting to be explored in all cultures. But alas, for reasons unknown, Native people don't have a particularly strong reputation for eroticism, which is not only unfortunate, but demonstrably wrong—a gross oversight about which something should definitely be done. For instance, we have the highest birth rate in the country, so we obviously know a few things about bumping canoes. So it's time to lift that blanket a bit.

Now, at a safe historical distance, it is known that many of our legends, particularly those involving Nanabush or other Trickster representations, were extremely erotic and graphic. In fact, some were downright bawdy, and enacted—ritually and otherwise—scenes that would put most porn stars to shame. Unfortunately, however, during what I refer to as the age of the CCE (Canadian Christian Era), many of these stories were discouraged, abandoned, rewritten, and even outlawed as being obscene, leaving many with the impression that all traditional Native legends were just cute stories for children. And while some were, many weren't.

These inaccurate perceptions about the hot and heavy Indigene need to be addressed, and in this day and age of instant media and communication, the sooner that happens the better. I have a few suggestions as to how to better celebrate and perpetuate (if that's the proper word) a better appreciation of First Nations sexuality.

First of all, almost everybody is familiar with the bikini wax known as a "Brazilian," because of those high-cut bikini bottoms they like to wear down in the southern half of the Americas. Let's Indigenize it, and give it a local cultural resonance in the northern half. Instead, let's get an

"Ojibway" up here, which would be in the shape of a dreamcatcher. (I know it would involve some intricate and detailed work, but Aboriginally well worth it). Or maybe an "Inuit," in the shape of an inukshuk, which traditionally stood as a guidepost for travellers. The metaphor works. Or how about a "Haida," shaped like a salmon swimming upstream to spawn. Once more, if the metaphor fits, why not wear it?

What's got me thinking about all this is that just a few weeks ago, the national media reported that there may soon be a Canadian "adult" cable network coming to a television near you, with at least 50 percent Canadian content. Pretty soon, "paddling your canoe" and "he shoots, he scores" could have whole new meanings. The Canadianizing of porn—it kind of boggles the mind, doesn't it? Will a "99" replace the popularity of a "69"? Will maple syrup supersede whipped cream? And will our national symbol ... the beaver ... change in our imagination? Anything is possible in our wired world.

Why should Native people be left behind in this digital revolution? Granted, this is a very sticky subject. Many in our community probably believe that porn may not be the best career choice to help re-establish our independence and fiscal autonomy. Is the illegal sale of cigarettes a better solution to our economic woes? Nudity versus cancer—I wonder if the Assembly of First Nations needs to have a referendum on this. Sadly, these economic opportunities do not actually reek of cultural significance. But then, simply put, vice pays. We all know that. Everybody does.

This new broadcast opportunity could also create a number of potentially lucrative series ideas for APTN (the Aboriginal Peoples Television Network). We could start running shows like *The Bushcombers* or *North of 69*. (Don't get me started on the *Poundmaker* and *Big Bear* mini-series.) Once more, anything is possible.

I know this is a controversial issue. But I once compiled a book about Native sexuality called *Me Sexy*, where I said that often the impression the dominant culture has about anything to do with Aboriginal sexuality is limited to dead hookers, high rates of STDs in our communities, and instances of residential school sexual abuse.

Unfortunately some of that is true, but that's also kind of like saying all White people are Latvian. And believe it or not, we Aboriginals tend to have a little more fun with sexuality than the media would have you know. If you don't believe me, I will personally prove it to you.

RACIAL PROFILING—THE LOGIC

Increasingly of late, the local media has been hounding the Toronto Police Department about its supposed tendency to racially profile certain members of the public. The practice is grounded in a belief that people of certain races are more inclined to exhibit anti-social and criminal behaviour in our society. And it's an accusatory stain that seems to follow our beloved men in blue. Much like UFOs and government involvement in the Kennedy assassination, the authorities say it doesn't exist, but most people believe the truth of the matter is out there for everyone to see. As do I.

Personally, I believe that denying racial profiling exists is the public's way of ignoring the truth. People are afraid to even contemplate the idea that there might actually be substance to this idea. I say this because I would like to take this opportunity to formally say that I believe in racial profiling. It works. There is a logic behind it. Dogs run faster than chickens. Pigeons fly better than trout. Accountants add better than writers. Kids play more hockey than professional hockey players. While there are exceptions to these rules, I dare you to argue this is generally not true.

So as an amateur student of history, it's rather obvious to me that certain races do tend to be more problematic or socially disruptive than others. I know it may be politically incorrect to say so, but sometimes you've just got to say what you believe. The facts don't lie. As a Native person, I can only look back to our long-vanished brothers from Newfoundland, the long-departed Beothuks. They were driven out of existence by a certain race of people—let's call them the colour-challenged—in the last half of this millennium. Now the Beothuks exist simply as memories. Were any alive today, I'm sure they would agree that racial profiling existed in their case.

Further out across the oceans of space and time, I look at the well-documented raping and pillaging of the British Isles a thousand years ago by an offshoot of that same northern pigment-denied population from that land across the water. The death of six million Jews, and several million others sixty-odd years ago, again were caused by those very same continental People of Pallor. Are you beginning to notice a trend developing here? The historic and ongoing abduction, removal, subjugation, and exploitation of several million African people for this blue-and green-eyed people's own economic reasons further strengthens my convictions.

Try and find a country on this planet that wasn't at some point, "discovered" and colonized by these very same people over the last several thousand years, its Indigenous people and their culture oppressed, depressed and suppressed, its resources appropriated, all in the name of Manifest Destiny. Many times, the country in question—thousands of miles away from their country of origin—finds itself renamed to reflect in some way the conqueror's birthplace. As you can tell, from the splendidly consistent example of these people, you begin to understand the historical substance behind racial profiling. I'm surprised they're still not all arrested on sight. Maybe that's because here in Canada, they tend to blend in with the snowy background too easily.

Now some might argue that I'm being unfair by lumping all the different cultures of Europe (rumour has it that's where they come from) into one big mixing bowl, and further, mixing my metaphors, painting them with too broad of a brush. Perhaps I should be a little more considerate, especially as a Native writer who has spent a career battling the concept of "pan-Indianism." However, it does occur to me to wonder if, when a melanin-challenged police officer stops a Black person, it ever occurs to them to ask, "Excuse me, are you Jamaican? South African? Third-generation Canadian? New Zealander?" (There are Black people in New Zealand. I know. I've seen them with my very own eyes. Call the embassy if you don't believe me.) Or do they even care? Somehow I don't think so.

Now don't get me wrong. I have nothing against White people. Some of my best friends are White, and should the occasion arise that I ever have a daughter, yes I would consider letting her marry one—provided they're not "too" White, if you know what I mean. We try to keep the raping and pillaging and conquering down to a minimum in my family. It brings the neighbourhood property values down quite a bit, and they are depressed enough as it is these days.

Though they are, as I've tried to point out, a troubled people, I do want to mention in all fairness that White people can, when exhibiting the quaint attributes of their Native ways, be charming and inquisitive, with good intelligence, a fine attitude towards life, a complex sense of melody and rhythm, and have written some excellent stories over the years. I've also heard their pastries and handicrafts are quite fabulous. So they can't always be as bad as their racial profile would have us believe.

So get off the Toronto Police Force's back. Read your history, people. Racial profiling does work, most of the time. Especially for people who do the racial profiling.

IT MIGHT EXPLAIN A LOT

I have a theory, but can't prove it. It's kind of weird, so bear with me. It's based on several recent visits to the United States. Specifically, going through American customs as you get ready to board a plane for that country. And I have a feeling the Iroquois lacrosse team that is stranded at the airport in New York is thinking the same thing.

On their way to England to play at the Lacrosse World Championships—a game, by the way, the Iroquois invented—the twenty-three members of the team were prevented from boarding the plane because they insisted, as always, on using a passport issued by the Iroquois Confederacy. Officials in England were afraid the team would not be allowed back into America on their way home, now that its airports have much stricter immigration rules. After some swift negotiations with the US State Department and in particular Secretary of State Hillary Clinton, an agreement for this particular event was worked out. Still, it was too little, too late. They missed their plane, and their chance to play. Getting in and out of America can be such a pain.

Ever since the tragic events of 9/11, crossing that imaginary border between our two countries has become increasingly difficult. Contrary to the popular understanding of how our legal system works, at the border you are now assumed to be guilty until you can prove yourself innocent. So, everybody now needs an official passport to go south. I was even informed by one customs officer that the Canadian Indian Status Card—I never leave Canada or home without it—is no longer accepted for crossing the 49th Parallel. Even Native people, on their own continent, must whip out their Canadian passports to prove who they are to travel across Turtle Island. I never knew Canadian Native terrorists were such a threat down there, Tyendinaga's Shawn Brant notwithstanding. His big claim to fame, if you remember, was blocking the 401 several years back, thus making a thousand or so White people late for work. Hardly an Osama bin Brant.

Of course, there's the memory of Oka. This very week was the twentieth anniversary of that pivotal event in Canadian Native sovereignty. The name and place now mean more than just smelly cheese. To put it into perspective, once all the smoke settled, the seventy-eight-day occupation and subsequent court challenges and inquiries caused more damage, including the life of Sûreté du Québec police officer Marcel Lemay, and cost almost half as much as the recent G20 conference. However, the siege did generate one okay made-for-TV movie, and managed to make one lone Canadian army corporal with a steely gaze a star. Granted, irate Mohawks can be troublesome, but the irony here was that most of the troublemakers (as the politicians would call them) had come up from the United States to Canada to join the party.

But I digress. I was talking about my theory. These American customs officers (or agents, or whatever they are called) are a dour bunch. I have travelled the world and have to say they seem a little more sombre than most customs officials I've ever met. They sit there in their booths—I call them booth people—looking over your passport and all kinds of other personal information, asking you what your reasons are for daring to come into their country. What you are bringing with you? Where are you planning to stay? How much money are you bringing into the country, or how much have you spent? How long are you planning to stay? My accountant, my agent, and my girlfriend don't know this much about me. And the booth people always have these seriously unimpressed looks on their faces—ones that are not exactly welcoming: more of a "Guantanamo Bay isn't just for Middle Eastern people. We know you Canadians like going to Cuba, which, by the way, is a communist country, in case you didn't know, so maybe we can help you out with a one-way ticket to our resort down there."

So this is my theory. It came to me as I was watching a bunch of people make their way through customs, all with varying levels of difficulty. "Geez, they should have had this in place 518 years ago. That would have solved a lot of problems," I thought to myself. Trust me, I'm not the first Native person to ponder these thoughts. Then I thought about the larger picture. What if there is a larger law of universal karma? And maybe reincarnation? And some sort of celestial sense of irony? That would explain a lot.

So here it is. What if all these booth people, in charge of keeping out all the unwanted people in the world from setting foot on the shores of America, were the reincarnated spirits of all the dead Native people that have, over the centuries, been killed off in America by colonial expansion, Manifest Destiny, epidemics, the Trail of Tears, Cavalry, American boarding schools, etc. Through some sort of eternal search for spiritual justice, they have returned from the beyond to protect their shores from invaders who are intent on hurting the people who already live there. They are trying to pick up the slack from five centuries ago.

I say this because if you look into the faces of these people of the booth, they do have this sort of disconnected, vacant look that is either born of processing several thousand people in an eight-hour shift, or travelling back from the dead. Yes, I know most, if not all, of them appear to be non-Native, but if you can come back to the land of the living, you can probably fudge some personal appearance details. When you hunt the mighty buffalo, you must look like one.

I am sure all this means very little to the Iroquois lacrosse team. They are stuck at an airport in New York.

Maybe they could canoe ...